TO BORROW FREEDOM

Riding Down a Dream on the Coast of Portugal

SHEILA GREENFIELD

First published in 2025 by
Trafalgar Square Books | TrafalgarBooks.com
An Imprint of the Stable Book Group
32 Court Street, Suite 2109, Brooklyn, New York 11201

Copyright © 2025 Sheila Greenfield

All rights reserved. No part of this book may be reproduced, by any means, without written permission of the publisher, except by a reviewer quoting brief excerpts for a review in a magazine, newspaper, or website.

Disclaimer of Liability
The author and publisher shall have neither liability nor responsibility to any person or entity with respect to any loss or damage caused or alleged to be caused directly or indirectly by the information contained in this book. While the book is as accurate as the author can make it, there may be errors, omissions, and inaccuracies.

Trafalgar Square Books encourages the use of approved safety helmets in all equestrian sports and activities.

Trafalgar Square Books certifies that the content in this book was generated by a human expert on the subject, and the content was edited, fact-checked, and proofread by human publishing specialists with a lifetime of equestrian knowledge. TSB does not publish books generated by artificial intelligence (AI).

Library of Congress Cataloging-in-Publication Data
Names: Greenfield, Sheila, -2024 author.
Title: To borrow freedom : riding down a dream on the coast of Portugal / Sheila Greenfield.
Description: North Pomfret, Vermont : Trafalgar Square Books, 2024.
Identifiers: LCCN 2024028286 (print) | LCCN 2024028287 (ebook) | ISBN 9781646012183 (paperback) | ISBN 9781646012190 (epub)
Subjects: LCSH: Women in tourism--Portugal. | Greenfield, Sheila, -2024. | Horsemanship--Study and teaching--Portugal. | Horses--Grooming--Portugal. | Hospitality industry--Portugal.
Classification: LCC G156.5.W66 G68 2024 (print) | LCC G156.5.W66 (ebook) | DDC 338.1/7611 [B]--dc23/eng/20240712
LC record available at https://lccn.loc.gov/2024028286
LC ebook record available at https://lccn.loc.gov/2024028287

All photographs from trail rides by Robert Lee and courtesy of Robert Lee and Sheila Greenfield

Cover and interior book design by RM Didier

Typeface: Canto, Cherry Blossoms

Printed in the United States of America
10 9 8 7 6 5 4 3 2 1

Thirty-five years ago, on a stormy Halloween night,
my life changed forever. Through the swirl of wind and rain,
my eyes locked with the piercing blue gaze of a woman cloaked in
mystery and magic—a beautiful witch, radiant and still.
In that instant, without a single word, she looked into my soul...
and I into hers. *We knew.* Somehow, impossibly, we already knew
each other. No words were needed, and from that moment on,
nothing would ever be the same.

This book is her story—our story—a life lived with wild courage
and wide-open hearts. It's about love, horses, freedom, and chasing
impossible dreams, about trusting your instincts and leaping into the
unknown. As Helen Keller once said, "Life is either a daring adventure
or nothing at all." Ours was that daring adventure.

Welcome to the ride—and thank you, Sheila,
for everything.

Robert

Região
Norte

Região
Centro

Região de
Lisboa

Alentejo

See regional trail detail on facing page

Algarve

1

*And God took a handful of southerly wind,
blew his breath over it and created the horse.*

BEDOUIN LEGEND

THROUGHOUT MY LIFE, animals, great and small, have always played a huge part. Growing up in Lisbon and the Algarve in the sixties and seventies, I had cats and dogs, rabbits and guinea pigs, a goat at one stage, and even a donkey. But the animal that truly captured my heart was the horse.

When I was four and a half, my younger sister, Monica, died from an electric shock from a refrigerator. I remember her little three-year-old body laid out in a beautiful white dress with her hands clasped together over her chest like she was asleep. I was convinced Monica was going to wake up. But she didn't wake up. It was the first time I saw my parents cry. They entered a black void of grief.

My escape from the seemingly endless sorrow was my Aunt Rosemary's house. It was she who introduced me to horses.

Penguin, a liver chestnut pony with a docked tail, was the first horse I ever rode. Pretty much immediately, we understood each other, and we bonded as quickly. I loved him and wanted to take him home. I wanted to connect one-to-one with him.

By the time I turned five, a knowing had developed deep inside me: I'd always have horses in my life. They were just as important to me as people.

Before I was thirty, my dream of opening a riding center was realized on an old farm on Portugal's Blue Coast—twenty-three acres of open fields and woodland in Europe's largest coastal park. For fifteen years it became my life. And still, all these years later, it's where my heart belongs.

I still dream of galloping down a deserted Malhão Beach, bareback, on a free-spirited Lusitano, holding mane, feeling the flight, the power, the connection. I let my mind wander back to the sound of hooves on the glistening shores of Portugal's coast.

THE EIGHT RIDERS on their horses had stopped beside me to take in the strange sight on the sand of the remote beach on the southwesterly tip of Portugal. To the west, crashing Atlantic waves sent clouds of salty spray cascading onto us. To the east, undulating dunes rose steeply toward rust-colored cliffs, which cocooned the beach. Center stage was the scene stealer: an oil-covered seabird, giving us the evil eye. So smothered was he in thick black oil that he had to stab his long beak into the sand to pull his body forward a few centimeters. Every time he did so, he pierced all of us with his blue-eyed glare. The horses skipped back each time the seabird turned his head toward them. Having likely dragged his tar-sodden body over a hundred meters through the soft dunes, it looked like his energy was drained.

I dismounted slowly, trying not to upset the bird, and handed my horse's reins over to the rider beside me. Leaving the creature there to die alone wasn't an option, but the question turned uncomfortably in my mind: *How do I catch, never mind transport on horseback, this traumatized oil-sticky seabird with a dangerously long beak?*

"Robert, I could so do with your help now," I muttered to the sand.

The other riders looked from one to the other, stroking their horses, trying to keep them calm. Nervousness is infectious. The horses were already starting to paw the sand and snort, ready to get away from the oily creature. I had to play for time; there was no way I could do this on my own.

Turning my back on the riders, I breathed in deeply and focused on mentally transmitting my message. Somehow, Robert was usually pretty good at picking such messages up.

I again faced the riders and horses. "Robert is on his way. He'll know what to do."

The worried eyes of the riders looked up and down the desolate beach.

Nothing but wind, sand, and the endless crashing of waves. They didn't look convinced.

Guests came to our farm for one-week, sometimes two-week, stays to explore on horseback the most sparsely populated region of southern Europe: the poor, beautiful, and remote Lower Alentejo. We did an average of twenty-two weekly trail rides a year, each consisting of six full days of riding—five to seven hours a day, twenty-five to fifty-five kilometers at walk, trot, and canter.

The Blue Coast Trail was two hundred and thirty-five kilometers over six days. But twice a year, over two weeks, we ran a trail we called "To the End of the World and Back." At almost five hundred kilometers, it was Europe's longest scheduled trail ride by a large margin. It could be grueling, even for accomplished riders, and we were just over a week into it.

I heard a different rumble to the crashing waves. From the corner of my eye, I spotted the Jeep hurtling over the dunes. I breathed a huge sigh of relief.

Thank God for telepathy.

The car jerked to a stop a few feet away and the door swung open. Robert emerged, all dust and smiles.

"Is everything okay?" he asked. I noticed the sweatbands on his wrists and forehead were all dark. He must have been helping the girls set up the lunch spot for our riding group. We would shortly arrive at a remote location with an amazing view to find tables, chairs, shade canopies, and all the horse paraphernalia we might need awaiting us. Like a stage set, it would look like it had always been there.

I jutted my chin out toward the bird. "Look."

The bird craned its neck back to fix Robert with a greasy eye.

"Ah," said Robert, smiling easily at him.

At six feet, three inches, everything about Robert was big. He had boundless dynamic energy and created easy bonds with animals and humans (who fell for his Irish charm). Naturally charismatic, he had a magnetism that drew everyone's attention. My senses opened to him; I felt that dense bond between us, like a highly charged wavelength.

He moved slowly toward the oily bird, assessing his condition, and then turned to the group. "Are you all okay?" he asked. "Don't worry, you'll be on your way soon enough." To me, he added in a low voice, "Just give me a sec, Sheila," which basically meant, *Relax, I've got it sorted.* Of course he did. My "Action Man" always knew how to save the world.

Robert walked back to the Jeep and returned carrying a big gray horse blanket and a rope. I held my breath. With a slight nod to the other riders, I put my finger to my lips. Everyone became quiet. The horses kept their eyes fixed on Robert, their heads following his every move. He crept up on the bird from behind, threw the blanket over him, and scooped him up in his arms. The bird squawked and tried to flap himself free.

For a moment, I felt like I was looking into a mirror. *Does safety always come at a price?*

Robert tied the rope around the bottom of the squirming bundle and placed the captive bird gently in a box in the back of the Jeep. I knew the bird was going to be safe now, whatever happened. Closing the back door of the vehicle, Robert winked at me before turning to the group of riders.

"I'll take your man to the local bird sanctuary," he said. " I'm sure they can help him there. Here, have a great ride, everyone."

And he was gone.

As the Jeep disappeared over the dunes, I closed my eyes for a moment and felt the breeze glide over my face. The past six years spun and whirled in my mind. It hadn't been easy, but then nobody had said it was going to be.

When Robert and I had bought the derelict farm six years ago, it had ticked most of the boxes: Location—in the protected parkland of Portugal's wild southwest coast, with unlimited access to hundreds of kilometers of riding routes, only six kilometers from the sea, and five minutes' drive to the coastal town of Milfontes. Land—enough to build a home, the big stable block, the clubhouse and pool, our guest rooms, and still leave big fields for the horses to roam in. Our business could grow organically with no need for compromise.

My original vision of an international riding center in Portugal, promoting the locally bred Lusitano horse, had been jumpstarted by an EU grant. Robert joined the adventure, and by the time a year had passed, he'd transformed it into a high-end profitable business, visited by riding guests from around the globe. So the boxes *had* all been ticked, but the ultimate test remained: Given the choice, would I do it all again? Fight against red tape at every corner? Share my partner with one and all?

I opened my eyes and signaled to the riders to move off over the sand.

It never ceased to amaze me how Robert was able to swiftly solve our life's daily dramas, yet the more mundane aspects of life bewildered and frustrated him. What was it that he was really afraid of? The compromise? Maybe he felt smothered by the routine and consistency that a life with animals demanded. I could cope with that.

The lapping waves smudged the edges of the hoofprints on the wet sand as we trod the line of the receding tide. Looking past the horses, I noticed the aquamarine horizon as if for the first time and felt shivers run down my back and arms.

I knew what my dream was, but what was Robert's dream?

2

You see a horse with your eyes,
you feel a horse with your soul.

AUTHOR UNKNOWN

THE RIDERS IN MY GROUP were made up of four nationalities. From France, we had Pascal and Jacqueline, both in their sixties, and married. Pascal was by far the fittest of the French section and was clearly held back by the flailing staying power of his wife, and his daughter and son-in-law, Dominique and Jean-Claude.

To come on any of our trail rides, a rider had to be experienced, but the Ride to the End of the World and Back tested a rider's mettle to the max. The distances we traversed were well out of the comfort zone of most riders, so apart from acting as guide, I very often had to be their coach, psychologist, and cheerleader, too.

Jean was our English guest. At sixty-eight, she was fit as a whip, and no matter the stage of the ride, she always managed to look as fresh as a pressed blouse. From America there was Marie, who'd been with us on eight different occasions. Marie was in her forties, made of tough stuff, and lived for adventure. And lastly there were the Swedes: Bjorn and Magnus, both in their twenties. Bjorn was a sleepy-eyed bean pole with shoulder-length black hair, while Magnus was a short stocky brick house with a cracking sense of humor and white-blonde bangs. Their effortless confidence and obvious virility were great for group morale.

The horses had all calmed down by the time we moved away from the shore and on toward the cliffs.

"Sheila, I feel so dizzy," said Jacqueline in her thick French accent. "I feel I will fall to the ground."

I turned and faced backward in the saddle.

"Jacqueline, it's okay. Look at me. Look up."

She did her best but was nosing exhaustion point.

"Don't worry," I reassured her. "Your horse is used to it."

I still forgot sometimes: this magical experience was not one people had the privilege of having every day. It deeply immersed the rider into the moment, into the salty water, into the seat of the self.

As the path narrowed ahead, we rode single-file and continued up a steep incline that leveled out onto the clifftop contours. The sun-baked clay was hard and unforgiving, and the small sharp rocks underfoot were taxing for the horses, so I called a halt and told the riders to dismount and prepare to lead their mounts for the last half hour.

Shading my eyes with my hand, I looked out toward the ocean. The horizon was a lapis haze—the dark blue Atlantic merged seamlessly with the sky—while way below us the frothy waves pounded the rocks, forcing spirals of salty sea spray up the side of the cliffs. I took a moment to breathe in the sun's heat and energy, and glanced back at what were, by and large, emotional, sweat-stained faces.

"Sheila, darling, could you please take a 'piccie' of the two of us?" asked Jean, the one exception.

"Certainly," I said, "of you and Bobby Darling, you mean?"

"Of course! Who else would it be of?" she countered, flashing her Elizabeth Taylor smile while gently rubbing Bobby's forehead.

How does Jean consistently look so amazing at the end of every ride?

Ten minutes—and a number of "piccies"—later, we arrived at our lunch spot. The location had been carefully chosen not least for its stunning view. We were to dine on a hill overlooking a crystal-clear blue lake. A small river fed into it, and on the other side, flowed through the dunes and on into the sea.

As we approached the shaded area under two medium-sized pine trees, the "horse support team" sprang into action. They directed each rider to a designated spot and helped them untack their horses. Once all the bridles were off and halters were on, I led the way to a big sandy area. Immediately, the horses started to pace around in small circles and blow at the sand with their nostrils, checking that it was clean. Then they bent their knees slightly, lay down on one side, and rolled vigorously over and over, throwing clouds of dust and sand everywhere.

Some riders were a little too nervous to stand close to the thrashing horses, settling instead to watch from a safe distance. I gave them a reassuring smile.

"Don't worry. This is really good for them. It stretches out all the muscles along their backs and gives them a great natural massage."

After the horses stood up and shook it all off, sending quivers rippling through their whole bodies and out through their heads, we led them to their individual spots where they were clipped onto stakes set out in a rough semi-circle around our lunch area. Ten days into our two-week trail ride, the riders knew the drill backward: wash down the horses, and check them all over for cuts and bruises.

Robert had devised an ingenious way to tether the horses, which he'd read about in an old library book on the Portuguese cavalry. It consisted of a long metal stake with a ring soldered to the top of it, which was hammered into the ground, and to which a two-meter-long rope, encased in a rubber pipe, was tied. The horses were then clipped to the ends of each rope-pipe. This allowed free movement with no danger of the horses becoming entangled or getting rope burn. Each horse had his own water bucket, bowl of feed, pile of hay, and saddle stand, which held the saddle, covered by its own saddle blankets, which were turned upside-down to dry out after the morning's ride. The bridle (once its bit had been rinsed) was also hung over one end of the stand, under the blankets.

Only when the horses were comfortable were the riders given an ice-cold drink and slices of watermelon—the horses came first (by a nose). I glanced over at the table to see what Fátima had prepared for us. I spied grilled sardines and red peppers, mixed salad, and tomato rice, with warm freshly baked bread, olives, and goat cheese to be served on the side.

Fátima smiled as she noticed me eyeing the olives. "How's your appetite?"

As the riders relaxed over lunch and relived the morning's adventures, I checked each horse thoroughly. By running my hands along each horse's back and legs, I could feel for any new bumps or lumps. A slight difference in temperature or increased sensitivity in a particular area was an indication of a sore or bruise developing. Each horse reacted differently. Some stamped the ground as I interrupted their meal. Others swished their tails, shook their heads, or even laid back their ears.

While I was lost in equine company, snippets of conversation drifted over to me from the table. Marie's personality and enthusiasm always brought a smile to my lips.

"I can't feel my ass, my legs weigh a ton, and I have dust in places I didn't even know existed!" she said, following with her infectious laugh. "But I wouldn't have it any other way." She must have noticed me smiling. "Hey, Sheila, where's that man of yours, and his bird?"

"Marie, your guess is as good as mine. Knowing Robert, I'm sure something dramatic has happened. He should be here soon."

Now that she mentions it, where the hell is he?

It was toward the end of the two-hour break that the Jeep reappeared at its usual top speed. Robert hopped out, his arms and jeans covered in oil, and his right forearm fully bandaged.

"Hi everyone. How was lunch?" he said, smiling.

How can he be so nonchalant? I raised my eyebrows at him and got a wink back. *Nothing to worry about.*

All the riders got to their feet and flocked around him.

"Are you okay?" said one.

"What happened to you?" said another.

"Where's the bird?" said someone else.

Fátima and I stood back with our arms folded, watching The Robert Show, while he turned to everyone with a twinkle in his eye.

"Everything's okay. The vet at the sanctuary said that the bird was a North Atlantic cormorant and that he would never survive. He said the kindest thing to do would be to wring his neck."

They all gasped, horrified.

"But," Robert continued, "he also said that if I really wanted, I could try washing the cormorant with Fairy Liquid." He paused and smiled incorrigibly. "So I thought we should give the bird a chance."

Sighs of relief all round.

"But what happened to your arm?" asked Dominique. "Did he bite you?"

Robert raised his bandaged arm and looked at it along with everyone else.

"There was just a wee misunderstanding about who was the boss, is all. Nothing a few stitches couldn't fix."

My face fell. *Stitches! That's just terrific. Smack bang in the middle of the hardest trail of the year and we've got an injury to contend with.* I turned away, while the riders clustered around Robert. *Typical.*

Over the course of our fifteen years at the farm, guests had suffered a total of two broken legs and one broken wrist. Accidents happen, and we were prepared to deal with them. But Robert was indispensable to the operation; I needed him fit and able.

I walked off and joined MC and Bela for the final horse check before we set off. MC had come up with a great solution for girth rubs. These were the sore areas that could develop around the girth, which held the saddle in place, and if left untreated could lead to a horse being out of action for a month. She found that if she wrapped a felt bandage round the girth on each side of the problem area, the girth would be raised away from the sore. And then, with the simple genius of inserting a sanitary pad between the two felt bandages, the rub was kept totally clean and could heal.

"Let's go through the afternoon ride, guys," I said when we had completed the horse check, opening up a map. "It's really long, so you're going to need your wits about you."

There were usually two groups of seven to nine riders on each trail ride, traveling about fifteen minutes apart, assisted when necessary by a support vehicle (and of course, if needed, the lunch-horse support team that drove ahead). MC was leading the second group today.

"I'm fine up to the drinks stop," she said, "but is it okay if we ride as one group after that? I'm a bit worried about crossing the river on my own. Especially after all the rain we've just had."

"Of course," I replied. "Good idea. I'll wait at the drinks spot for you."

MC smiled. She was a stunner, and in many ways, my right-hand woman. She'd been with us a few years now and had become a treasured part of the team. At twenty-six, she had the kind of looks that could easily have launched a successful modeling career. She had the height, the sleek black hair, and the searing blue eyes, but more than this, she had an elegance that was all her own. I often wondered what our kind of life did for her. Was there something she wanted to get away from? Or, like me, did she just belong around horses?

I turned to Bela, who'd been working with us only a few months. She had a lot to learn about horses, though she had a natural affinity for them. Whether she had the stomach for some of the more trying aspects of horse management remained to be seen. In many respects, she was busy being twenty.

"Bela, are you happy to do the backup and the drinks spot? The horses will need loads of water, electrolytes, and salt by then."

"Sure thing," she said, nodding readily.

"And maybe have some sugar handy as well, please."

"No problem."

It was only as Bela and MC walked off that I noticed the yellow and purple cotton strands plaited through Bela's hair, and her bright orange shirt with a sunset across the back of it. I loved how she was growing more and more into herself.

WHILE I WAS LEADING THE FIRST GROUP OUT, Robert ran along-side me and put his hand on my leg. He studied me intently and spoke in a soft voice.

"Sorry about that. I couldn't get away back there."

I brushed off his hand. "It's okay. Part of the job, I guess." I could feel him calibrating his measure of my mood.

"Sheila—"

"How are we going to manage with the bird? I thought you were going to bring it somewhere, not adopt it."

"Hang on a minute—"

"And your arm...how many stitches did they put in?"

He put his hand back on my arm.

"Sheila, calm down, will you? Only five, and without a bother. Anyway, what would you have done?" He knew the answer. "Come on, you know we'll get him right again. At least we'll give him a chance."

As we walked past the Jeep, I noticed a big bird cage in the back and caught a glimpse of something black and angry moving about. My frustration melted as I glanced at Robert's dark blue eyes, so full of care and concern. There wasn't an animal in the world he wouldn't save from the gallows.

"I guess you're right. We'll manage. It's just hard, you know? We're still a week away from home, and sometimes having to share you with everyone isn't easy..."

"How do you think I feel all the time?" he said, squeezing my hand, punctuating the moment with tenderness. "I'll go and help the crew pack up. Have a good one."

I walked on, followed by my half of the riders. *Focus on the ride. Forget about the bird.*

We only did the Ride to the End of the World and Back twice a year—in March and October when it wasn't too hot. The aim was to reach Sagres, a small seaside town on the most southwesterly point of mainland Europe. Sagres has an "end of the world" feel to it, with its sea-carved cliffs and looming wind-whipped fortress perched high above the ocean. It was in Sagres that Prince Henry the Navigator—*Infante Dom Henrique*—founded his school for navigation in 1419, a center for nautical and astronomic studies. Renowned sailors and cartographers came from far and wide to study at the school, whose importance in the Age of Discovery is comparable to Cape Canaveral's during the early years of space exploration. Its most famous alumnus, the renowned Portuguese explorer Vasco da Gama, was the first European to reach India by sea in 1498.

I hoped my riders had recovered enough of their energy for the three-and-a-half-hour trek ahead of us. They were all in high spirits, so I led us away from our lakeside retreat with optimism.

3

Until one has loved an animal,
a part of one's soul remains unawakened.

ANATOLE FRANCE

EEP INTO THE STIFLING AFTERNOON, our track meandered its way into the welcome shade of a forest of mushroom-shaped umbrella pines. Though the heat largely remained, I could see the respite from the glaring sun registered on every face in the group—even the horses'—when I turned around in my saddle to speak to the riders.

"Look at these trees, guys," I said, putting my "tour-guide hat" on. "Their pinecones are the ones that produce the really fancy pine nuts. All harvested by hand. It's no wonder they cost an arm and a leg."

Marie, who was right behind me, had her mind on other things. "Can we just stay here in the shade, please?" she asked. "That red bark beside the white sand and pine needles looks very inviting. What do you say, Sheila?"

I breathed in the warm balmy air and slowed my horse slightly. "Next time, maybe. How's the backside?"

Marie's grin was never far away. "Yeah, I'm fine now, which is more than I can say for our French friends," she noted quietly, stealing a glance back at them. "Check them out."

As I looked at the four stragglers bringing up the rear of the group, Marie leaned forward giggling, trying to hide her face in her horse's mane.

"This will not work," I said with a sigh as I turned my horse around and rode back alongside the line until I reached the amblers. They looked like they could expire any moment.

"*Alors, Pascal. Ça va?*"

Pascal was probably coping as well as any of the riders in our group, but his family's withered stamina was dragging down his morale. Hailing from the "horsey district" of Camargue in southern France, he was a seasoned rider and a stalwart, but his wife, daughter, and son-in-law looked like flinching rag dolls. Though they were riding my three most comfortable and reliable horses, it was obvious from the way they were moving around in their saddles that the additional gel and sheepskin seat savers they'd been given weren't helping.

"Yes, I am good, but them! Ah!" Pascal shrugged like only the French can, his look of contempt telling me everything. Jacqueline and Dominique panted exhaustedly while Jean-Claude groaned in time. I smiled encouragingly at them. Somehow, I had to get them all to the night's camp without ruining the ride for the rest of the group.

"Don't worry," I said cheerfully. "Soon we'll dismount and walk a bit."

Jacqueline looked close to tears. "No, no more walking... I cannot!" she proclaimed. "I must go in the car—now!"

"No problem, Jacqueline. We'll be meeting the Jeep soon; then you can have a rest."

"*Nous aussi!* We cannot go on any farther," added Jean-Claude.

I smiled at them as reassuringly as I could. To go on the remaining miles of the day with three loose horses following us just wasn't an option.

"Don't worry. We'll sort it out," I said, and then raised my clenched forearm to rouse their strength. "Come on—*courage!*"

Within minutes, we were out of the forest. I called a halt at the bottom of a hill.

"Okay, everybody, we are going to lead the horses up this hill. Please dismount, cross your stirrups over the saddle, and let's go."

I stayed back to help the French contingent, who looked at me like they were being tortured. "Just up the hill and then you can rest. *Allez!*"

The three of them limped along so pathetically they were slowing their horses down.

"Look, try this trick," I suggested. "It really helps." I let my horse's lead go, and moving behind him, wrapped a thick handful of his tail around my hand. Then as he followed the other horses up the hill, he effortlessly dragged me along behind him. I turned back around to see hope taking hold in several faces.

"Go on, try it," I said. "It doesn't hurt the horses. They're used to it."

The three took hold of their horses' tails and the relief began. Dominique even managed a little laugh.

Every deck has its aces.

"It'll be our little secret," I said with a wink.

Five minutes later we arrived at the top of the hill behind the rest of the group. I gave the stragglers the thumbs up and turned to the others, who were all red-faced and puffing. While leaning on his knees, Pascal eyed Jacqueline suspiciously.

After they'd all caught their breath, I brought the riders' attention to an old tree stump.

"Okay, everyone, please use this mounting block to get back on. Let me know if you need help."

In just a few minutes everyone was back on board and appeared to be revived enough for the next stage.

"As you can see, we're on the clifftop plain. This will eventually link into the valley beside Alzejur, where we'll be spending the night..."

A whoop and a holler from the Swedes inspired a collective, if slightly shattered, laugh.

"Now," I went on. "I've got a little challenge for you: To get through this endless plain—"

"Pain!" shouted Magnus, producing another ripple of laughter.

"That too," I agreed, laughing myself, a little. "To get through this endless plain—and pain—we'll be doing a half-hour of continuous trot. Let me know if you're dying, and we'll take a break."

"Sheila, you trying to kill us or what?" said Marie, lifting an eyebrow in the direction of the stragglers.

"We'll be fine," I replied confidently and sidled up to the three in question. I lowered my tone as I moved in close to them. "Remember, this is only about endurance; you'll be changing your pressure points and position all the time. You will get through this!" *Even if it kills me*, I added internally, hoping my telepathy skills only extended to Robert.

I faced the whole group now. "Okay, listen. Just a couple of tips: I want you to keep alternating your diagonals about every forty strides—count them in your head if that helps. You'll find your horse will favor one side, but just keep trying. When you feel your legs and knees getting too tired to post, just stand up in the saddle, lean forward, and grab a handful of mane. Try to balance there. Keep your backside up and off the saddle, and don't come back down onto the horse. It'll give you great relief. The trick is to keep changing position. Let me know if it gets to be too much, and we'll have a break."

I was fully aware that most of the riders were about to be pushed well past their comfort level, but what the hell—*What doesn't kill you...*

As we walked out together, a thick honey-like scent filled the air and pervaded our senses. Marie, who was next in line behind me, had shut her eyes and was quietly singing to her horse, Maya, while gently stroking her neck. Over the last ten days, the two of them had been getting closer and closer. I'd noticed at the last lunch that Maya was aware of where Marie was at all times. I smiled to myself as I pictured Maya retiring to the United States. That would be a first. So far, our retired horses who'd been bought by former guests had gone to live like royalty in the England, Ireland, Germany, Switzerland, France, Wales, Scotland, and Norway.

"What is that soft, fruity smell?" asked Marie, awakening to her senses' delight, and looking curiously around her. Scattered left and right and up beyond the vanishing point were splatters of white, which broke up the otherwise inhospitable landscape.

"Gum cistus, or rockrose," I said, pointing to the copious shrubs around us. I always enjoyed this passage because of their scent and aesthetic and how they enveloped the groups' senses. "When they get hot in the sun their scent is very strong. Look at their papery white flowers—they all have a maroon spot in the center."

"Are they used for anything?"

"Yes, see the leaves? They're covered by a brown resin called *labdanum*, which is used in herbal remedies and perfume. They also use it to make a cistus essential oil, which is used for meditation. Quietens the mind, apparently."

A cheeky smile crept up the left side of Marie's face. "I can think of two or three people who could use some of that."

I turned in my saddle and looked back at the line of riders. The two Swedes were just behind us, chatting away happily, their horses as relaxed as they were. I had to smile. Bjorn, whose shoulder-length hair was probably his most notable feature, was riding Max, a big black horse whose face was totally covered by his abundant forelock. And Magnus was riding Kaya, a chunky palomino, whose white-blond mane and tail were a perfect match for Magnus's hair.

The little things we notice.

I turned my horse and walked down past the others. Just past the boys was Jean on her Bobby Darling: perfect makeup, flowery shirt, immaculate jodhpurs. She looked like she was on her way out to dinner.

"You look as perfect as ever, Jean. Are you and Bobby Darling ready to carry on?"

"Ready as we'll ever be," she said, and then with her dark mischievous eyes twinkling, she nodded almost imperceptibly toward the group at the back.

"They'll be fine," I said, trying to sound confident as I walked down to them. "*Ça va,* Pascal? Everyone ready?" I gave them a meaningful look of encouragement.

"*Oui,* we are ready. *Allez!*"

Moving back to the front of the ride, I raised my hand to signal the trot. I was glad to be riding Damastor. He set a perfect pace and needed no rein contact. By standing up in my stirrups and leaning forward slightly to keep my balance, it was easy to keep turning around to check on everyone.

After about fifteen minutes, it looked like we needed a breather. Marie's open smile had turned into a determined scowl. Jean was slightly flushed. The two Swedes were focused on some distant point on the horizon and strangely silent. Pascal had pulled his cowboy hat down over his face and was holding onto the horse's mane with both hands as if in a trance. The three at the back, though coping extremely well and determined not to complain, looked like they were serving a sentence in hell.

I touched my horse's neck, raised my hand, and slowed us to a walk. I then crossed my stirrups in front of me, twisted the reins round each other to secure them, and slipped off Damastor, who walked on, leading the ride on his own. I went back on foot to check on each rider.

"Well done, guys! You're doing brilliantly. Just another ten minutes to go. Does anyone need to get off?"

"*Non, non,* we just want it to finish..." moaned Jacqueline from the back. She looked a little better now that she'd poured her bottle of water over her head.

"Okay, great. Hang in there," I said, and turned and caught up with my horse.

Time seemed to stretch mercilessly over the last miles as the relentless trotting tested everyone. I had to cajole, bully, and bribe all the riders, who'd no choice but to dig deep into their last reserves of energy. Just as it felt like it would never end, Damastor slowed down imperceptibly and stretched his neck down toward the ground. I immediately put my hand up to slow the ride to a walk. Sure enough, in the next clump of trees, I could just make out the support car.

As one, all the riders dismounted and tried valiantly to keep their balance on unsteady legs as the horses dragged them to the long line of prepared water buckets, which they plunged their heads into. The sweltering riders could only gasp dryly as they waited for their own refreshments, watching Bela as she went from horse to horse with electrolytes and sea salt in the palm of her hand, which was quickly slurped up.

Finally, trays of freshly cut pineapple and watermelon and cool lemon drinks were passed around to the parched, dusty riders, who seemed unable to utter a single word.

I found my way to a half-filled bucket of water and poured it over my head. MC rode in with her group, every one of them parboiled.

"We survived," said MC a little exhaustedly, giving me the thumbs up. While MC's group joined the others for refreshments, Bela and I went around, checking every horse and every rider, adjusting saddle blankets, topping up water bottles. We were nearly there—just another five kilometers. One more hill, one more river, and we'd reach the night spot as one group.

Before long, I led the ride out again, and not even a half hour had passed when we reached the narrow, deep, and fast-flowing river on the outskirts of Aljezur: the last challenge of the day.

"Try and stop briefly in the middle of the river so the horses can cool their legs down," I called over my shoulder as Damastor plunged in. "But please take care they don't roll on you. Bjorn, you be especially careful—your horse is a specialist!"

Bjorn's smile disappeared quickly, as right on cue, Max started pawing the river, drenching Bjorn, and began to go down.

"Kick him, kick him!" I cried, quickly turning Damastor around to face Max. A sharp wallop from my hand on his backside did the trick, and Max leapt out of the river onto the far bank.

MC went about rounding up the rest of the horses who'd started pawing the river. "Let's go!" she ordered. "Move on. Don't let them lie down!"

I stood Damastor upstream while MC stood her horse downstream, and we rallied them all through. "Come on, guys," I said. "Five more minutes and we're there."

The night spot was waiting for us like a treasured oasis. Drenched, muddy, and dusty, the horses and riders filed in, having earned their rest. After the guests had unsaddled and rubbed their horses down, they were driven to their hotel by MC and Fátima. I stayed to do the final check with Bela. Any slight swelling on the fetlocks or hocks was plastered in a thick layer of clay, or *argila*, then covered in a few layers of cling film and loosely bandaged. By the next morning when all the dried-in clay was washed off, the horses' legs would be cool and all the swelling gone. We took our time. An hour later, all the horses had been fed, watered again, and left to recover.

After checking the saddles and bridles, and replacing the sodden saddle blankets, I eventually sat down on a bale of hay with Bela. She was camping out with the horses tonight.

"I've a feeling they'll let you sleep tonight, Bela."

"Yeah, don't worry. You go home and rest. You must be shattered after all that."

I smiled at her. "It was a long one, all right." We all took turns between camping with the horses along the ride and going back to base. Thank the Lord it was my turn to go home tonight.

It was only as I was driving back to the farm that I remembered the bird. Had he survived? And Robert and his stitches—how had it even happened? It all felt so long ago.

Battling fatigue as the day's adrenaline wore off, I drove with the window open while slapping myself hard. *Stay awake, Sheila!*

Half an hour later, I drove up our driveway under a silver crescent moon and the shelter of the tall eucalyptus trees. I got out of the car, closed my eyes, and listened. To the silence. And then, as my ears adjusted, to the steady symphony of the cicadas. I stood there absorbing the deep sense of peace I always felt after returning home. The night sky was a thick, black velvet blanket decorated with thousands of glittering stars. The distant snorting and snuffling sounds of the wild boar drifted up from the valley as I walked up the long, cobbled path to the clubhouse, where the lights were still blazing.

Through the kitchen window, I could see Robert holding the cormorant's beak with one hand, and its wings with his other hand, while Fátima darted around the bird with a sponge, scrubbing and drying him. The kitchen walls, floor and ceiling were splattered in thick black oil, but the cormorant was actually looking like a bird now. Maybe it was the manic energy of the bird, or possibly Robert's determined tongue-twisted expression, or even my exhaustion descending into delirium—whatever it was, I just stood there and laughed.

4

*There is not one big cosmic meaning
for all, there is only the meaning
we each give to our life.*

ANAÏS NIN

I'VE ALWAYS FELT THAT EVERYTHING has a reason for being and that we're all connected to each other at some level. Our tiniest actions appear to have an effect on the whole, and like ripples in a pond, they spread forever outward until all life forms have been touched and even changed. I often wondered why the guides who worked with us picked such a lifestyle. And why our riding guests chose this particular riding holiday when some of them could have gone anywhere in the world. Perhaps they were subconsciously looking for something—a need for some air and a space to breathe, to have time to think, or to not have to think at all. No mortgages, no subways, no crowds, no stress. To have their soul massaged, cosseted, and accepted by a humble horse. To be with people with whom they could talk freely about horses all day long. To go home after a week, fully revived, and then maybe come back again—for more.

Although the guides we were fortunate to have working with us were from all walks of life, I felt they were all connected at a deeper root level. Bonded by a thirst and desire for adventure, they were addicts. The twenty-four hours in the day were never long enough to spend with the horses, and if they couldn't be with them all the time, then they wanted to be able to "talk horse," guilt-free, all day long.

Perhaps they were out-of-time spirits seeking their spot in life, seeking themselves. It seems that even the sunniest of us carry dark shadows from our past, and the way we deal with them can help us walk toward the light, or move sideways into blackness.

As a child, one of our guides had had a near-death experience when she was hit by a truck while crossing the road. The incident had left her with a pronounced limp and a massively scarred thigh muscle. She first came to us as a riding guest, and after many return visits, ended up staying in Portugal. There was one horse in particular who seemed to understand what she'd gone through and was somehow able to connect with her and help her. Poeira, the mare in question, was highly sensitive and difficult to ride, but the empathetic way she behaved and the understanding she appeared to show was touching to watch. For this rider, she became the "dream horse."

Another guide had found the dead body of her twin after his suicide. She too started her journey with us as a guest, but after finding some kind of peace with the horses, ended up staying for an extra six months as a trail-ride leader. Again, it was a particular horse, this time Max, who seemed able to reach out to this rider and facilitate healing.

One guide, who, as a child, had suffered terrible sexual abuse at the hands of a family member, came to work with us as a trainer and trail-ride leader. She was soft-spoken with an ability to make any horse look like he was floating effortlessly beneath her. Within two years the young and flighty Allegra bonded with her, and the healing began.

Strangely, I found it was never the horse you would have imagined for a particular person that ended up making the connection. Being such highly sensitive and socially intelligent beings, horses react to and have a memory for human emotions. Humans have been in partnership with them for over five thousand years now, so maybe it's no wonder that they seem to know and feel exactly what we need. They can form lifelong and mutually beneficial, deep emotional connections with us. It's a unique relationship.

But how do they do it?

It's as if we can only hear part of the music, and they can hear the whole symphony, and identify the broken chords and notes. Their bonding with us makes it possible for them to then tune the instruments and fix the score.

In her book *Saved by a Horse*, Mary Berkery puts it perfectly:

> *Having no agenda, they hear you, see you, and feel you on a deeper soul level, sense emotions lurking beneath the surface*

and mirror them back to us, and show us what we have been avoiding. They know when a person is in harmony.

FOR US, THE SUMMER was always a time to get away and escape the dense heat that inhabited the country like a physical beast. When the sidewalks were haunted by dust, when the sun steam-dried the wet clothes on your body in less than half an hour, and when the laundry was hung up to dry outside overnight to stop it getting too stiff, it was time to escape. Initially, we wanted to be able to run our rides all year round, with no extremes of temperature. We worked through the hot summers before eventually learning to respect them. We realized it made sense to take a month off and give the horses plenty of downtime, allowing us to recover and cool down in Ireland. As they say, "In the summer, the song sings itself"—we didn't need to be there.

Although it had been a major factor when deciding where to base our trail riding business, we never fully realized that climate would become our greatest ally and most formidable adversary. As I've mentioned, there were certain essential criteria we considered when deciding where to have our home base, and first and foremost was location. There was so much on offer: Portugal is divided into eleven provinces, from the *Minho*, the "garden," in the very northwest, to the *Algarve* in the very south. The latter, which is separated from the rest of the country by a low mountain range, has its own mild microclimate, and is renowned as Portugal's main tourist resort center.

Slotted in between, the remaining districts all have their distinct characteristics: The *Trás os Montes* and *Alto Douro* in the far north have very long cold winters, hot dry summers, and wild untamed nature parks. The *Douro Litoral* is bisected by the famed River Douro—literally its backbone—with the city of Porto as its heart. To its south is the coastal *Beira Litoral* with its industry and commerce, bordered by *Beira Alta*, the ancient province, situated in the interior, featuring the highest mountains in Portugal, the *Serra da Estrela*, home of the only ski resort in the country.

Farther south is the historical *Beira Baixa*, followed by *Estremadura*, the cultural, commercial, and political center of the country and home to Lisbon, the capital. The *Ribatejo* is situated along the River Tejo, and, being rich in alluvial soil, is ideal for cattle and horse breeding.

South again, the *Alto* and *Baixo Alentejo* are the biggest provinces, occupying forty percent of the country's total area, stretching from the Atlantic coast in the west to the Spanish border in the east. These provinces make up the breadbasket of the country and produce sixty percent of the world's cork. It was in the *Baixo Alentejo*, or lower *Alentejo*, that our spirits felt the most at home and could roam the freest. The location was ideal for riding out in any direction with no constraints, fences, rules, or urban development of any kind. We wanted to be based in a place that offered a real mixture of natural beauty and diversity of nature. Our riding terrain ranged from rugged mountains to open flat plains to beautiful seascapes to river valleys. It had it all.

We also required space for all the horses to live outside in the most natural environment possible. Our property allowed for five big fields around the stable block where all the horses were able to "be themselves" in individual herds. (Their motto, like ours, was to work hard and play hard.)

Our ideal location would have been within an hour's drive of either Faro or Lisbon airports. The journey ended up being two hours from Faro, and two and a half from Lisbon, with a good kilometer of driveway that led to the entrance of the farm. Although it was drivable all year round, it had to be closely monitored for flooding and repair. We also required connections to electricity and water. Generators and a wide range of solar power were sourced to fill our energy needs. With the help of a "water diviner," who walked the whole property with his forked stick, we found the best place to dig for our eighty-meter-deep borehole, with water found at thirty-eight meters. Situated at the top of the property, it supplied water with plenty of pressure for not only the horses, but also for the running of the whole operation. The force of the water from this underground supply was such that it filled a ten-by-five-meter pool overnight without its level dropping. For watering the extended garden, we dug a seven-meter well at the bottom of the land. A round brick well was built from the bottom up—quite a challenge, as it was continually being fed by a small river. The plants loved its muddy water. On top of this, the run-off from the clubhouse kitchen, baths, and showers was fed directly into the plants, adding to their irrigation. The garden became a blooming, blossoming oasis.

What was most important about our place was its individual spirituality. Nearly everyone that came, stayed, and rode with us felt it was a place of healing, of finding yourself, and of simply *being*. I think the spot we found and the center we built affected the humans, the horses, and all other animals in the same way. In this respect, it hugely surpassed our every expectation.

This was its main strength and gift.

5

A horse doesn't care how much you know until he knows how much you care. Put your hand on your horse and your heart in your hand.

PAT PARELLI

WRITER JOSEPH CAMPBELL is credited with saying that myths are the dreams of a society, and that dreams are the myths of the individual. Every horse I ever met was a living myth to me. Even as a child, I recognized the horse as the most mythic of animals, and that was before I'd ever opened a book of fairy tales. The horse's attributes are myriad: Speed. Strength. Grace. Beauty. Nobility. Intelligence. Passion. Power. The list goes on. Horses' archetypal place in human consciousness gives them an ethereal presence in our lives. It's little wonder, then, that they pervade my dreams the way they do.

Looking back, I would have liked to have been able to look forward.

December 1999 came around like a cracked whip. All through the month, I'd been walking up a steep hill, balancing the expectations of twenty-odd "Millennium Riders" on my shoulders. And now it was the end of December, and my knees were in danger of buckling. Riders had booked for this ride a whole year in advance, and we'd fifteen guests still on the waiting list. I knew them all, which was mostly a good thing—save for the terrible Tania. My stomach clenched again and again as I thought of the week ahead. Could we match their massive expectations for this event?

I hoped the twenty-eight horses I'd carefully prepared would be enough. Twenty for the guests. Two as leads. Six spares. What could go wrong? Past scenarios drifted through my mind in thick colorful clouds: Lame horse. Sick horse. Horse with colic. Swollen tendons. Lost shoes. Sore backs. Rubs. Rider with a broken leg. Rider with a dislocated thumb.

Rider with a concussion. Rider needing head stitched up. Rider with the runs. Hungover rider. Rider in bits.

The only predictable thing was unpredictability.

I'd fallen asleep on the sheepskin rug in the clubhouse and into a dream where the guests for the Millennium Trail Ride were all standing around me in a circle, dressed in their breeches, raring to go...with Tania standing nearer to me than anyone. *Are her breeches really shimmering silver? So weird.* As they all looked at me expectantly, I could hear the horses whinnying. *Are they laughing at me?* And then my name being shouted by someone not in the group. Someone unseen. Urgently. Insistently. A voice I knew well.

"Sheila! Wake up!"

I opened my eyes, startled, to see MC standing over me in a panic. Her hands were tight balls of white knuckles pushing through skin. Her oval face was drained of color and wild-eyed.

"Come quickly, Sheila! There's been an accident."

We bolted outside and ran down to the stable yard. In the main field I could see two horses down. I sprinted to the tack room and grabbed a couple halters.

"What happened? Did you see it?" I asked MC.

"Mistral and Íntima were galloping around, you know, excited with the cool weather, and Mistral slipped and crashed into the big cork tree. Íntima was too close. She just went head over hooves into her..."

I sensed Bela hovering. I glanced at her briefly: she was beside herself, completely undone. *This is no time for blubbering.*

"Quick, Bela," I snapped. "Get two of the stalls ready. MC, come with me."

We raced into the field. Íntima was now standing, shaking her head, looking dazed. The other one, Mistral, had her two front legs stretched out in front of her and was sitting up like a dog. We began to walk slowly up to them.

"Just breathe for a sec," I said to MC. "Get your heart rate down if you can."

Horses are hypersensitive animals and react to the slightest shift and nuance in our mood. In a stressful situation like this one, it was crucial that we control the rhythm of both our breathing and our heartbeat, and keep them as low as possible.

Íntima was closest to us. We could see blood spilling out from a gash above her hock.

"Look," said MC. "It's her near hind."

The horse took a step toward us, putting her weight on her injured leg.

"At least she can walk," I said. "That's really good."

Mistral was still sitting there like an oversized Labrador.

"MC, can you please lead Íntima in slowly," I said in a low voice. "Get Bela to hose her leg gently with cold water, and then come back here straight away."

I watched Íntima walk away, cautiously placing each hoof in front of the other. From what I could see, five or six stitches should do the trick.

Mistral whickered softly. I moved toward her and eased her halter on. Then I rubbed her forehead and caressed her ears. Suddenly, she rocked her body onto her backside, heaved herself forward, and stood up. As MC appeared by my side, the horse tried to take a step forward. Her near hind dragged along the ground at a strange angle. Her left hip bone was protruding forward. Step by step, she hopped toward the stable on three legs, dragging the injured one behind her.

Bela's ashen face lingered in the doorway.

"Have you hosed Íntima?" I asked her. She barely nodded. "Get my phone, would you, so I can put a call through to Mike," I said, trying to keep everything moving. But Bela just froze. "Please, Bela, I need the phone now!"

The phone in hand, I called Mike, our vet, and described the situation. Mike was in Spain, so couldn't come. As he gave me precise treatment instructions, I closed my eyes and bit my lip. *A dislocated hip? I've never heard of a horse with a dislocated hip. How are we going to manage this?*

"Okay, Mike, thank you. We'll try and do that. I hope it works." I ended the call and took several deep breaths again to slow my beating heart. I didn't want Mistral to realize I felt way out of my depth with what was about to come next—she'd know immediately.

Like two statues, MC and Bela stood watching, waiting.

"Bela, could you run up to the forest and tell Robert to come down immediately?"

She darted off like she'd heard a gun.

"MC, could you grab the first-aid kit from the fridge and prepare a needle and thread? We'll have to stitch Íntima up first, while the cut's fresh."

A line of horses stood at the edge of the field, watching intently. Their ears twitched as they nuzzled each other. I closed my eyes and steadied my breathing. *It'll be fine. I can do this.*

MC had finished cleaning Íntima's wound thoroughly and was now cradling the mare's head in her arms, crooning to her in a gentle tone.

"She's ready for you," she said quietly.

"Thank you," I said. "At least it's a nice clean cut. Try and keep her still."

I pulled the loose skin together and got six swift stitches in before Íntima pulled back and started to paw the ground.

"Okay, I think that'll do," I said. "You did a great job with her. She doesn't seem too upset at all." MC winced as Íntima started to rub her forehead up and down the young woman's back. "Just to be on the safe side, maybe give her twenty mils of antibiotic. Give it to her in the chest. It'll be less likely to swell up and bother her."

MC smiled and breathed out. "No probs, Sheila. Then I'll leave her to rest in her stall."

I touched her arm. "Thanks. Will you put some aloe vera on her later? There should be a new batch on the shelf."

I'd recently picked some of the juiciest-looking leaves from our crop of aloes. After removing the outer skin and spikey edges, I'd blended them into a slimy green jelly-like substance—the best cure for burns and flesh wounds.

As I now walked out to where Mistral stood, my stomach turned over. Her head was hanging down. Her eyes had glazed over. Her tail was limp. Even her lower lip drooped.

Where the hell are you, Robert? I need you here now!

Out of the corner of my eye, I spotted him racing down the hill. *Why is he carrying an axe?* I moved my hand up and down to slow him down. He slowed it to a walk. I could see him looking the horse over while trying to get his breath under control. His face had gone pale. I watched him, knowing he was already working out all the possible ways we could help fix Mistral.

"It's okay," I said in a low voice. "She's dislocated her hip joint. Mike's in Spain, but he explained how to put it back in."

Robert nodded at this information and placed the axe down below the pepper tree, out of the way. As he looked at Mistral, I noticed his blue shirt clung to his torso like a second skin, and bits of bark stuck out of his hair.

He turned to me, clasping my forearm in his huge hand. "Don't worry, Sheila. I know we've never done this, but we're going to be fine. Now tell me exactly what the vet said."

It took just a few minutes to get us all in position. MC held the horse's head steady. Robert and I stood beside her back leg. Bela wasn't up to helping.

Robert slowly raised Mistral's injured leg and stretched it back as far as it would go, then moved it forward so that it was parallel to her body. Nothing. Then we both tried to shoulder the hip joint back into its socket. It wouldn't click in.

Suddenly, Mistral lunged forward. MC was sent flying by the horse's strength. The mare hobbled off on three legs while Bela covered her head with both arms and started crying. Robert looked stunned.

"That didn't go too well, did it?" said Robert. He turned to Bela. "Here, do me a favor and go up to the clubhouse and make us all a cup of tea? Yeah?"

As Bela dashed off, I glared at Robert, shaking my head.

"She's just a kid," he said.

MC stood up, rubbing her backside, and I went and caught Mistral. I wound her lead rope around a pole, and between the three of us, we maneuvered the poor horse back into position.

"Are you good to go?" I said to MC and got a nod back. "Right, can you hold her again? I don't think she'll get away from you this time."

I turned to Robert. "Look, we have to push much, much harder this time. Her hip joint is huge."

"I know," he said, rubbing the horse's forehead. "I just don't want to hurt her."

I touched his arm gently and looked into his cobalt eyes. Not for the first time, I was amazed at how they changed color, depending on his mood.

"The quicker we do this, the better for her," I said quietly. "Come on, you'll be fine!"

Robert pushed his full weight into the hip joint; we heard a loud hollow *clunk*. Instinctively, Mistral lashed out backward with her leg, catching me right on the side of my head, knocking me face down into the sand. Robert rushed over and picked me up. His face was chalk white.

"Sheila, talk to me! Are you okay?" He was supporting all my weight.

My legs were made of jelly. Mistral looked at me quizzically. I noticed all four of her legs seemed to be firmly on the ground.

"Yeah, fine, fine. A bit dizzy. How is she?"

Watching from behind the stable door, Bela let out a squeal. "Sheila, there's blood on your head! It's bleeding down your back!"

Robert gasped. He hadn't noticed the blood trickling and splashing onto my yellow T-shirt. "Stand still, will you? Let me have a look."

I dissolved onto the stool MC had placed beneath me. Stupid stinging tears prickled my eyes.

"I'm fine...leave me alone," I mumbled.

He carefully pulled my hair apart and examined the cut.

"Shut up now, Sheila, and stay still a moment. Jesus, what next? These goddamned horses are just far too dangerous!" He turned to MC. "Could you please get the human first-aid kit from the Jeep? And you," he said, pointing at me, "do not move."

I did as I was told.

He cleaned the cut, snipped some hair, and applied butterfly stitches.

"There, all done," he said. Then he focused on me like a teacher might. "Look, Sheila, you've got a big cut at the top of your head. Now do us all a favor and go home and put your feet up. But *don't* lie down yet. Do you hear me?" I saluted obediently. He turned to Bela. "Here, Bela, will you walk up with Sheila? Make her a cup of tea with loads of sugar, and just stay with her. I'll be there in two minutes."

Poor Robert. Lines of sweaty dust streaked and sectioned his face.

I steadied myself on Bela. Halfway up the hill, we stopped and looked back at the horse field. Robert and MC were beside Mistral now, checking her over. The tree shadows had elongated significantly, deformed by the white winter sun. Three horses were lying flat, basking in it, for all appearances dead, save for the occasional ear twitch. Mistral was at the water trough, dunking her head and violently jerking her muzzle from side to side as water poured onto the ground. She seemed to be recovering well. I wondered if she might, after all, be able to do some work toward the end of the coming week. She was a hot favorite. Three different Millennium Riders had requested her.

From outside my fuzz bubble, I felt Bela looking at me.

"Wasn't Robert brilliant back there?" she said softly.

"Mm-hmm." My Action Man. What would I ever do without him?

Then again, what would I ever do *with* him?

6

*Every person, when riding,
reveals his inner self.*

AUTHOR UNKNOWN

THE HORSE OBSESSION is a bit hard to explain. It actually transcends obsession. Just as a blues musician doesn't develop a love for the blues—the blues are already inside—my relationship with horses is encoded in my DNA. It's not like it was ever a conscious decision to spend time with horses. The force connecting us is akin to the power of gravity. I'm convinced it is linked to genetic memory and hereditary imprinting.

My first real instruction in riding came at the age of five from Senhor Fernando, a larger-than-life riding master with twinkling blue eyes and a drooping black mustache. He had an intuitive connection with both his students and horses. The occasional touch of a whip's lash across my back and the broom-handle-behind-the-back-and-through-the-elbows treatment improved my posture no end. I didn't once question his no-pain-no-gain approach.

In my rucksack of memories, I carry the mutual respect that can be forged between humans and horses through authenticity, and the lack of pretense that was etched onto me. There's zero room for pretense with horses—they instantly see through it. The sensory world of horses teaches you quickly to know your heart, and to access and trust your intuition.

As I grew up and into a woman, the horse-ache remained the same. Boyfriends came and went; they were always secondary. Even after studying in the United Kingdom and France, I returned to Portugal with one objective: to learn as much as I could about horses. So I went to Lisbon to learn the classical art of equitation. There is no better way to learn to train a horse than to teach promising young stallions to bullfight! I admit, however, that immersion in such a male-dominated world proved a little challenging.

I'll never forget the first time I had to ride a horse into the ring to face a bull. The black stallion in question, Mágico, had been trained for a full four years to bring him to this moment: his first contact with a live bull—a tame bull, but still. As we entered the ring, the stallion held the bull's scent in his upturned lip. Glancing around, I realized quite abruptly that in a circular arena, there is no escape.

When the massive animal turned to look at us, my horse's body condensed into a tightly coiled spring. I held my breath and waited for his next move. Did Mágico want to run as much as I did? Instead of feeding my fear, I entrusted myself to Mágico, to his training, and to his total commitment to his rider. He faced the bull, every cell of his being alert and ready. The bull pawed the ground then slowly lifted his head and moved toward us. I was hypnotized by the advancing bull. In an instant, I felt Mágico cantering *toward* the bull, and then at the last possible moment, he leaned to his right then to his left, circling round the back of the animal. It was magic.

Three years of riding stallions at this level and intensity resulted in a collapsed spinal disc, which required urgent back surgery. Through the post-op fog of pain, all I wanted the surgeon to tell me was when I could ride again.

I'll never forget his sober expression when he told me that first I had to learn to walk again.

One year later, I started my two-year instructor's course in Germany. I found the horse care and riding methods highly structured and demanding, and I grew to love the focused German work ethic— quite the opposite of the Portuguese way I was used to. A combination of both methods, perhaps—German and Portuguese—would be the best way to keep horses, I decided. It was when I returned to Portugal in 1989 that I started a destination trail riding business: *Caminhos do Alentejo, Alentejo Trails*.

I also met Robert.

HALLOWEEN ISN'T USUALLY CELEBRATED in Portugal, so I'd been of two minds whether I should go to the party. As I got closer to the venue, I could see big black storm clouds piling up on the horizon. Maybe the party would be canceled. But as I walked from the parking lot, I could hear the band in full swing, and though it was the end of October, everyone was outside dancing.

The smell of freshly cooked piri piri chicken hanging in the air made my mouth water. I grabbed a passing plate loaded with chicken and salted, roasted chestnuts, a specialty at this time of year. Looking at the costumed couples on the dance floor, I couldn't help smiling. They were all pushed as close together as possible while trying to keep a fully blown balloon wedged between them, no hands allowed.

After greeting some friends, I amused myself by watching the waiters serve drinks to the writhing mass of witches and werewolves. This party's theme was definitely new to them. I squeezed my way through a throng of sweaty drunk bodies, then suddenly had to stop and catch my breath.

I'd just entered a different force field.

The hairs stood up on the back of my neck as all my senses intensified. I closed my eyes and tried to capture the signal. Twisting around, I felt a wave of energy pulsating toward me. I looked up to see a pair of intensely blue eyes teasing and burning deep down into me. They belonged to a stranger perched on a bar stool. I was totally shocked to hear my mother's voice echoing inside me: *You'll know him immediately*.

Wearing a long, knotted black wig, which hung down his back like a clump of wet seaweed, he looked the worse for wear and had clearly been at the party a while. His big frame draped over his stool while he sat nonchalantly, smiling at me. Then, in a lilting Irish accent, he said, "Can I get you a drink?"

My legs shook as I weakly leaned against the sticky bar top, drink ignored. While I absorbed his energy, the whole room became blurred.

The music faded into the background as my subconscious mind ticked off the usual boxes: *Height—very tall. Demeanor—exceptionally confident. Looks—extremely presentable. Eyes—exciting and dangerous. Figure–very sporty; huge shoulders.*

I barely listened as he talked on, his voice carrying me like a small fragile boat on a swirling torrent of words.

Suddenly, a clap of thunder reverberated through the building as heavy raindrops splattered on the ground. The balloon dancers ran for cover while the band played on defiantly.

On an impulse, I leaned across to this stranger. "Do you want to go to the beach?"

"Sure," he said. "It's perfect beach weather. Why not?"

He took my hand in his and towed me through the crowd to a car as streaks of lightning crisscrossed the sky and warm rain pounded down around us. Our saturated clothes clung to our bodies as we slid into the vehicle.

Five minutes later, we were parked at the beach, watching in awe as the lightning illuminated the surging waves, turning the sea foam momentarily silver before blackness descended once more. I got out of the car and pulled off my clothes.

"Come on, hurry," I called. "Before the rain stops!"

I ran toward the surf, hearing him shout after me. "You sure about this? There's a huge swell running...this is nuts!"

Reluctantly, he stripped and ran down to the breaking waves, wading in beside me. We held hands so tightly, trying to keep our balance in the dark swirling water, each acutely aware of the other, of the voltage between us, and the electrifying situation we were in. A fork of lightning lit up the sea and beach all around us while a deafening crack of thunder exploded right above our heads. He pulled my hand toward him.

"Let's get out of here now. We'll go for a swim another time."

I grinned at him. "Yes, another time. That's a good idea."

Driving back to the party, wrapped up in a big towel, I just knew it was right. I'd felt totally safe at the beach and had a sense deep inside me that I'd now always walk in the company of this big and bewildering Irishman.

I hopped out of his car when we reached my own in the parking lot and clutched my towel around me, desperately hoping this man would want to see me again.

"Well, that was an interesting first date," he said with a mischievous grin. "I can't wait to see what you'll want to do next time."

My heart went skipping down the street.

"What's your name, by the way?" I asked. "I'm Sheila."

"Sheila," he repeated slowly. "It was good to meet you. I'm Robert."

7

*A lovely horse is always
an emotional experience of the kind
that is spoiled by words.*

AUTHOR UNKNOWN

THE INSISTENT HOOTING OF A PYGMY OWL piercing the darkness startled me awake. I inched my way toward the edge of the bed, but Robert's heavy hand, draped over my belly, instinctively tightened its grip, reeling me back in.

"Not yet," he mumbled. "Not yet."

"Shhh," I whispered. "I'll be back later." Using both my hands, I lifted his heavy arm and placed it down slowly on a pillow, then sat up over the side of the bed. As my eyes adjusted to the dark, I looked around the sanctuary of our little home. When we'd started this ten years ago, we'd decided that work stuff was always to be left outside, in the cold.

Robert had converted an old donkey stable on a little hill into our cozy house, with an orange orchard on one side and the pastures on the other. During the day, if I looked through the French window frame beside the bed, I'd see a live painting of the horses grazing in an open field. The bed, which was right in the middle of the room, was big enough for four. The walls were deliberately rough, and in the far corner, a "snug"—smooth and oval like the inside of an egg—had been excavated into the wide outer wall, and on its floor was an oversized sheepskin. The second bedroom sat empty. Expectant...

I crept out of the bedroom and dressed in front of the warm fireplace. The three dogs sprawled across the floor were out for the count. One of them gave me the feeblest tail wag I'd ever seen.

Outside, in a beautiful play of light, a pink hue magically haloed the mountain top. My boots crunched dark footprints into the freshly frosted track while each breath took form as a thick white cloud that clung to my face. I walked by Robert's beloved banana trees—they looked barely alive—and went straight into the main stable block to check on Íntima. A soft whicker greeted me.

Her dark shape was nestled into a deep straw bed. Murmuring softly, I crept into the stall and curled up between her front and back legs, and laid my head on her belly. Íntima nuzzled my hair, then rested her own head in the straw, instilling a warm glow inside me. *Such a privilege.*

Robert and I had spent months all those years back, planning the layout of the stables. A "horse spiritualist" had helped us with the optimal orientation for the stable block. U-shaped, it could stable twenty-four horses. The bays, or holding areas, where the horses were tied up to be fed and prepared for the guests to ride, were separated by purpose-made metal dividers. We both wanted an open-plan design, allowing the horses to see each other, while also giving the staff easy access to each individual stall. At the front of the divider and in line with the horse's head, two metal rings had been soldered. A rope passed through these rings and attached to the horse's halter on each side. The rope had a clip on one end, and the other end was fed through a solid wooden ball, slightly bigger than a tennis ball. As the horses moved their heads up and down, the wooden balls kept the tension on the rope, preventing the horses from getting their legs tangled in the rope.

In the middle of the U-shaped building was the tack and feed room. A big hay barn was built on the floor above this structure, with storage space for three thousand bales.

For some weird reason, although I didn't mind our house being messy, I felt the tack room had to be immaculate. Rows of gleaming bridles, all individually labeled with names, hung on one wall, while polished saddles took up the entirety of the opposite wall. I loved some of the names: *Menina, Quo Vadis, Damastor, Dominó.*

Robert had been in his element when planning the layout of the fields. The four big fields fanned out from the central stable block, which made caring for the horses as labor-efficient as possible. Each field had a large water trough in the shade, and at their farthest end stood two big hay feeders that were always full. The majestic cork oaks in every field were protected from the horse gnawing by a low wooden railing around them. With a touch of genius, Robert had also added small triangular frames, made of eucalyptus poles, at the corner of every field. Measuring five meters per side, they prevented a horse from ever being cornered by another and hurt.

MC and Bela came down to the stable half an hour later to find Íntima and me curled up, still fast asleep, though the clanging of the horses' breakfast being dished out from the wheelbarrow woke us both. Moments later, all the horses came thundering in from the fields, straight to their own spots, and thrust their muzzles into their morning meal. MC and Bela then clipped the ropes on to their halters.

I stepped out of the stall, picking bits of straw from my hair.

"Good morning, guys. How's everything today?"

Bela took a step back. "Sheila, how's your head?" she asked, looking at me, wide-eyed. "Shouldn't you be in bed?"

"Ah, no," I said. "It's not sore. Looks worse than it is." I brought my hand up to the bandaged gash on my head and massaged it gently. "Don't worry about it. How are all the horses?"

MC narrowed her eyes. "Well," she said a little circumspectly, "Mistral seems to be fit, no sign of lameness, and all the others are happy. Bel and I are just doing the rounds... Anything special you need today?"

"Don't think so," I said. "Everything looks great. If you could oil everyone's hooves and trot Mistral out, that'd be great."

MC nodded with her arms crossed, still keeping up her slit-eyed thing. "Does Robert know you're in the yard?"

"No. And he won't either," I said definitively. "I'll take Íntima for a walk now and check her stitches. Relax. Big day tomorrow."

I could feel their stares stabbing me in the back while I led Íntima down the driveway. The pale winter sun had dragged itself up from behind the mountain; the air was crisp and cold. The horse rubbed her velvety muzzle on my shoulder, her thick gray lashes and chin whiskers beaded with cold dew.

Behind us, a few slinking dog-like shapes appeared. As we walked by the overgrown riverbed, Íntima shied, wide-eyed, and leaped sideways. I listened: muffled grunting, snuffling, and trampling sounds rose from the dark river valley. Wild boar. *I should have guessed.* Every single one of the horses was terrified of them.

I placed a calming hand on Íntima's neck and let her tune in to the steady beat of my untroubled heart. I explained in a quiet voice that the wild boar would not attack, however much her instinct told her to run. I would protect her. And she calmed. This was the magic of the peerless bond between horse and human.

The sun rose higher. In the distance, a long snake-like cloud sat low, mirroring the river as it flowed into the sea. A sure sign of good weather. I walked faster until Íntima was nearly trotting, her stitches still intact. Two kilometers later, we entered the property through the gate on the north side. I stopped, stood still, and closed my eyes, allowing that feeling of absolute peace and oneness wash over me. But there was something almost imperceptible missing.

We'd achieved so much over the last five years, but I couldn't get Robert to sit still for a single moment. I felt like an incomplete circle that needed filling in. Literally. Yes, we were busy, but surely, this was the time, the window. What was Robert afraid of? That our lives would be changed forever? Maybe that I wasn't competent enough? Or that maybe the horses would always have priority? In my heart of hearts, I'd wondered about that myself.

Back at the yard, Fátima had arrived with Leonel, the smiliest and possibly most benevolent person I'd ever met. All four staff were now grooming the horses and oiling their hooves.

"*Bom dia.* How's the head?" said Leonel. "We have two loose shoes. Better get the blacksmith to check them out."

"Thanks, Leonel, will do," I replied. "Bela, would you please hose Íntima's leg down again for a good five minutes?"

I went around to each horse for a closer inspection. Speaking to them continuously in a low sing-song voice, I first checked that their eyes and nostrils were clear. Then I ran my hands along their backs, feeling for any knots or bumps. With the halter in both hands, I then turned the horse's head all the way round to the left, and then to the right, until touching the flank on either side. Any resistance could be a sign of pain.

Legs next. I felt my way carefully down each one, my hands searching for any sign of heat or unusual swelling. Then I pressed down on the horse's spine, starting at the withers, the base of the neck, all the way down to the base of the tail, kneading the tail vertebrae with both hands as I worked my way to the very end of the dock. Finally, I wrapped each long tail around both hands and leaned backward with my full body weight. The horses automatically stretched themselves forward, giving their backs a good stretch.

I loved the way that most of the horses' tails swept the ground. Why would anyone want to cut or trim them? In the winter, the horses tucked them in between their buttocks, keeping the hairless bit between their legs warm. And in the summer, they whipped and swished them into the best fly swats. From the position of the tail, you could usually tell what mood they were in. When tucked in and flattened, you knew the horse was afraid and could act violently. When up, lifted over the back, the horse was highly excited and usually hard to control or reason with. A switching tail meant the horse was either very irritated, in pain, or reacting negatively to the rider.

Boémio was the last horse for me to check. As he looked at me full on, memories of his past engulfed me. Five years before, my good friend, Raina, had begged me to give Boémio a home. She'd described him as being emotionally traumatized. He'd suffered terrible abuse in the bullring. She said he deserved a second chance and she would entrust him to no one else but me.

From the minute I saw him being unloaded from the opened truck, my heart melted. He showed none of the usual emotions—joy, expectancy, excitement, fear—just dread. He knew what resistance meant. Pain and punishment.

Back then, he had been a cold white sculpture. I had inspected him all over when he arrived. Unforgiving spurs had etched a myriad of long black lines into his flanks. Thick skin on his withers showed where ill-fitting saddles had rubbed him raw. But it had been when I examined his head that my eyes had filled with burning tears. His poll, the sensitive area immediately behind the ears, had been totally hairless, gouged with thick ugly scars. The front of his face had been a mutilated tic-tac-toe board—he'd been ridden with a *serreta*, a metal contraption with a serrated edge, designed to "control unruly horses." When I had gently slipped two fingers into the side of his mouth, he'd instinctively opened it, pushing out his tongue. I'd gasped. It was shaped like an hourglass. I'd only ever heard about this kind of thing. The horse had been ridden with a barbed wire in his mouth, which had nearly severed his tongue.

I smiled now as he rubbed his forehead vigorously up and down my back. He had come such a long way.

As soon as the horses had all been checked and cleaned, they were let out again into their respective fields, and I wandered up to the clubhouse for a quick coffee with Fátima. I sat down at a table on the terrace as the sun's heat made wisps of curling white steam rise up from the pool and the flat-leaved cactus plants.

After a few minutes, Fátima arrived with two steaming mugs of freshly brewed coffee, her small wiry frame, unruly dark hair, and square capable hands oddly incongruous with her gentle demeanor.

"At least you can tell *me*," she said, leaning in confidingly. "How are you feeling?"

"Fine," I said.

"Will you be up to riding tomorrow?"

I felt my head gingerly. It was still very sore.

"I hope so. I don't think Bela will be up to it on the first day. MC is fine. Even if I only do half the ride and then swap. We'll see. Don't say anything to Robert."

She nodded while frowning. She knew exactly how protective Robert was of me.

"Okay," she said half-heartedly. "Just don't take any of your usual crazy risks. Please!"

"I'll try not to, really," I said. "Look, I think something's up with Bela. Could you keep an eye on her? I need her to function this week."

Fátima emptied her lungs impatiently. "What's wrong with her now?" There was little sympathy in her tone.

"Not sure yet. I just feel she's not quite with it somehow—who knows what it is? Anyway, are you all set for tomorrow night?"

"Yeah," she said, letting her sangfroid settle back in. "I'm looking forward to doing something really special."

I nodded discreetly at Fátima as the two girls walked up in our direction. "I'll catch you all later," I said. "I'm going to have a wee lie-down."

It was nearly ten by the time I stole back into bed. I thought for a moment I'd get away with it and pulled the covers over my head.

"You didn't say you'd be this long. That was much, much later," said Robert sleepily. "Come here, you."

That night, Robert called a last-minute staff meeting for all six of us in the clubhouse. He wanted everything to be perfect for the week ahead. The clubhouse looked very inviting. The cozy couches in the corners, covered in cushions and throws, all earthy browns and beiges, blended perfectly with the clay walls, under the traditional layer of bamboo canes lining the ceiling.

Leading off from the main area was the industrial kitchen we'd added on to the original structure where Fátima could prepare meals for up to forty guests. Although it was already dark, I saw the pool lights were on and their blue light shone round the landscaped gardens. The wood-burning stove in the corner roared and sizzled, fanning the smell of eucalyptus oil into the room. For a second, it all came back to me...

> *I had noticed that all the horses were on high alert when I gave them their evening feed. Looking round constantly, they'd flared their nostrils and curled their upper lips, trying to capture the scent. Darkness had fallen so we couldn't see the smoke. The local radio warned of a huge wildfire approaching from the south—with a four-kilometer-wide front. All local fire brigades and firefighters had been*

summoned. Robert had gone through the emergency plan with us.

"If the wind changes to an easterly, the fire will come down the mountain straight toward us," he'd said. "It will not stop. All the horses must be brought in and kept calm. If we have to, we'll lead them all in small groups across the main road and toward the river. They should be safe in the middle of the paddy fields."

The wind had stayed steady. We'd watched helplessly as the angry red flames raced and cracked their way across the mountains. Firefighting helicopters and planes loaded with water crisscrossed the sky, dumping their loads on the raging front. Robert had worked with the firemen all night, beating out flames and showing them the best access routes through the mountains.

We were spared that night, but I'll never forget the way I felt when I watched Robert leave to battle the fire. I knew then I never wanted to feel that scared of losing him again...

The six of us sat around the open fire, sipping Fátima's pumpkin soup, which, with a sprinkle of fresh mint on top, was mouth-wateringly good.

"I'm all set food-wise for tomorrow," said Fátima. "It'll be a great *Ano Novo*. I know it."

"Yeah, and I'm all set drink-wise," said Robert. "Hopefully, fifty-odd bottles of champagne will do the trick." He turned to Fátima. "Are you going to tell us what we're eating?"

"Ah, no," she said, grinning, "only that the main dish will be one of our boar friends from the valley."

Leonel sat in the corner chair, arms crossed behind his head and legs stretched out in front. His perma-smile and ability to deal with Robert's eccentricities and workload made him irreplaceable. Only the week before, while on his way to work, he'd misjudged a sharp corner and turned his truck over, sending his false teeth flying out the window and onto the road. He'd simply got out, picked up his teeth, and with the help of some passers-by, straightened up his truck again. He was still on time for work.

Bela was hugging her legs in toward her chest, looking off at some distant point on the floor. I remembered that this was going to be her first experience with such a large group of riders with huge expectations. I hoped she'd be up to it.

MC was sprawled across the couch, looking into the blazing fire, absorbing it all. She turned her head to me and smiled. She was good.

"Goodnight, guys," I said. "Try and get a good night's sleep. See you in the morning."

Robert stood up first and led me outside.

"Come here, chicken," he murmured. "Just sit down with me for a bit."

I sat on the ground in front of him and felt his warm arms wrap around me. It was the best feeling in the world. I knew that, somehow, he'd make everything all right.

8

*My celebration is incomplete without yours.
It's sweeter when we share the podium
than when I stand there alone.*

ABIODUN FIJABI

W E'D BEEN TRAVELING FOR OVER A WEEK, and I still didn't know why he'd brought me along. Apparently, it was all to become clear the day we visited the Uffizi Gallery in Florence. Starting in Lisbon, we'd first visited Vienna, where I'd been lavishly treated to the best *Wiener Schnitzels* and *Apfelstrudel* in town, and then completely spoiled with the most luxurious hotel. To top that, I was brought to the private training sessions of the magnificent Lipizzaner stallions of the famed Spanish Riding School, and even to visit the horses' stables. A privilege at only twenty years old.

From Vienna, we flew to Venice, Italy's magical floating city. Again, I was treated like a princess, wined and dined as I learned about *La Serenissima's* past and origins. The city was constructed in the year 402, and rests on one hundred and eighteen islands, separated by one hundred and fifty canals. There were no cars in Venice, and I had to laugh when I witnessed a high-speed chase through the waterways: a getaway boat followed by a siren-blaring police speedboat—007, eat your heart out.

The buildings, such as Saint Mark's Basilica, seem to be sculpted in intricate lace, and the four hundred bridges that linked the city to itself were carved out of stone, iron, and wood, each more beautiful than the next. Although some of the canals were deeper, they only averaged about two meters to bottom, which eased the job of the gondoliers. Everything felt fluid. I was floating through time and history with no connection or affinity to the present.

Despite the fact that I was deeply aware of the privilege of being treated to the magic of the trip, I grew increasingly uneasy about the purpose of our shared adventure. After all, I didn't know him very well, and although I hadn't been put into any compromising situations, there was a palpable feeling of fervid anticipation about him as we made our way to Florence.

I had never been there before, but as soon as we arrived in the city, I knew that, somehow, *I had*. It felt like coming home—the smell of leather mixed with incense and fish and sulphur, the street names, the food. I knew my way around without having to ask anyone.

At breakfast our second day, he said, "Wear your nicest, most favorite clothes today. Everything will become clear."

He and I headed for the Uffizi Gallery. We wound our way through the twisted streets, and I took the lead toward the *Palazzo Vecchio* with its unforgettable arched bridges, pressing on toward our destination.

However, as soon as we entered the gallery, I lost sight of him. *Maybe he's met a friend,* I thought, *or mingled into one of the groups of tourists.* I continued on from room to room, marveling at the exquisite exhibits and wondering, *What am I really doing here?* Then suddenly, my stomach turned upside down. I staggered over to the bench in the middle of the room and clasped its edges while bending forward as I clutched my heaving belly. Sweat prickled my brow and arms. I kept my head down until my breathing evened out and the burst of nausea passed.

The room was silent. All the tourists had left. I stood up and there it was—Botticelli's *Primavera*. Sensual and full of springtime joy. Breathtaking.

"How are you feeling?" I heard his voice behind me as his warm hand draped over my shoulder.

"Upside down and inside out. I don't know what's wrong with me. Maybe I've eaten something funny. Look—I can't stop shaking."

"I knew it," he said, his eyes alive with excitement. "Come on, I'll explain everything."

He took my hand and led me outside. We stopped for a moment in the *Piazza Degli Uffizi*, savoring the cool March air. It was only about ten degrees Celsius.

"There's a perfect café for us just round the corner," he said, still not letting go of my hand. The sky's cerulean canvas backdropped all the buildings, outlining them in all their magnificence. Flights of snowy-white doves cooed and strutted around in their persistent fashion as they clustered around people sitting on the square's benches.

We sat at a table at the very back of the café and waited until the waiter brought our order. He said nothing for a while, just sat there, his big shape spilling over the small chair.

"Do you remember, the first time we met about three years ago?" he said gently. "I told you then that you were the one I'd been looking for all this time. I was right."

I remembered him bringing some fabulous purebred Lusitanos down from Lisbon for a prospective client. I remembered a group of us going out for dinner. And I did remember him saying that, but at the time, I hadn't thought anything of it.

He leaned toward me now, lassoing me in with his energy.

"That painting, *Primavera*, was painted by Sandro Botticelli between 1470 and 1480. I know they say it was to decorate the bedroom of a Medici bride, but that's not true."

"What do you mean?" I asked. His hands gripped the table edge now, as if in an effort to stay calm.

"I know that I lived here at that time. And so did you." He paused, as if testing my response. I met his eyes fully. "We were lovers and cousins," he went on, "which was not well accepted, but at any rate, that painting is a portrait of *you*. You were a princess then. You loved horses and you had that beautiful black stallion that you'd ride through the streets of Florence. Do you remember meeting me down by the river?"

I said nothing, but continued to meet his intense gaze.

"I've spent years tracing my family tree and it all makes sense," he said. "Everything I love, all my interests, they've been handed down to me through generations. It has to be the same for you."

"No...yes....I don't know," I stammered, unsure, but entranced by his conviction. "All I can tell you is that Florence and everything about it feels like home. And also, I feel that I've known you forever..."

"But your feelings for me are different now," he said, interrupting me, a sad expression now crossing his face. "It's a shame. In this time, we are no longer lovers. Just platonic. But that's okay. At least I've found you again, and I feel at peace. Like me, you have dedicated your life to horses. They're not our whole lives, but they make our lives whole. It's the same for you, isn't it?"

I just smiled at him, basking in his love, energy, and grace. He was one of the greatest architects in Portugal, and he was a founding member of the Portuguese Association for Purebred Lusitanos, and a highly successful breeder. I pinched myself. *How can this be happening to me?*

Our connection going forward was a lifelong one, living, as we could, for the special, magical moments that cannot be put into words.

I was lucky to have been his friend.

9

"An emblematic bird of passage..."

PATRICK LEIGH FERMOR

ECEMBER THIRTY-FIRST, 1999.

Just before dawn I gave up trying to sleep and padded down to the stable. On autopilot, I dished out horse feed from the wheelbarrow. Then, zombie-like, I began muttering to myself while adding in all the supplements.

"A pinch of garlic powder and vitamin C for winter colds... a spoonful of sunflower oil for shiny coats...a pinch of salt for dehydration...and a small black beer for the newbies, get them up to scratch." *Hmm. Why did I tell the girls to sleep in again?*

As the twenty-four horses ate their breakfast, I wandered over to the barn noticeboard where we posted communications to each other. A note from MC: *Qomplexo has a weeping left eye—could you check it, please?*

In a small, disinfected bowl, I mixed a spoonful of powdered cuttlefish bone with distilled water. Then, using a clean bird's tail feather, I gently pulled out the horse's lower eyelid and brushed the salty mixture into his eye. He didn't move. It was as if he sensed that this old wives' remedy would help him.

An hour later, I turned all the horses out and started for the clubhouse. My head was beginning to throb. I wondered vaguely how I was going to get through the day. The dawn of a new millennium. It was always going to be a long one.

I spotted Fátima walking toward me armed with a steaming cup of coffee.

"Here you go," she said, handing it over. "You look a bit better. How are you feeling?" Her warm smile washed over me, radiating motherly concern. I gave her a one-armed hug.

"Much better, thanks, Fátima. Please don't worry. How are the girls today?"

"I think you're right. There's something up with Bela," she said, more serious now. "Something more than her 'usual,'" she added a little dismissively. *No love lost there.*

I went into the clubhouse and found MC and Bela sitting close together at the table in the far corner of the room, their cereal, toast, and tea laid out around them, untouched. Bela's face was blotchy, her eyes were red, and she kept wiping her nose on the sleeves of her fleece.

"Hey, what's wrong?" I said, sitting down beside her, taking both of her hands in mine. They were ice cold. She squeezed her lips into a thin white line, shook her head and shut her eyes.

MC's eyebrows and shoulders rose in unison. "She says she's okay... doesn't want to talk about it now."

Bela's tears trickled down her chin. I gently curled her hair back behind her ear.

"It's okay, Bela," I said softly. "Everything's going to be fine. Shall we just get through the week, then talk about it?"

Bela nodded quickly.

"Of course, we can talk about it now if you want..."

She shook her head just as quick.

"Okay...I'm always here if you change your mind," I said gently. Then work mode kicked in. Time to get everyone organized for the day. In a firmer voice, I continued. "Now, the guests will be here around one. Please make sure you have an early lunch. Get the horses in, fed, groomed, and tacked up. I've left the group lists on the noticeboard."

I turned to MC, who was focused and ready. "MC, you'll be on Pash with the slower group. I'll ride Menina with the other group. Bela, you'll be helping Robert do the backup, and then getting set up back here. Okay?"

She nodded, her tears dried up.

"Be really positive. Remember: nothing is ever too much trouble for the guests. I know you'll both do a great job. I'll have a nap now and then come down to help you. Any questions?"

MC was doing her squinty-eyed thing again.

"How's your head?" she said.

"Getting better."

"Shouldn't you be on an easier horse? Riding Menina is like riding a bomb with a lit fuse...and no brakes."

"I know, I know. I'll have a chat with her before we start. I'll ask her very nicely to look after me."

Who am I kidding? But who else can I trust to ride her?

Menina, Mini, Little Girl, had stolen my heart from the moment I laid eyes on her, nearly four years ago. I'd heard of a horse through the grapevine, and asked Robert to come with me on the two-hour trip to the heartland of the *Alentejo* to check her out.

The rare moments Robert and I had together were precious. I loved having him all to myself and not having to share him with endless guests, staff, dogs, horses, or problems. As we drove—just the two of us—I burrowed my left hand under his right thigh. The wind rushed by, tangling my hair. I held it down with my free hand and watched the fleeting countryside. I felt a rush of emotion as the undulating plains and open spaces beckoned and claimed my soul, giving me a feeling of infinity and freedom I only ever felt here. *Does he feel it too?* Although he'd lived here for nearly nine years now, I always felt a part of him was still somewhere else.

He glanced at me and reached over to caress my cheek.

"You love it here, don't you? It's wild and beautiful. Just like you."

That telepathy again. I knew it was way different for him. Different backgrounds. Different expectations. The wide-open spaces invited soul searching of the kind that didn't suit everyone. *Is he ready for this? Is he able to do it? Is he able to do it for me?*

A few minutes later, we were driving by dark green paddy fields. Robert strained his head around, nearly driving off the road.

"Look out for any black storks, will you? I brought the camera along. They're so well camouflaged, they're really difficult to see. They love rooting around in the paddy fields."

"Sure," I said. He was fully alive now with his antenna up for the storks. "Did you know the *Alentejo* is the biggest rice producer in Portugal?"

He barely shook his head.

"It exports to loads of countries, including the UK." He wasn't really listening. "You know you can grow rice in salt water? Fascinating, huh?"

"Yeah, yeah," he said distractedly, still searching for storks. "Look! On the left, I think I saw one."

He swerved and braked suddenly, and pulled onto the side of the road. We quietly slipped out of the car and crouched down behind a bush. A pair of black storks were busy feeding only a few meters away. Robert soundlessly focused the camera and started shooting. I smiled. He was in his element.

From this distance, it was easy to differentiate these birds from the common white storks. Their beautifully black heads, wings, tails, and long necks shimmered with an eye-catching purple and green gloss. And the contrast between the white of their bellies and under-tails and the bright scarlet of their beaks and elongated legs was dazzling.

Ten minutes later, I prodded Robert.

"Come on. Horse is waiting," I whispered.

We crept back to the car and left the storks to their paddy field. Very soon, we were driving by the famous "Stork Motel," a massively overcrowded tree, tilting toward the road.

"Would you check that out, Sheila? It looks like a madhouse!"

I looked up. The gigantic tree was weighed down by stork nests balanced on its outstretched branches. I counted at least twenty of the huge stick structures, each measuring well over a meter across. In every single one stood a one-legged, contemplative stork, guarding its family home.

I grinned like a child.

"Hey, look!" I announced. "'City storks,' over on the aqueduct. The turn to the farm must be just around the corner, like the guy said."

As Robert turned off the road onto the worn track, I wondered if today was a good time to talk about it. About my incomplete circle. The timing had to be just right.

"Robert, we need to talk," I said intimately.

The Jeep immediately accelerated on the sandy forest trail, the back end spinning out slightly as we swung round the trees. A dark shadow crossed Robert's face. The last time I'd mentioned "The Talk," he'd walked out of the house, slamming the door behind him, and he hadn't come back till much later that night.

Now in the car, we sped through an endless forest of huge cork oaks. Small droves of Alentejo black pigs ignored us, far too busy stuffing themselves with acorns to be bothered by a speeding vehicle. No wonder they were prized for their succulent meat and *presunto*.

"Where the hell is this place?" said Robert five minutes later. "Sure we're going the right way?" His voice was clipped and edgy.

My heart quickened. This was definitely not the right time.

10

*For one to fly, one needs only
to take the reins.*

MELISSA JAMES

THERE ARE DAYS IN OUR LIVES that feel beyond any question predestined. Who knows? Maybe all of them are, and the tedium and boredom are as locked in place as the significant meetings and milestones. Or perhaps we're just rafts of chance on endless oceans of chaos. Whatever the case, when you connect with another being on a soul level, the experience is unforgettable.

It was a dry and dusty morning in June the day I met Menina. Robert and I had driven two hours to get to what we'd understood to be a "hillside farm." Visions of lush and verdant fields with rolling hills and weathervanes had filled my mind on the journey. What we encountered were details of quite another picture, more in keeping with a bad dream than a fantasy.

"That couldn't be it, could it?" I said a little doubtfully, catching sight of a dilapidated shack through the thinning trees.

"Let's have a look," said Robert, turning up a narrow dirt track. He stopped the car just inside an open gate and tightened his lip. His glance at me said only one thing: *Wrong place.*

Scrawny chickens pecked and scraped at the parched soil while two scarred and savage yard dogs barked ferociously at us, their short metal chains attached to a rusty oil drum, cutting into their necks. The shack was a crumbling whitewashed cottage with traditional blue bars painted around its windows, and three clear plastic bags filled with water hanging in the doorway.

"Let's just go, Sheila," said Robert, slipping the car into reverse. "This can't be the right place."

"Wait a minute," I said, "I think I heard something."

Before he could object, I was out of the Jeep and approaching the little house. I passed a well with an old double laundry sink beside it, half-filled with steeping clothes, next to a worn-out scrubbing board. A wire washing line hung with an assortment of multicolored plastic bags, neatly pegged up to dry. On a low wall by the front door was a red plastic basin full of washed dishes, carefully covered by a gingham cloth. I noted no telephone or electricity wires overhead. It was clear this house had no power or running water.

I stopped by the three hanging water bags and looked beyond them to the unlatched door. I nearly gagged at the smell of spoiled cabbage while noticing two copper coins lying at the bottom of each water bag—designed, perhaps, to keep more than the flies out.

I reached past the bags and knocked twice on the door.

"Who's there?" It was grumbled rather than asked.

"*Senhor Maurício*, I've come about the horse. I asked your son-in-law to pass on the message..."

There was no doubt I'd been heard, but nobody came to the door. I waited a couple of minutes, studying the cracks in the terracotta tiles under the door. "*Senhor Maurício?*"

A grunt, then nothing. I breathed out and considered the rest of the yard. Past the barking dogs was an old barn where swallows flew in and out.

The door creaked open behind me. I turned around to see, of all things, a stork emerge from behind it. The bird stopped to look me up and down and then proceeded to march over to the car to check on Robert.

Then a small wiry old man appeared and squinted at me from behind the water bags. He wore a broken straw hat and a blue cotton shirt buttoned up to the collar, tucked into gray trousers, which were held together by patches and held up by a frayed leather belt. He had a round swarthy head, stubble on his chin, and dark bags under his eyes. His right hand rested on a crooked wooden staff.

He shook his head regretfully while scratching his Adam's apple, choosing to fix his gaze around my feet.

"A woman," he said derisively, shaking his head again. "I was expecting a man." His breath smelt of decaying teeth.

"Yes, Senhor Maurício," I said, looking directly at him. "I'm a woman."

He raised his head and looked at me with a mirthless glint in his brown eyes, giving a definitive wave of his hand. "She is a man's horse."

"Very well." I shrugged. "Can I see the horse now?"

His eyes sank back down to my feet.

Robert was out of the Jeep by now, rubbing the stork on the nape of its neck. The bird had closed its eyes and was swaying slightly from side to side.

"Robert," I called back to him, "I could do with a little help here."

"You're doing grand," he said, engrossed in communing with the bird. "Me and old Beaky here are just getting to know each other."

"Fine," I said, a little exasperated. "Thanks a lot."

Senhor Maurício grunted at me, "Stay there and wait, woman." He shuffled across the yard, muttering obscenities, as the dogs cowered into their tin shelters at the sight of him only to leap back out afterward, straining at their chains, barking as vociferously as before.

Out of the corner of my eye, I noticed three huge geese waddling purposefully in my direction from the opposite end of the house. I knew how aggressive and protective they could be.

"Rob!" I cried. "Help!"

Before I could even register if Robert had heard me, Senhor Maurício appeared round the corner leading the horse I had come to see.

Everything slowed and shut down around me: the barking of the dogs, the honking of the geese, Robert, the stork, even Senhor Maurício—they all went out of focus. I breathed in sharply and felt my heart accelerate. Nothing could have prepared me for this.

There she was: a dark mahogany bay with black points extending down her legs, black tail and mane. She stood completely still, except her ears, which flickered as she snorted gently, taking in my unfamiliar scent. Dark intelligent eyes set far apart scrutinized me from head to toe. *She is reading my soul.* Her powerful neck curved majestically and was held high. I took in her perfect proportions, her imposing presence, while she held me in a direct gaze.

An overwhelming sense of oneness with this proud, magnificent animal washed over me as I took a step toward her and gently cupped my hand on her neck. Instantly, an electric surge coursed through my body. The horse lifted her front leg.

This was the moment: *I was being tested.*

I brought my breathing and racing heart under control and felt the undeniable connection between us. She kept her leg suspended for a long minute before banging it down hard on the dry earth, creating a little cloud of dust, which rose up and dispersed across my leg. Her dark muzzle jerked so close to me that when she snorted, her hot breath diffused over my face.

Come on, she seemed to be saying impatiently. *You and I know each other. We're the same.*

Powerless to move, I felt the horse inch closer. She stretched her neck forward. Thick velvet lips gently touched their way over my head, along my hair, and around my face. When she drew back, we caught each other's gaze and held it. *We are going to be friends.*

When I looked back at Senhor Maurício beside me, he was staring at me with an expression I hadn't seen in him before. Bewilderment, maybe. He turned around to Robert.

"Well, what do you think?"

"Let's go and talk business, Senhor Maurício," said Robert. "I think we'll leave the two women to it."

Driving home afterward, I sat in silence, dreamily looking out the windshield, somehow altered from meeting Menina. A number of times, Robert looked like he was going to say something but stopped himself. He kept lifting one hand in the air, glancing at me sideways, then exhaling and looking off into the distance through his side window. Then he suddenly pulled off the road and stopped the car. He turned to me with an expression of a man lost at sea.

"Will you please explain to me what the hell happened back there? It was something else!"

His eyes had turned to the deepest, darkest blue. *Come on,* he seemed to be saying impatiently. *You and I know each other. We're the same.*

I just shook my head slowly, rubbing my forehead with both my hands. My voice, barely a whisper.

"I haven't got a clue."

11

*What matters most
are the simple pleasures so abundant
that we can all enjoy them.*

ANTOINE DE SAINT-EXUPÉRY

WHILE THE DAWN OF A NEW DECADE is an exciting threshold to cross, the beginning of a new century is a much bigger deal. But the event of a new *millennium*? Dealing with my own excitement as we approached this significant milestone was fine; it was the expectations of twenty visiting riders and the pressure of having to deliver an unforgettable blast into this much-anticipated time period that troubled me. My stomach always clamped at the prospect of a new group of riders, and now, as I curled up in my bedroom snug, I had a throbbing headache to deal with on top of it. I sat still and focused—on my breathing...on getting my heart rate as low as possible...on riding the route that reeled out in my mind.

And on Menina.

She was something else. What had started out as a battle of wills only four short years ago had grown into a unique and special partnership. This intelligent horse had shown me that my patience and experience were no match for her power and integrity. After a year had passed, the penny finally dropped that she couldn't be forced to do anything against her will, so I opted for a less-is-more style of riding.

Menina taught me to sit as quietly as possible and not interfere with her innate perfect balance. Gradually, I started realizing I could affect her mood and focus by breathing slowly and deeply from my stomach. Like a vine stretching upward to the sun, this feeling grew organically into thought transmission, from my mind to hers, which she captured and reacted effortlessly to. Leg, hand, and weight aids—the "normal" means of influencing a horse—were unnecessary as riding became an encounter of body and mind controlled by the breath. Not only did this discovery change my perception of horses and people, it brought my riding to a whole new level. Being "plugged into" the horse's mind was akin to an out-of-body experience. And Menina was the one to whom I owed this new way of seeing.

I smiled to myself. Robert wasn't half bad at it either. I ached for him to be with me to bandage my head, give me one of his huge bear hugs, and tell me that it was all going to be okay.

HALF AN HOUR LATER, dressed to ride, I walked down to the stable area to help the girls get the horses ready. But everything was already done. All twenty-two horses were cleaned, tacked up, and looking very relaxed. With a little *wicker,* Menina called me over—she didn't tolerate me talking to any other horse first.

I stood in front of her, wrapped my arms around her neck ,and burrowed my face into her warm sweet smell. "Look after me today, Menina. I'm going to need your help," I whispered.

I went round to all the other horses, speaking to each one while handing them a bit of chopped-up carrot. Behind me, MC and Bela were giving a last sweep before the riders showed up.

"Thanks so much, guys. You did a great job. Everything looks perfect. Did you remember to put water bottles and an apple in everyone's saddle bag? And a first-aid kit in mine and MC's?"

"Yeah, all done," said Bela. "Uh-oh...here they come. Showtime!"

I took a deep breath and forced myself into "client mode" while excited visitors quickly surrounded me, all clamoring for attention. As the air shrank around me, I could sense the horses eyeing up their new riders. Did they feel as nervous as I did?

From the corner of my eye, I spotted Tania gushing up to Robert, all blondness and red lipstick, armed to seduce. MC and Bela desperately bit their lips and looked in the other direction. I turned away from Robert.

Is he actually enjoying this?

I thought about making Tania ride Menina.

Our old friend, Jean, sidled up beside me, as perfectly presented as ever. "Sheila, dear, please tell me I'm seeing the new millennium in on my Bobby Darling."

"Of course, Jean. Look, she's right there waiting for you."

And so it went on, until practically everyone had the horse of their choice. Then the riders led their horses up to the arena where the staff helped them to mount up, checked their positions, adjusted their stirrup length, and tightened their girths.

MC looked calm and in control as she set off with her group of ten riders—the less experienced of the group. I'd made damn sure it included the terrible Tania. As I followed with my group ten minutes later, Robert walked alongside me, as was his way, his hand on my thigh.

"Sheila, listen—will you please take your time with the ride? No more accidents, especially not today."

I brushed his hand off.

"No, *you* listen. What's with *that woman*? The two of you?"

He was jogging now to keep up with me.

"Do you think I enjoy it? She thinks I'm her boy toy, for Christ's sake."

"It's not amusing," I said, shaking my head.

"Ah, give over, will you? It's just part of the job and you know it."

I looked down at him. Was he trying to be funny?

"Look," he said, "it's four o'clock now. Aim to be back at seven-thirty. That should give us plenty of time to set everything up here."

He put his hand back on my thigh. I ignored it.

"Won't it be dark by then?" I said, my mind back on logistics.

"No. Remember, we ordered the full moon for tonight especially? It should rise behind the mountain around a quarter past six." He squeezed my thigh gently. "You'll be okay," he said, and dropped back, talking to each rider that followed me as they passed him. "Looking lovely, Jean. First prize for turnout! John, have a good one. Look after Max for me. Stella, on the lovely Cladda...enjoy! Francesco, looking great. See you later."

God, the Irish really do have the gift of the gab.

I laid my hand gently on Mini's neck and dropped the reins. The horse responded by lowering her head, snorting, and relaxing into a carefree walk. After a couple of minutes, I doubled back along the line of riders to check them all. Robert's banter had eased everyone's nerves. I overheard John, a tall Englishman with impeccable manners and probably our most nervous rider, whispering to Max as he leaned forward and stroked the gelding's ears: "You'll look after me on the long gallop, won't you, Max?"

Once back in front, I gathered up my reins and raised my hand, signaling to start trotting. The track wound its way through the eucalyptus forest, giving us all the chance to inhale its aromatic smell. The long line of horses and riders settled in. A few minutes later, I spotted the river ahead, and, putting my hand up, slowed the group down to a walk. Mini tensed her back slightly. She snorted. I looked more closely at the river. With the recent rains it had swollen so that it was at least ten meters wide. The water roared as it rushed by, crashing over rolling rocks, creating mini rainbows in the foam and spray.

I looked down at the fresh hoofmarks. MC's group had turned left upstream, where there was a bridge. *Probably a good idea. What would Robert do if he was here in the saddle? He'd risk it, of course.*

"Just let me check how deep it is," I said to the group. "Wait here."

Taking a deep breath, I turned Menina into the turbulence. I pointed her head toward the far bank, gently urging her on. She lifted each front leg high in the air before stretching it forward to find a safe footing. I concentrated on sitting very still. Focusing on the far bank, I breathed deeply as the rumbling water level rose to the top of the horse's legs. I glanced back at the group of white-faced riders. Nobody said a word.

The roar of the water was deafening. Glancing down into the gyrating whirlpools, I felt sick. I looked up and encouraged the horse onward. Moving forward gingerly, Menina felt firm ground and leapt out onto the far bank. I dismounted and did a quick check of the mare's legs. *All clear.* But would everyone else manage this?

"Are you all happy to try that?" I shouted over the rumbling. "If not, we'll go 'round the long way."

They all looked at each other for a brief moment.

"Yes, let's do it!" Stella yelled back. "Can you guide us?"

I smiled. *Oh, God, please get them all through this—no drownings!* I made my voice sound upbeat and positive. "Okay. Just one at a time. Jean, you go first."

Jean was easily the most experienced of the group. I hoped her self-possessed riding style would inspire confidence in the others.

"That's it, nice and steady. Let her find her own way. Take your time. Well done!"

Jean and Bobby Darling splashed through and joined me, Jean somehow still immaculate. *How does she do it?*

"Ooh, that was jolly exciting, Sheila. Didn't my Bobby Darling do well?"

"Brilliant. Well done," I congratulated her, then shouted, "John, you come next with Max!"

The powerful black horse crossed slowly, pausing between each step. John was rigid, staring straight ahead, but when Max heaved himself out of the water, John's face creased into a huge smile. He slid to the ground, reached his arms around the horse's neck, and buried his face in the gelding's mane.

One by one, the others splashed through until only one was left. Francesco, everyone's favorite Italian, looked a little uneasy.

"Hey, I think Morena's feeling a little nervous here on her own!" he shouted in a high-pitched voice. "How do I calm her down?"

The horse had tuned into his anxious energy. She was prancing about, throwing her head in the air.

"Okay, listen," I called. "Keep calm. I want you to breathe nice and deep and evenly. Lower your tone. Point her at the river. Put a hand on her neck. Let her do the rest. She'll carry you across. Relax."

For a second, it looked like it might work as they started toward us, but then Morena crouched down and sprang headlong into the middle of the raging river. She made a huge splash, and all I could see was the horse's black head as fast-flowing water swirled around. Then Morena uttered a piercing neigh as Francesco wrapped his arms tightly around her slippery neck.

"Help! Help me!"

I instantly turned Menina back into the river. She needed no instruction. She bounded up to Francesco and stood downstream of him, her powerful chest facing the tugging current. Morena's head looked close enough, so I leaned over and tried to catch hold of her reins. *Damn!* I missed, then steadied myself. Grabbing a handful of Mini's thick black mane with one hand, I leaned my upper body across the raging river, and stretching down, I was just able to grasp Morena's soaked reins.

"Gotcha! Francesco, hang on. We're okay...nearly there!"

Slowly, I coached and pulled the bedraggled horse and her shaky rider to the safety of the far bank. As we landed, the others broke out into spontaneous applause.

"Well done, Francesco," cried Jean. "What a relief!"

I dismounted, and leaving Mini to graze, went to the sodden Francesco, who was sitting on a log beside his horse, looking terribly defeated.

"Are you okay? Did you get hurt? Let me look at you," I said gently. Putting a hand on his knee, I studied his pale face. His heavy-set eyebrows gave him a comical mien, particularly now, as he was so forlorn. I removed a small sachet from my jacket pocket. "Here, suck this. It's glucose; it'll help. You're just a little shocked. It's totally normal."

"I'm okay," he said. "Really. So sorry about that. I just lost my nerve back there." His voice was apologetic and small. "Is Morena okay?"

I felt down the horse's legs, checking for any obvious damage.

"She seems fine, Francesco. Thank God you're both alright. Let's carry on. We'll get some dry clothes for you at the break."

I walked over to Menina, and with my back turned to the riders, let out a sigh of relief. *Thank you, God. Stupid me. And Menina, you're a star!* I gave her a treat, then slipped a small cube of brown sugar into my own mouth. I could feel the adrenaline wearing off as I shot another quick look at Francesco. It hadn't taken him long to recover. He was chatting to the women in his melodious Italian accent. They all loved him.

The slippery mud-covered track snaked along the river's edge as we continued on. To the left, the hillside rose steeply, completely covered with *medronho* bushes. John rode up beside me.

"Good work back there," he said, smiling. "Your horse knew exactly what to do—I'm impressed." He reached out to stroke Menina's neck but was given an ears-back look of contempt, which made him instantly draw back.

"Sorry, John. She doesn't know you. Don't take it personally. She can be very antisocial," I explained, secretly love-bombing Menina. And then, to divert his focus: "Have you seen these berries before?"

"Arbutus, aren't they?"

"Yeah, they're called *medronho* over here. The berries are used to make a lethal type of schnapps. A handful of them and you'll be on your ear."

He grinned at me like a naughty schoolboy.

As the track began to climb steeply, I stood up out of the saddle and leaned forward, twisting a handful of my mare's mane around my hand. The horse's lower back was free now to help her hind end push. I wondered how Robert was getting on and wished he was with us. My head was killing me.

We'd made it into the middle of a cork forest before the track leveled out, and I called a halt. The red bark of the twisting trees, the white sand, and the snatches of blue sky enveloped us like an ethereal checkered blanket. The riders used the break to make any adjustments needed: sipping water, shortening stirrup length, ensuring their saddle bags were done up tight. I raised my hand to get their attention.

"Is everyone feeling okay?"

Murmurs of affirmation all around.

"You all did brilliantly back there. Way to go. Now, we have our big canter coming up, so can you get into your order as we walk out? I'll trot first, then signal the canter. Any problem at all, let me know. Then, hopefully, Francesco, we can find you some dry clothes. Are you warm enough?"

He nodded and gave me the thumbs up.

For once, everyone was quiet—focused and, I hoped, ready. I led the trot out of the forest, trying to keep a steady pace as Menina stepped higher and higher in anticipation. I inhaled her salty, sweaty smell, laying my hand on her glistening neck.

The stately cork oaks gave way to tall eucalyptus trees on one side as the track opened onto the plain. Menina coiled her body in readiness for the canter signal, and as soon as she got it, surged forward, her explosive power breathtaking. Instinctively, I made a bridge with both reins, crossing them over each other at the base of the horse's neck, which then acted as a lever—my only chance of controlling her.

I glanced back over my left shoulder. *All still there*. I increased the pace slightly, and Menina settled into her stride. As the corner approached, she moved over to the other side of the track, swishing her tail. No one was going to overtake her. Two kilometers later, after another quick glance behind, I raised my hand and slowly waved it up and down, gently bringing my horse down to a trot and then a walk. I did a head count. *All there*. Pure relief every time.

"Well done, everyone! We'll dismount now. Please cross your stirrups, take the reins over your horse's head, and we'll lead them in for a drink."

Jean was soon at my side, beaming.

"Oh, Sheila, that was so exciting. And we all survived. My Bobby Darling was just amazing!"

"It must be love," I said. And I wasn't kidding. It was a joy to witness a genuine bond between a human and a horse. "Come on," I said. "Let's go and have a drink." *And a painkiller for my pounding head.*

MC, whose group had arrived earlier, raised her eyebrows at me when she spotted Francesco and Morena.

"We're fine now," I said. "Francesco decided to go for a swim in the river... something about an Italian tradition on New Year's Eve." I smiled at Francesco while nodding toward Bela. "There's a pile of dry clothes for you in the emergency kit."

Leaving Menina to graze, I snuck off to the Jeep, which Bela had parked to the side, just out of the riders' way. I broke open a freezer pack and pressed it to my throbbing head while downing a couple of painkillers. *Just another two hours*. I couldn't wait to lie down.

The sun was starting to set as we helped the riders mount up. All twenty-two horses would now be together in one group, with me leading and MC bringing up the rear. I glanced westward. The copper sky turned purple toward the horizon, giving my heart a little whisper of nostalgia. The door on the twentieth century was closing, and we were right on the threshold of a new millennium. My excitement for dreams to come eclipsed my wistfulness, but I held it for the fleeting moment it rose up in me.

Riding out, the *whish* of a nightjar flying close by briefly startled the horses, and as the group naturally grew tighter, crunching sand and snorting filled all the voids in conversation. A pale glow backlit the mountain, etching its crooked contour against the starry backdrop. Then it darkened and the moon rose.

On cue, the horses stopped, and as one, they turned their heads toward the mountain. As the moonlight spilled onto us, horses and riders stared at the full moon, which was blood red. I was goosebumps all over. And looking around at all the stunned faces, it was clear I wasn't alone.

An image of Robert smiling flashed across my mind's eye. *Remember, we ordered the full moon for tonight especially.*

Touché, Robert.

When the group clip-clopped off a few minutes later, I sensed Jean sniffling at my side. "My dear, this is truly magical. Do you have a spare hanky?"

"No, Jean, sorry. But look, we're nearly home."

As the long line of horses wound its way down the driveway, Mini raised her head, curled back her top lip, and snorted loudly. To my amazement, the track was lined with dozens of flickering candles, all protected from the wind. Glowing pinpricks of golden light flanked the next bend and the path all the way up to the clubhouse. I glanced at the riders, every one of them bewitched. They sat on their horses, haloed by a rare calm. *Were all these candles Robert's idea? Did he do it all on his own?* Not possible, even for him.

Moving down the path, I became aware of a cracking and hissing sound. In front of the clubhouse, a roaring bonfire burned bright orange. *So this is what Robert has been chopping firewood for over the past few months.*

We rode into the stable yard in groups of five, and Bela and Leonel helped everyone untack, rub down, and feed the horses.

"Thanks, all," I said, looking at their tired faces. "I'm sure you're starving. Go on up. We'll follow you shortly."

As I turned away from the group, my legs melted beneath me. Bela caught me before I hit the ground.

12

*Some horses come into our lives
and quickly go, but others leave hoofprints
on our hearts that will never fade.*

AUTHOR UNKNOWN

M Y HAND REACHED FOR MY TINGLING HEAD. Though still sore, the persistent thumping had reduced to a more manageable throb. I seemed to be in my bed. *How did I get here? Where is everyone? And what is that noise?* A rhythmical drumming... I opened my slitted eyes to see Tippex, my dog, looking up from the floor by the bed, his tail a wind-up propeller. The gorgeous little guy was clearly worried about me.

"Hi, Tippy," I said, my hand pushing over his cold black snout to stroke the rough hair on his head.

I sat up to see a single wild rose on the pillow beside me and smiled despite my head. My internal taskmaster came to life: *Get up. Find clothes. Take painkiller.*

The bathroom flickered in the light of a spruce-scented candle as I bent over to splash cold water on my face. Straightening up slowly, I noticed a lipstick-scrawled message on the mirror: *C U at the party XXX ps. Luv U* encased in a heart.

A quick dab of makeup, no time for a shower, a spray of perfume. I'd have given anything to crawl back into my cozy bed.

Tippex hovered by my feet, willing me to stay. I crouched down and gently stroked his bat-like ears. "Sorry, Tippy, I've got to go now," I said, standing up. "You can come if you want." He just looked at me with his devoted brown eyes. I thought about the day MC and I had found him.

The annual horse fair was always held in Golegã, a small town situated an hour and a half north of Lisbon. MC and I had gone on our annual pilgrimage with two full van-loads of guests, who we'd checked into a small local hotel. While we'd gone about making a comfortable bed for ourselves in the back of the van, we'd noticed a skinny little black-and-white dog, scuttling about on three legs, his fourth dragging behind him. Though far too mistrustful for any kind of contact, he was happy to eat leftovers from a plate MC left out for him.

Three days later, once the fair was over, I was able to lift the dog into the van. He'd squeezed himself under the driver's seat for the six-hour drive home. I'd decided to put off telling Robert. He never liked being presented with change, but if you allowed the change to happen gently, he always accepted it.

It was two years before the little dog with the sonic ears and paint-brush tail was brave enough to enter the house. He'd since been fitted with a new hip and survived being shot at by the local hunters, which had happened once on a ride. I could still taste the acid fear when I thought of the shot ringing out and a dog's yelp ripping the air. I'd wound a bandage tightly around his stomach to stop the bleeding and scooped him up in front of me on my horse. Holding him with one arm, we'd galloped home. And the vet had taken care of the rest.

BY THE TIME I MADE MY WAY up to the clubhouse, the party was in full swing. I'd dressed in my black jeans and a multi-colored silk Indian top, while long red horse-themed earrings completed the outfit. I paused for a moment behind the palm tree and scanned the area for Robert. I longed to be held by him. The bonfire was still roaring and illuminated the entire garden area. Clusters of animated guests sat around it, their faces glowing amber in a soundscape of chatter and laughter. Hopefully, there was some food left. I was starving.

I could smell the *caldo verde*, a traditional vegetable soup spiced with *chouriço,* and the *leitão*. The remnants of roast boar, multiple salads, potato and rice dishes, and two types of *bacalhau* platters decorated the long trestle table. The salted cod was a staple of the local diet—I'd read somewhere there were three hundred and sixty-five ways of preparing it. For tonight, Fátima had chosen *bacalhau spiritual* and *bacalhau à braz*—one prepared with cream and onions, and baked in the oven; and the other mixed with eggs, onions, and black olives.

Fátima appeared out of nowhere, her eyes fixed on me with motherly concern.

"Are you okay?"

I smiled at my friend, clasping both her hands in mine.

"I'm fine, thank you, Fátima. This looks amazing. You've outdone yourself!"

"What can I get you to eat?"

"May I please have some *Bacalhau Spiritual* and bit of salad?"

"Of course," she said, picking up a plate.

"Where's Robert?"

"Trying to dodge the Terrible Tania, as per usual. She's something else, that one." She leaned in confidingly. "You wouldn't believe what she told me this afternoon..."

"Go on."

"She described last night at the disco as 'dancing amongst a sea of erections...'"

In unison, we threw our eyes up to heaven. "Look," said Fátima, nodding at the pool.

Tania had cornered Robert and was edging ever closer to him while laughing seductively, her strapless black dress creeping up and sliding down, leaving zero to the imagination. I scowled.

"Umm, I'll get your dinner," said Fátima, and disappeared.

I stalked my way 'round the pool like a she-wolf closing on a turkey. As soon as Robert spotted me, he lunged forward, giving Tania the erroneous impression he was moving toward her. Presumably delighted that he'd finally succumbed to her charms, the poor girl tottered toward him, only to be brushed aside as he moved swiftly past her into my arms. As she turned to see where Robert had gone, her heel slipped over the edge of the pool, and with waving arms and a flung drink, she fell backward into the deep end.

Robert hugged me tight, ignoring the splashing water behind him.

"Hey, I was so worried about you, you crazy lunatic. Why do you always push the envelope?" He lifted me in the air and twirled me around. *This is where I belong.* Laughing, I squeezed his shoulders.

"You owe me one," I whispered.

"Yeah?" he said, pulling me closer to his ear.

"I just rescued you from the T.T." I smiled at him and blew his hair off his face.

"Don't talk to me about her. In fact, the water might just cool her down. Have you eaten yet?"

"Not yet. I'm going to now."

Robert slowly released his grip on me, and I slid down until I was on tippy toes, arms looped around the back of his neck. One lingering kiss...

"I'd better do the rounds. Will you be okay with her?"

His mouth was a straight line, his eyes playful. "I'll just have to, won't I?"

I forced myself to walk away. Robert placed his hand on his heart. "I'll be right here, with you."

On the way up to the clubhouse, I spotted MC, Bela, and Leonel hiding behind the pool's well-clipped hedge, bent over in complete hysterics, while the disco queen clambered up the pool steps, heels and all. Only Fátima, bringing me a full plate of aromatic fish, managed to keep a straight face.

"Enjoy. I hope it still tastes okay," she said, smiling, and then, jerking her chin at the pool: "Nice work."

I couldn't help smirking. "This is perfect, thank you. What time is it?"

"Eleven-thirty. Don't worry, you still have plenty of time. And I don't think Robert has a clue!"

I sat down beside John on the long wooden bench. He'd progressed to the drinking-champagne-straight-from-the-bottle stage and slung his spare arm over my shoulder. In between hiccups, he focused on me with bloodshot eyes.

"How's our fearless leader doing?" *(Hiccup.)* "Great party! Here, have some champagne!" *(Hiccup.)*

Somehow, a full glass appeared in my hand.

Alcohol brings all sorts of sides out in people. With John, it was funny-melancholy.

"*Saúde*!" I said.

"*Skol*!" said John, faster.

"Cheers!"

"*Brost*!"

"*Egeszegere*!"

"*Salut*!"

"Chin-chin!"

"*Nostrovia*!"

"What the hell—down the hatch!" I shouted and clinked with him. We drank, and then John fell silent. I sensed he wanted to be alone with himself, his bottle, and the huge moonlit sky. I wandered over to the girls, who looked amazing, standing beside two handsome young men.

"Looking great, guys. How's the party?" And then to the two boys: "*Olá, sou a Sheila.*"

The girls smiled at me. "Hi, Sheila," said MC. "This is Manuel, and this is José, our friends from the village. They're teaching us Portuguese. How are you feeling, by the way?"

"Much better, thanks. Are you set up for midnight? Did you have time to get him ready?"

MC nodded, smiling at Bela, who winked at me complicitly.

"He looks great, don't worry, Sheila," she said.

"Well done, thank you. Could you sneak him around the back for about twelve-thirty?"

"*Sim, senhora*," said Bela in her best Portuguese.

Five to twelve. It was time.

I WATCHED ROBERT SQUEEZING HIS WAY through the guests toward me on the clubhouse terrace. *Hmm, no sign of the T.T.* What was she up to now?

I felt magnetized toward Robert as he joined my side. He clasped his fingers through mine, and the countdown began.

"Ten! Nine! Eight! Seven! Six! Five! Four! Three! Two! One..."

He held me so tight. His voice softened. "Happy New Year, my darling. To us."

"To us, and to our future together."

Where had the last eleven years gone? Looking into his warm protective eyes, I'd never felt closer to him. Was tonight the night? I made up my mind: *Whatever happens later, he has to hear me out.*

Robert leaned over and, tipping my face up toward him, kissed me. I felt that the world had stopped and nothing else existed.

A tap on my shoulder made me reluctantly pull away. It was Francesco.

"Hey guys, Happy New Year! Happy Millennium!" It was impossible not to smile in his company.

"Your prediction was wrong. The world didn't end," I said to him, teasingly.

"I know. Thank God!" he replied and moved on to the dance floor where within moments he was leading the conga, followed by a long wobbly line of admirers. On cue, Jean appeared out of nowhere.

"How are you, my dears? I do believe I'm a little tipsy," she said, waving her full glass of champagne around obliviously, splashing me in the face... just a little.

"Go on, Jean," I said. "Join the dance. Here, I'll hold your glass."

She weaved unsteadily in her stillettoes before kicking each one of them off and lurching herself into the conga line.

Robert took my hand and led me toward the clubhouse but stopped as he noticed Fátima making frantic signs at him from the kitchen. She was right on cue.

"Don't move," he said softly. "I'll be right back for you." And off he went.

Then, I heard the bell ringing and turned just in time to see Boémio entering the dance floor.

The dancers became stop-motion frames. The whole group gasped, amazed to see a horse in their midst. They gathered round as he walked unaccompanied into the middle of the crowd and stopped, surveying the confusion. His flowing mane and tail were intertwined with silver and red tinsel, and *Happy New Year, Bom Ano,* and *2000* had been artistically painted across his flanks, shoulders, and neck. He looked directly at me, snorted, and tossed his head in acknowledgment.

My heart skipped a beat. The gamble had paid off. This horse had just made the transition into the new millennium one that no one would ever forget.

Across the terrace, I saw Robert, whose jaw had dropped. He looked straight at me and raised his glass in a toast: "To Boémio, our superstar! A Happy Millennium to everybody!"

I squeezed my way toward the horse and flung my arms around his neck. He hugged me back, bringing his head down toward his chest, trapping me in his embrace. Immediately, the hairs stood up on the back of my neck. I absorbed his special sweet smell and intense body heat.

Boémio, for his part, was reveling in all the attention, chomping away on an endless supply of carrots. Everyone crowded round, stroking and patting him amid a hubbub of fuss.

"He's so soft and furry, like a huge bear!"

"I love the graffiti on him. Very cool!"

"Can I sit on him?"

Through it all, the horse just carried on eating, his hazel-colored eyes occasionally flickering over his adoring groupies. I glanced at Fátima, who raised her eyebrows toward the far corner of the room. The T.T., now in a short metallic purple number, had spotted the two young men, and was making a beeline for them.

"Come on, you," I said to Boémio gently. "Let's take you home."

I put my hand on his neck, and we walked into the moonlight. Robert's footsteps crunched the sand behind us, then we all stood side by side, bathed in liquid silver. A gift of nature.

"Sheila, that was perfect. What an amazing idea—Boémio made it unforgettable."

It felt like the right time.

"Robert, you know...we need to talk," I said, slipping my hand into his.

"Yes, I know. But no, Sheila. Not yet." He released my hand and put both his hands on my shoulders, turning me toward him.

"But why?" I felt my chest tightening and turned away. "Can't we even talk about it? What are you so afraid of?"

Robert turned me toward him again and held me at arm's length.

"We're not ready...well, *I'm* definitely not ready. Come on, Sheila, look at the moon. Let's just enjoy the *now*. We can talk next week, okay?"

"Okay."

LATER, WHEN I WAS SURE Robert was asleep, I tiptoed into the bathroom and lifted the slim box of pills out of the medicine cupboard, then slid it deep into the little bin under the sink and placed some tissue across the top to cover it. If you allow the change to happen gently...

13

The sun sees your body.
The moon sees your soul.

ANCIENT PROVERB

I T WASN'T ALWAYS EASY FOR US, especially at the beginning when it came to buying the right horses for our guests. Guineu, who'd later become our film star, came from an abandoned old farm in a deserted part of the southern *Alentejo*. The floury dust there rose so thick that you could chew it as it coated your mouth, while it clogged your nostrils and smeared your eyes shut. Shimmering heat lines rose up in the haze of a blurred horizon. Completely forsaken, this place had once been a well-known stud farm for purebred Lusitanos. The herd that remained had, for the most part, learned to fend for itself.

Pasture in spring was enough to keep all the new foals and mares going, but the summer months were challenging, to say the least. Scrappy dried-up grass and low-reaching tree leaves simply weren't enough to sustain the group of horses, and many succumbed to tick fever. This tick-transmitted disease caused the infected animals' limbs to swell, their temperatures to soar, and their appetites to disappear. The condition itself was easy to identify, as the horse would stand with his front and hind legs as far apart as possible. If not treated early, the symptoms ended up reappearing after seven days, and the disease inevitably killed the horse.

I remember very clearly the day we went to collect Guineu. There were sick horses everywhere, standing in sad wide stances with clusters of swollen ticks hanging from their underbellies like bunches of grey grapes. I was promptly sick out the Jeep's window.

Our horse was standing under a cork oak apart from the main herd. Fortunately, he was not infected.

We were utterly unprepared for our first-ever group of clients. My childhood friend, Liuliu, had agreed to help me for the week with whatever was needed—leading the rides, driving the Jeep, setting up camp, entertaining the guests. Our tight relationship rendered words and explanations unnecessary: we worked as one. And what we lacked in experience, organization, and planning, we made up for with blind enthusiasm and a fierce determination to give our guests the time of their lives.

I had no way of knowing it then, but the group of six French friends who first came—seasoned *randonneurs*—were to teach me the essence of trail riding. They managed to show me that peace and utter fulfilment come from being at one with nature and with your horse; that less is always so much more; that the simple things in life are the important ones, like delicious homemade food and endless laughter shared by friends; and that pranks must be as inventive as possible.

I should have seen it coming when I picked them up from Lisbon airport in the UMM Alter, aka the *Umfi*. Ex-Portugese army, the *UMM* stood for *União Metalo Mecânica*, a Portuguese metalworks factory and auto manufacturer, based in Lisbon; the *Alter* stood for one of the best-known breeds of Portuguese horses, the Alter Real. The *Umfi*—the most uncomfortable, and by far the loudest, vehicle I have ever driven—was a soft-top with a raggedy tarpaulin cover over its roof and most of its sides. Bench seats in the back faced each other, seating up to ten people. In the space between the benches, everything from a small pony to a full kitchen had been known to fit. When the *Umfi* could be persuaded to get up some speed on the motorway, a separate gearstick for its overdrive mode could be deployed. Although it was then able to go only marginally faster, the engine became so loud that any attempt at conversation became impossible (aggravating at times, incredibly useful at others). Nonetheless, the bright yellow Jeep was my pride and joy.

The group of riders had brought along their own chef for the week, but at the airport, Dési was nowhere to be found. None of the group appeared remotely worried. They carried on smoking and chatting and sinking espressos, telling me not to worry, that Dési would soon present himself.

Sure enough, an hour later he materialized, carrying two overflowing bags of food and a crooked smile.

And so it began.

Liuliu and I took turns leading the ride while the other traveled in the *Umfi* with Dési and set up camp for the horses and riders at each stop. Apart from preparing all the meals, Dési became increasingly interested in Liuliu. As the week progressed, he'd spend hours courting her in French, trying to convince her to be his mistress in Portugal while his wife remained none the wiser miles away in France. Of course, Dési explained, this was totally normal. Needless to say, Liuliu and I made a pact to always sleep very close together on our tiny air mattress, just in case his ardor led him to make an advance in the night.

The group of friends turned out to be excellent riders, and our first dust-encrusted day concluded on the shores of a large inland dam. A welcoming camp came into view when we arrived, with Dési putting the finishing touches to a deliciously fragrant dinner. While every rider tended to his own horse—washed him down, fed and groomed him—the sun exchanged places with the full moon.

The sun, *o sol,* is masculine in Portuguese, whereas the moon, *a lua,* is feminine. When in her "full" phase, she exerts a strong pull on us, as she does on the tide, and enhances our qualities, whatever those may be. It's a time for intuition and tuning in to the "cosmic flow." It's no secret that more babies are born when the moon's pull is at its strongest, or that women and the moon share a similar cycle. At least, it's not a secret in Portugal.

After dinner, I moved away from the group to the water's edge. My heartbeat pounded in my chest as I watched the moon claim the starlit sky. She seemed to be whispering a secret to me through the darkness: *Mystical states are experienced in the flow.* Her powerful truth coursed through my body. Silver light hovered over the water, denser at the edges where it met the earth, a spirit-blanket protecting those who embraced it. My skin tingled all over and I became aware that I was no longer alone. Spellbound, all the riders sat at the water's edge in humble silence, and for the first time that day, I longed for Robert. He too would have understood her message and been captivated by her beauty.

At that time, Robert was still living and working in the *Algarve* as an architect, honing the craft that he was so very gifted at. He would move up to the *Alentejo* about six months later when it became clear that I couldn't run the growing company on my own. Back at the moon pool, I hung on to the knowledge that we'd be meeting up with him at the end of the week.

At some point, the unique whooping of a male pygmy owl split the silence and brought me back to my senses. Everyone, including Liuliu, had melted away except for *Le Doc*. He'd been waiting to light his forever pipe, and now the floral, spicy aroma rose up in little white clouds around his head. Because he was the group's most experienced rider, we'd decided he should ride Guineu, and they'd bonded immediately.

"*Ça va*, Sheila?" he said, his John Lennon spectacles balanced precariously halfway down his long aquiline nose. "*C'est merveilleux. Un vrai cadeau.*"

I nodded, not trusting myself to speak over one of those condensed moments that would inhabit us forever.

Getting to my feet, I bade the bossman *bonne nuit* and left to find Liuliu and our shared bed. It seemed that all the riders had decided to sleep beside their horses. Very *français*. Liuliu and I needed to get a good night's sleep so we were set up on the camp's opposite side. I glanced over at our shared horse, Akbar, who appeared delighted by his own company. Liuliu didn't budge as I got into my own sleeping bag beside her. *Out for the count.* Feeling embraced by the stars' canopy, I drifted off, grateful for the perfect end to our first-ever day.

A sharp rock jabbing into my back woke me up. *What the hell?* Our mattress was flattened. I rolled over onto Liuliu. It looked like the plug had been pulled out.

"Agh… what's happened to our lovely bed? There are rocks everywhere," moaned Liuliu, less than half-conscious. The sky was just lightening to pink. I figured it must be around six in the morning.

"I don't know," I said, clawing around for my riding boots. "Liu, did you move my boots? I'm sure I left them right here…"

Liu sat up now, her white-blonde hair projecting outward in all directions, and squinted into the rising sun. "What? No. Borrow mine. I'll have a look around."

Liu and I had always shared all our clothes, shoes, and socks. In fact, everything except bras, which wouldn't have gone well for either of us—I'd be left gasping for breath while she'd be left swimming in a vast empty ocean of fabric.

I got dressed slowly, then ambled off into the bushes. No boots to be found.

"Look up," Liu cried suddenly. "In the tree!"

Sure enough, there they were, hanging like Christmas decorations, just out of reach. *Very funny.*

We decided to ignore the Frenchmen's shenanigans while we fed and checked all the horses. We scanned each Gallic face as they appeared one by one to greet their horses, but no one was giving anything away. Each rider led his own horse down to the edge of the dam for a drink and a splash. Some of the horses made the most of this and rolled around in the knee-deep water. Unlike us, they all looked well rested and were raring to go.

Dési magically whisked up some delicious crêpes and proper coffee. I glanced around at all the faces again. Chatty and relaxed as usual, there was no sign from any of the riders that the game was on. *Nada.* Maybe I could speak to Dési in the afternoon when it would be my turn to ride with him in the *Umfi.*

The sun had begun to beat down on us by the time I set off with the ride. *Le Doc* rode alongside me up in front of the group, his pipe already lit. He held it in his right hand, which dangled down below the saddle, close to the horse's saddle blanket. Guineu didn't seem remotely bothered by the aromatic smell or the smoke, which puffed up around him.

It was while I was checking on the back of the ride that I caught a whiff of burning and heard loud cracking sounds. *Le Doc's* pipe seemed to be exploding in short bursts, which had somehow ignited his horse's saddle blanket.

"*Attention!*" I cried as loud as I could. "*Arrêtez! Du feu!*" I galloped up to the front of the ride, leaping off as I reached Guineu and banging out the fire in the saddle blanket with an old rag from my saddle bag. *Le Doc* poured his water bottle all over it. Weirdly, his pipe continued to spark away, detonating an extended series of mini explosions.

His horse began eating grass as soon as we put the flames out, and we checked him for burn marks. Not a bother on him. Meanwhile, *Le Doc* emptied out his pipe and checked the contents. He said nothing, but it was later disclosed to me that tiny bits of dynamite had been mixed through his tobacco, which had caused the explosions.

Poker-faced again, the other riders gave nothing away.

At lunchtime, I found out that someone had loosened the ties around the gas bottles that kept them secured in the back of the *Umfi*. As the back gate of the jeep was very low, all the gas bottles had bounced out onto the road when Liuliu had accelerated around a bend. *Grâce à Dieu*, no one had been hurt, nor had the bottles been stolen. The *Umfi's* growl had, of course, drowned out all the clanking. When Dési drove back to find them, he discovered all three bottles side by side, upside down in a ditch.

It was a silent war.

Jean-Pierre always wore his camel-colored sombrero pushed back on his head. Sandy-toned hair poked out round its edges, framing his oddly unsymmetrical face. Full lips and a proper-sized nose took nothing away from his disconcerting green eyes. I found myself constantly drawn to their underwater quality and devilment. He was riding Tango, a cheeky chestnut. They seemed to make the perfect pair.

Turning his head toward me, Jean-Pierre pushed his torso up from the ground where he'd been doing *downward dog*, and crossed his legs, yogi style. I bit my lip, trying not to fall into his green light.

"*Ça va,* Sheila?" he said in his thick French accent. "You look so tired. Are you okay?"

"*Oui. Ça va, merci.*" It had to be him. Or was everyone in on it? "How's Tango? You like him?"

"Bah, *il est parfait*. Very perfect. Maybe he likes to come live *avec moi en France*?"

No effing way. "Maybe. Not yet. In a few years, *peut-être*."

He turned away to look at his horse grazing, loose, about a meter from him. They'd come to an understanding already.

Tango never would make it to France. About ten years later, I was leading the first group of a week-long trail ride and had just finished cantering along a windy track through an umbrella pine forest. We'd slowed and dismounted, then led our horses into a shady area where we'd planned to have our break and refreshments. The backup Jeep was already there waiting with a long line of buckets to welcome the thirsty horses while drinks and chopped-up watermelon were handed out to all the riders. The second group was due in about ten minutes later.

Suddenly, all the hairs on my arms had risen like electric antennae. I'd pulled Robert aside. "You have to go, quick. Something's happened to the other group. Something's wrong."

His swift intake of breath said it all. He'd been here before. He knew that what I was feeling wasn't a false alarm. His eyes turned the darkest blue of concern before he snuck into the jeep and was gone. No one in the my group had noticed as we mounted up and continued riding toward the lunch spot. There we would learn that Tango had collapsed at the beginning of the canter and was dead before he hit the ground. Thankfully, the guide who had been riding him was unhurt, but she was so traumatized she couldn't get in the saddle for over a month. Robert had unearthed an excavator, which he used to bury Tango's body there and then.

Later, our vet explained how a sudden heart attack was not uncommon in horses, especially in very fit ones. Tango had one of the biggest, cheekiest hearts ever.

I SPENT THE AFTERNOON WITH DÉSI as we cleared up the lunch camp and stacked everything into the Jeep, making sure to leave the area cleaner than we'd found it. Then we drove the *Umfi* to our night location. It was situated in a pine forest just behind Sahara-like dunes that obscured the view of the sea. Immersed in the smell of pine, heat, and tangy sea air, we set up camp. Nothing was said about all the pranking—it was almost as if it had never happened. I wondered if Dési was hatching some plan. I kept peeping at him as I prepared the horses' dinner, and he prepared ours.

By the time the ride came in an hour later, I had my own plan for what Liu and I should do. As I ran my hands over each horse, checking for any sensitive areas or signs of heat, I shared my idea with her. She just grinned.

The afternoon ride had gone seamlessly—not a single explosion.

Judging by the length of the tree shadows, I knew the sun would stick around for another hour and a half. *Plenty of time.*

The riders led their horses to a clearing and stood back to watch them roll over and over in the soft sand. Smudged dark by the dust, they were then led back to ties on the high line where they were groomed, checked once more, and fed. Liu and I circulated through the group, bandaging the horses whose tendons tended to swell up overnight with *argila*, or clay mix, and then leaving them to rest. Later, we'd top up their hay and water.

The riders lingered around their horses, finding any excuse not to leave them. *Le Doc* was brushing Guineu's tail, gently separating the strands so as not to pull out a single hair. Jean-Pierre was sitting on the ground, cross-legged, telling Tango a story, and some of the others were busy oiling the outsides of their horses' hooves to help keep them hydrated.

I walked up to *Le Doc.* "Would anyone like to go to the beach? *Nager, à la plage? Voulez-vous?*"

He peered at me through his gray tail curtain. "*Oui!* Yes, *absolument*!"

Dési and two other riders stayed at the camp while the rest of us walked the ten minutes down the hill, ending with a sprint over the majestic dunes onto an empty unbounded beach. A fine mist of sea spray rolled off the breaking waves to greet us, while beyond, turquoise sea beckoned, insistent as anything.

Liuliu and I dropped our towels and ran for it. The waves were perfect, and soon everyone joined us, bodysurfing like it was going out of fashion. I glanced around and nudged Liu.

"Go," she said. "I'll make sure they stay here for a while."

On the beach, I changed quickly, then grabbed Jean-Pierre's pile of clothes, leaving only his hat behind. I scampered back to camp and hid them under one of the back seats of the *Umfi.*

Long shadows cast by the setting sun melted into the evening shade on the sand while Dési and I hurried to turn the camp lights on. Twilight was short in Portugal—half an hour later it would be pitch-black.

I hovered by Dési as he put the finishing touches to the night's stew. Freshly chopped coriander was sprinkled into the simmering pot as he gently stirred it through before passing me a spoonful to taste. *Ooh la la*— to die for. He grinned and told me his secret recipe: sea bass, ray, mussels, octopus, squid, potatoes, red and green peppers, onion, garlic, laurel, tomato, and white wine (and lots of the latter).

Lured by the tantalizing aroma, the swimmers started drifting in. Liuliu seemed deep in conversation with *Le Doc* but was able to give me a quick thumbs up.

Jean-Pierre, the last to arrive to camp, sauntered right by me, *sans slip*, with his hat covering his manhood. I could rather easily imagine him passing through all three hundred and three stations of the *métro* system wearing the same expression.

Much later, snuggled woozily in our sleeping bags, I got the full story from Liu.

"Well, we finished surfing, then Jean-Pierre just stood there naked on the beach looking at all of us—laughing his head off, I might add, as if it were totally normal. I didn't know where to look until he picked up that hat of his and hung it on his tackle."

"*Hmm*," I said, sleepily. "I've a feeling tomorrow will be an interesting day for me."

Echoes of the pounding surf sifted through the trees, giving an offbeat rhythm to the cicadas' lullaby. Moments later, I was fast asleep and dreaming of mermaids riding giant seahorses side-saddle as they surfed the waves alongside a pod of dolphins. Robert was surfing with them.

An inhaled hint of a presence made me open my eyes, but all I saw were the tendrils of mist-covered treetops linked in a silver web, keeping us safe under their canopy. I smiled, cozying a little deeper into my still-inflated bed.

It was the last day of our first-ever week. By evening, the horses would be back home again. And best of all, tonight I'd get to see Robert.

Every bit of me ached for him. Incommunicado all week, I had so much to tell him.

Liu and I fed, watered and checked all the horses, removing bandages and washing off *argila* from two of them. Meanwhile, Dési had whipped up another *petit-dej*: coffee, fresh croissants, and a huge fruit salad. *Perfect.* Although Jean-Pierre was, in fact, wearing clothes today, he gave nothing away. Maybe he'd called a *détente*.

Our route took us along the beach, then inland through the cork oak forests directly back home. With the tide fully out, the compacted wet sand mirrored perfectly reversed images of all the riders. Our upended doppelgängers.

Jagged rocks marked the end of the beach as we rode in single file up the dunes, each of us in our own way impacted by the power and raw beauty of the ocean.

Akbar imperceptibly shortened his stride, compacting his muscles. He knew what was coming. I'd have to stay in control. I doubled back to have a quick word with all the riders, while my horse, quivering with anticipation, threw his head about, his long dark mane whipping me in the face—there was no talking to him. Four kilometers of wide sandy trail opened up before us: a veritable racetrack. Before I could raise my hand to give the signal, we were gone. Pounding hooves drilled the ground. I glanced backward: euphoria beamed from the faces thundering along behind me. The thrill of flying when all four hooves are in the air simultaneously.

After what seemed like only a few seconds, the track started up a slight incline. *Time to slow down.* I started to shorten my reins, but there was no contact. They'd come loose from my horse's bit and now flapped wildly in the wind.

Someone had undone the buckles, but left the ends tucked in under the keepers so I'd miss them.

Breathe, breathe, just breathe, I told myself as the suddenly useless reins swung around in my hands. *If only I was on a different horse.* Akbar was dominant... unforgiving. I crouched and reached forward, trying to grasp his bit so that I could then pull it sideways and get him to slow down. But he yanked his head away. We were going too fast. *Someone might get hurt.* I eased myself back up into the saddle and waved my arm up and down in the hope that the group would get the message and slow down. There was more of an incline now and the horses were getting tired. When I looked back again, I saw that they'd all dropped back.

Finally, my horse slowed to a canter, then to a trot, and at last, a walk. I slung my arms round his neck, slid to the ground, and as he walked along, I reattached the reins to the bit. Everyone clapped.

Though not a word was spoken about the ordeal, the plain, simple, and loathsome truth was this: I had lost the prankster competition. But at least only my pride was hurt.

Later, as we led our horses into our final stop, I spotted a tall figure talking to Dési. My heart jumped into my mouth.

"Rob!" I yelled and ran toward him, abandoning my horse, my wobbly legs barely able to carry my weight. *Of course!* He was joining us tonight for our last meal together. Jumping up into his arms, I snuggled into his neck, overcome by his familiar sweaty, dusty smell. I knew everything was going to be all right. I was home again.

14

A horse is the projection of people's dreams about themselves. Strong, powerful, beautiful, and it has the capability of giving us escape from our mundane existence.

PAM BROWN

THE LETTER WAS EMBOSSED with a wax seal, the return address written simply in gold print:

Lady Rosamund Gladstone
Hawthorn Castle
Wales

I looked at Robert. "Do you know a Lady Gladstone?"

He squinted at the official-looking envelope. "No, I don't think so." He opened it and took out the letter.

The Riding for the Disabled Association (RDA) in the United Kingdom, it said, was commemorating its fiftieth anniversary, and was looking to celebrate by taking a group of ten riders for a week's riding abroad. Ten of the centers they'd contacted in Europe had been unwilling to accommodate them. Would we be interested in hosting the week? They'd provide their own trained helpers, physiotherapist, and nurse.

I put my hand on Robert's arm.

"How do you think they heard about us? I've always dreamed of doing something like this with our horses. What do you think?"

He stood up, brushing my hand off, and walked over to the window.

"No idea." And then, "I'm not sure..."

I inhaled and squinted at him. *Why the hell do I always assume he'd agree with me on all things horsey?*

Although his broad back filled most of the window frame, I caught a glimpse of what he was looking at in the field. A herd of ten gray horses was galloping around at top speed, stopping and turning on the spot, rearing up, biting each other and racing off again.

Robert snorted. "What would these guys make of it? Look at them! They're not exactly tame. *Or* safe. I'm really not sure..."

Clearly, this was going to take some persuading. I walked over to him and wrapped my arms around his waist. Leaning my chin against him, I squeezed affectionately.

Nada. Explaining this to the horses would be simple by comparison. I knew they'd understand.

I squeezed a bit harder. "I think it could work. We could change their food. Less protein, more volume." This usually worked for decreasing the horses' energy. It took the edge off. "We could even borrow some super-safe ponies from someone..." Still *nada*. "You know I helped set up the RDA in Portugal a few years ago? There's nothing like it."

I didn't add that I still felt sick when I thought about it. My job had been to escort the RDA supervisors and interpret for them when we drove inland to some remote villages in the Serra do Caldeirão. The idea was to meet families who lived in these secluded mountain areas and promote the huge benefits that contact with horses can have on children with physical and mental disabilities. It hadn't gone well.

One of the families we'd visited had their disabled son chained up outside like a dog. They threw him food a couple of times a day, rationalizing that he was too dangerous to be let loose.

Another young man was left to spend his days running along the railway tracks, trying to catch trains.

But it was a fifteen-year-old girl called Clara who'd broken my heart.

Bedridden since birth, she'd said her legs didn't work. She lay alone in a dark, airless room with bare walls crowding in on her. She'd never once seen the light of day. Her huge dark eyes filled her pallid face as she listened to us speak. She would have benefited to no end from equine therapy, but her parents had other ideas. "God," they said, had apparently inflicted Clara on them as a punishment, and they intended to keep her hidden away.

For the next year, Clara's plight had haunted me. *I had to go back*. When I got there, a single candle's flickering glow penetrated the damp stale air while Clara lay bunched up on her bed like she hadn't moved since I'd last seen her. Her tiny pale frame seemed to have shrunk, but it felt like her soul brightened when she saw me.

"The horse lady," she'd whispered. "I knew you'd come back."

I'd sat on the edge of her narrow steel bed and cupped her hands in mine. Though cold, they throbbed to the beat of her pulse, and the silence between us dissolved. We talked in whispers until Clara fell asleep, exhausted.

That was the last time I saw her.

There was so much the RDA could have done for Clara. Until Lady Gladstone's letter, I'd tried not to think of the bedridden girl, but now it all came flooding back. I buried my face as Robert turned himself around in my arms to face me. He tilted my chin up and flicked my tear away with his finger. His dark blue eyes bore deep into mine. His words were a soft cradle.

"If it's important to you, go ahead and call them. We'll take it from there."

The next day, I faxed Lady Gladstone and suggested meeting her in two weeks' time beside the castle in Milfontes, which I reckoned would be a kind of home away from home for her. The fortnight went quickly, and when the day came, Robert and I drove in early and parked on the headland beside the lighthouse. Built where the Mira River flowed into the wild Atlantic Ocean, Milfontes—*a Thousand Springs*—was aptly named as hundreds of freshwater springs bubble through the surrounding sea cliffs and trickle into the sea. Founded in the fifteenth century, it was originally populated by prisoners. *Some prison!*

I glanced at Robert. He'd parked the car, but his white-knuckled hands were still glued to the steering wheel and he looked worried.

"What's wrong?"

Chewing the inside of his lip, he looked at me briefly with stony eyes. "I don't think you realize what we're getting into here. You seem to think it's all going to be easy." He paused and looked straight at me. "As usual."

He got out, slammed the door, and just stood there, breathing deeply. Then, as quickly, he opened the door and stuck his head back in. "Look, I don't want anything to go wrong. Can you get that?"

"I get it," I said gently.

He let the door close and moved off to a low wall where he sat down and hugged his knees. I got out and sat behind him, held him close, and wrapped my legs around either side of his body. I rested my head on his back and exhaled. "You know, we don't have to make any decisions today. Let's just meet Lady Gladstone and see how it goes." I felt him relax.

"Okay," he agreed, softened.

Milfontes is one of my "magic places." The wide river estuary is bordered on both sides by the most pristine white beaches, which morph into steep orange cliffs. Sporadic clumps of *girões* are splashed around, spilling clusters of magenta, white, and yellow flowers down its steep walls. And, oh, my God, *the smell*. The fragrance of brackish sea plants seasoned by the sun, tossed with the scent of wild garlic and flavored with the sea's sharp salty spray—*intoxicating*.

"Let's just stay here," I said, licking the moisture off my lips, "forever."

Robert turned around, his eyes reflecting the aquamarine sea. He looked right into me so that I felt fully naked yet utterly complete.

"You really want to do this, don't you?" he said in so gentle a voice I wanted to kiss him. Not for the first time I was aware of the effect the sea had on him. I felt it the night we met during the storm. I knew his whole family loved the sea; the wilder, the better. It was some kind of mysterious Irish connection to the ocean.

"Yes. I really want this," I said. "Come on, let's go. It must be nearly seven by now."

As we walked toward the square, I slipped my hand into his, linking and tightening our fingers. Before we'd taken ten steps, Robert squeezed my hand.

"That must be them."

If you'd asked me to picture a more adorable elderly couple, I don't think I could have. Our hearts connected on a soul level as soon as we made eye contact.

Lord and Lady Gladstone stepped toward us with their hands outstretched.

"You must be Sheila and Robert," said Lord Gladstone. "Ros and Willie. It's a pleasure."

A few glasses of sparkling *vinho verde* later and we'd agreed to run the RDA holiday for them the following spring.

I looked at Robert, sitting back, arms crossed behind his head, while he and Willie discussed the irrelevance of the monarchy. Willie couldn't have picked his subject better.

"I want you to come to the farm tomorrow," I said to Ros. "Just to make sure you're happy with the setup."

She nodded with laughing blue eyes. "Of course. Good idea. Will we be able to have a ride as well? Nothing too wild—I don't bounce back as well as I used to!"

After agreeing on eleven o'clock the next morning, I wrote the directions down and we said goodnight. I snuggled into Robert's big shape as we walked away under clouds of tiny pipistrelle bats while the sun slipped into the sea.

"How do you feel about the whole thing now?"

He tightened his arm over my shoulder and I knew.

"Yeah, let's do it," he said. "What special people. But let's see what they say tomorrow after they've seen the place."

Now that Robert had agreed, the whole thing seemed entirely possible. As we drove home slowly, I slipped my hand into its usual position under his thigh. Two cylindrical tunnels of light lit up the night ahead of us, giving me that journeying-through-space feeling. We turned off the tarmac road and onto our driveway.

"Stop! Look!" I cried. The bushes to our left shook and parted as the Jeep skidded to a stop. A huge male boar bolted out and crashed into the bull bars. Two red pinpricks glowered at us for a split second in a mass of tusks and bristles. Then he charged and rebounded off the fence on the other side of the track. He glared at us accusingly, reversed, pawed the dust, and with his head low, attacked again. This time the triple-barbed-wire fence twanged apart, and like a bullet, he was gone.

"What the—? That's the biggest one I've ever seen!" exclaimed Robert.

Looking at what was left of the fence, I shook my head. It was destroyed.

"No wonder the horses are scared of them," I said. I noticed Robert reaching for the door handle. "Hey!" I put a restraining hand on his arm. "Don't get out, Rob, please. There's probably more."

He was itching to go after it, fearless adventure flashing in his eyes. He relaxed his hand reluctantly and gave me a playfully bold look. "Spoilsport."

Still, he slowly wound down the car window expectantly. Nothing. A bit farther down the drive, a familiar nightjar crouched, waiting to pounce. He kamikazed toward the Jeep until the last second, then flapped off into the night. A rare and secretive bird with brown and black camouflage plumage, the nightjar hunts only at night. This one seemed to have learned that to wait for a vehicle to light up his potential meal of insects and moths was a great idea. He always waited for us on the track.

"What next?" I said, and then in an instant my face drained with the realization of a forgotten promise. "Oh, shit, shit, shit. I completely forgot to speak to Bela!"

"Why, what's wrong with her?" asked Robert with concern in his voice. "She seemed fine during the week."

"Not sure. Fátima was worried about her as well. She's just not her usual bouncy self. I'll go and see if she's still up."

"Okay, I'll do the final horse check."

BELA'S LIGHT WAS STILL ON. I crept along the cobbled path, which twisted its way through the lemon geraniums and rosemary bushes. Their competing scents, intensified by the night's humidity, were overpowering. Small solar-powered lights beaded the path and helped me avoid stepping on Robert's beloved cactus garden.

Candlelight cast soft moving shadows on Bela's cream curtains. I knocked twice on her door.

"Can I come in, Bela? It's Sheila..."

I heard a sniffle, then a weak voice: "Yeah...come on in."

Heaped muddles of jodhpurs, riding chaps, jackets, bras, and sweatshirts paved the floor. Bela was a tiny orb curled into her quilt up near her pillow. I sat down on the edge of the bed beside her and gently rubbed her back.

She sniveled and became even smaller. "Oh, Sheila, what'll I do?"

"Do you want to tell me about it?" Her eyes answered me with one look. And then I guessed. "Are you pregnant, Bela?"

She drew back a little and nodded.

"I don't understand," she said, her forehead crumpling. "I was so careful. Mum's going to kill me! My life is over."

I could feel her panic inside me, deep down. I put my arms around her and rocked her gently, stroking her tousled hair.

"Shhh, no one's going to touch you. It's going to be okay." I held her tight while sobs racked her body. In a heartbeat, it all tumbled over me in a jumble of twisted dark memories that I'd locked away for fifteen years. I'd thought the key had been thrown far away. The acrid smell of the dingy street before dawn. The sound of the prearranged knock on the door. The dark secrecy. The feeling of utter aloneness and vulnerability at being left with the brutish woman who shoved me into a back room full of plastic crucifixes and weeping Jesuses and broken-hearted Virgin Marys looking down at me from their perches. The terror of looking at the bare narrow bed covered with a used sheet. And the horror of realizing that the huge syringe with the thick needle sitting alone on a table, filled with bright yellow liquid, was for me.

Bela whimpered into my arms. I thought of my mother, and how she'd known what to do. And then, intuitively, I hummed a Portuguese lullaby, *Menino d'Oiro*, until Bela became quiet. She gently pulled back and peered through her swollen eyelids—exposed and so, so vulnerable.

"What shall I do, Sheila? Help me..."

I brushed the damp hair off her face, held her arm's length, and spoke firmly.

"The first thing you need to do is decide. Do you want to keep the baby or not?"

"No, of course not. No way!" She looked distraught.

"Okay, next thing: how far are you gone?"

"Five or six weeks, I think," she said, knitting her brows and counting, mouthing the numbers. "Why?"

"Well, then we can travel to Lisbon and sort it out. I know someone. You'll be fine."

"You mean..." She opened her eyes wide and pulled back from me.

"Yes, have an abortion...if that's what you decide to do." I put a hand back on her knee while she scanned the room.

"Oh...isn't that illegal? And dangerous? And...painful?" Then, rubbing her nose into her sleeve, she lowered her voice to a whisper. "Will you come with me?"

"Of course I will. It's not illegal or dangerous. Just a bit painful," I said, trying to sound reassuring while my inner torment expanded and grew. I got up slowly, but Bela grabbed me around the waist.

"Please don't tell Robert. Or the others..."

"No, of course not. You can do that. Or not. Sleep well, sweetie. We'll talk in the morning."

She released me very slowly. "Thank you, Sheila. Thank you so much!"

I waited by the door while she curled back into her fetal position and her breathing became slow and regular.

I pulled my scarf up around my neck; it was colder outside now. The moment I closed the door, stubborn stinging tears erupted. Bela's plight had stirred up my past.

Back when I was eighteen, my gynecologist had told me I was infertile and could never have kids. And then, surprise, surprise...I wasn't infertile after all. The procedure I then experienced had been illegal, extremely dangerous, and absolutely agonizing.

My mum had been amazing.

I stood outside Bela's room, shivering. Maybe I was now truly unable to conceive. *Perhaps I should have another scan when I go to Lisbon with Bela.*

A hint of silver shimmered in the closest field, and I heard an urgent nicker. Boémio, the king of the millennium party, always knew when I needed one of his special hugs. This otherworldly intelligence never failed to disarm me. As I walked slowly toward his outline, I caught a glimpse of myself riding him years before with my leg in a full plaster cast, strapped to his neck. He was the only one I'd trusted with it. Tonight, as I cried into his warm neck, he absorbed my pain once more.

Robert was breathing deeply when I snuck into bed later.

"Is Bela okay?" he muttered semi-consciously, wrapping his arms around me and pulling me close.

"*Shhh*...yeah, she's fine. Sleep now."

AT ELEVEN SHARP, Lord and Lady Gladstone appeared. We got on so well I felt we must have met in a previous life. While Robert and Willie went off to check on all the "technical stuff," Ros and I went out for a ride. And it was perfect. I knew that whatever happened, we'd be friends for a very long time.

15

Happiness is strange, it comes when you are not seeking it. When you are not making an effort to be happy, then unexpectantly, mysteriously, happiness is there, born of purity, of a loveliness of being.

KRISHNAMURTI

OR ME, PURPOSE AND PASSION add up to one thing. We all need it, and when it comes right down to it, it's really what life is all about (that and the "KCC Rule"—be Kind, Caring, and Compassionate). Theologian John Wesley probably said it best: *Light yourself on fire with passion and people will come from miles to watch you burn.*

I believe that a *raison d'être* is what keeps us focused, driven, healthy, and interested in life, whatever stage we're at. Some of us can lose our purpose along the way; it could be when we retire, or lose a lifelong partner, or even succumb to old age. Or something entirely different. Our purpose and drive will change as our life circumstances and priorities do, but striving to keep an open mind while accepting people for who they are and where they're at goes a long way toward keeping us on track.

Being involved with animals—in particular, with horses—has always given me a real sense of purpose. It's my passion. Rescuing, rehabbing, rehoming...it all just made sense. Animals have always taken center stage in my life. They give unconditionally and accept us just the way we are. They never hurt us intentionally. They never ask pointless questions. Is it the same unconditionality as between a parent and child? Not quite. But they're as spiritual as humans.

Our farm was, in so many respects, a portal for countless animals, and seemed to magnetize them from the most unlikely places and then somehow connect them to where they were perhaps meant to be all along.

We found Rags by accident. He was a tiny brown puppy, being fed and brought up by a family of foxes. One day, he followed us home. A riding guest fell in love with him, and he ended up going to live in Los Angeles with her. She even paid for one of our staff to fly him over.

We came upon Maxy completely by chance. The Retriever was curled up in an alleyway in Milfontes with blood pooling around his front legs. A motorcycle had run over his front paw, which was splayed out like a pancake, as big as a dinner plate. With careful bandaging and help from our local vet, the paw was rescued. Maxy went to live on a farm in Sweden. He got a lift there from some friends in their camper bus.

Pipa, a small brown-and-black bitch, hopped into the yard one day on three legs. She'd clearly been nursing and was swollen with milk. A deep ridged gash had nearly sliced off her hip bone, probably from where she'd been caught in a snare, and somehow, she was still walking. The vet was unable to save her, and we never found her puppies. But she was by far the bravest animal I'd ever met.

Fino turned up one day, a gentle custard-colored mutt. It appeared he'd had distemper as a puppy and still had uncontrollable shakes in his limbs whenever he sat down or relaxed, but he liked nothing more than to go running through the fields with all the horses.

There were so many more creatures that we had the privilege of helping, if only temporarily. The essence, *a essência,* of life is surely to feel you're part of a bigger whole. That you're needed. That you're loved. That what you do actually matters. That we are, in our own small significant way, making the world a better place for our children to live in.

For me, being immersed in and in tune with nature is what brings about pure happiness. I'll never be able to find the same feeling in a city. It's a place to visit slowly and leave quickly, and that inevitably leaves me with a bad taste in my mouth. It must be the same for animals.

16

Events are lived the way we interpret them. Life, essentially, is lived in our minds.

CHARLES DE KUNFFY

ELA AND I TRAVELED TO LISBON the following week. For the two-and-a-half-hour train journey, I focused on keeping her relaxed and my own memories locked away, deep inside. I did this by droning on and taking endless cues from the passing landscape—from the bounties of the rice paddies to the gathering of varnish and turpentine from the pine trees—and pointing out each town that hurtled by. As we crossed the *Sado* river, I looked at Bela to see that she'd dozed off. *Mission accomplished.*

It felt fitting to sit into the silence as *Alcácer do Sal* whizzed by outside. It felt like a lifetime ago that I'd worked on a ranch there; I'd been only twenty at the time. I closed my eyes and let the movie in my mind roll out in full color: the endless golden plain with a single cork tree interrupting the horizon. The ramshackle farmhouse where water had to be pulled out of the well by hand. Kerosene lamps as the only form of electricity. The pungent smell of the goat tribe still lining my nostrils. The four-hundred-strong herd of *Mertolenga* cows with their huge curved horns and gentle temperaments. And the Marlboro-man charisma of the ranch owner everywhere around me throughout each day. I had felt so at home there, sitting on a horse all day, herding cows across the land; dust-caked and sweat-lined, I'd reckoned I'd been born in the wrong century. The inevitable affair with the ranch owner had been raw and wild, and of course forbidden. I was so young then. In the end he'd walked away.

All locked away in a compartment in my mind.

The new train line went all the way into Lisbon city center. A train line had been added to the iconic *25 de Abril* suspension bridge over the River *Tejo*. The city sprawled out below us as the train pulled to a halt. Bela woke with a jolt and took in the enormity of the bridge's structure.

"Wow! It looks like the Golden Gate Bridge," Bela said as we stood up and gathered our things. "Sheila, I'm so hungry and thirsty, I think I'm going to pass out." She reached for the water bottle.

"No, Bela, you can't. Not yet," I said and snatched it out of her reach.

We took a taxi from the *Estacāo do Oriente* to "The Place." My heartbeat quickened as I knocked on the door of the familiar old building. As the nurse ushered us in, I could sense Bela slipping in behind me like a sticky shadow. I turned to her and smiled. "Are you okay, Bela?"

Her face was white and expression locked. "Yes, thank you. I'm fine. But you'll stay with me, won't you? At least for a bit?"

"Of course I will. Come on, let's go and fill out the paperwork."

The interior of "The Place" was unrecognizable. Gone was the dank, faux-religious aura. The windows in the waiting room were open now and sunlight shone onto paintings of bright yellow sunflowers that covered the walls.

Soon, Bela was ushered from the waiting room. I closed my eyes. *Please, please let it go well for her.* I had arranged for my own tests, while there, and after went to the café next door for a *bica* and a *pastel de nata*—bitter black coffee and a traditional custard tart, smothered in cinnamon powder. *Oh, my God. So good!*

I checked on Bela afterward and the nurse told me to come back in an hour and a half when she'd be awake and ready to go home.

I hopped on a passing yellow tram, which made its way up to the *Castelo São Jorge*—St. Jorge's Castle. I'd come here with my parents when I was a child for picnics. They'd loved its history and the fact that it was built in the sixth century. Now, leaning against the castle wall, I closed my eyes and tuned into the city. Though I was born in Lisbon, I'd never really spent much time here. It was huge, spanning seven hills with a population of almost three million. It had a lazy I'll-do-it-tomorrow-or-maybe-the-next-day kind of feel to it. The deeply ingrained café culture, the uneven cobbled streets crisscrossed overhead with crowded washing lines, the heat simmering up from the ground in curvy waves, and the smell of fresh octopus being grilled on the street corners—it made me smile. I breathed it all in and exhaled slowly, soaking in the sun.

In the background, a group of American tourists listened attentively to their guide. She was pointing out that the narrow road leading to the main castle entrance had been constructed with a sharp one-hundred-and-eighty-degree corner, preventing attacking enemies from employing battering rams or leading cavalry charges.

Before I could get lost in any more castle details, I glanced at my watch. *Shit! Bela.*

I jogged down the steep hill, following the tram line the whole way and nearly bumped into Bela in the doorway of The Place. She looked like herself again...and at peace.

"Sheila, I'm done," she said. "I'm so relieved."

"You look great," I said, hugging her. "Let's get out of here."

I took her hand and led her across the road to the café where I bought her a meal. She wolfed it down. I couldn't believe how much things had changed since my own ordeal at eighteen—no pain, no blood. Bela told me she'd be able to start light work a few days later. By contrast, my own test results wouldn't arrive for another two weeks.

Bela recovered as quickly as she'd hoped, and she never mentioned it to anyone. But, of course, Fátima knew. Her, "All okay?" to me when we arrived home said it all.

17

There is nothing I would not do
for those who are really my friends.
I have no notion of loving people by halves,
it is not my nature.

JANE AUSTEN

WHEN SHE LEFT THE ALENTEJO for the last time, I was sure I'd never survive, as she'd been my go-to—the glue that held everything together.

She and Robert had been friends in Ireland for a long time before I met him. Both crazy about their water sports, they'd competed side by side in countless kayaking and surfing competitions over the years and had formed a close bond. I'll never forget the first time I met her: Our business was in its infancy. Robert had just given up his architectural job in the *Algarve* to work full-time on the commercial side of the trail riding. Short-staffed as we were, he'd asked her if she'd be interested in working with us for a while. At the time, we were based in the small inland village of *S. Luis*, about six kilometers from where we'd eventually buy our farm.

The horses were kept in a single field and were brought inside every night to a long barn-like building, previously used as a cowshed by a local farmer. Two continuous low mangers ran in a parallel line down its center, set apart by a walkway about one meter in width. At night, the horses were tied to the mangers facing one another and separated by a series of hanging wooden barriers. Not the most ideal set-up, but it was all we had—these were the early days, after all. Despite our best efforts, most mornings we'd open up the stable to find a loose horse or two wandering around, and smashed barriers and other carefully-thought-out contraptions lying useless on the ground.

That September afternoon, the air was heavy and compressed as the entire *Alentejo* choked on a thick layer of dust. Robert and I had just returned from a cool, green month in Ireland—the ideal country to escape to during the relentless summer. If countries could be identified by colors, I imagined Ireland as a soft palette of grays and greens, whereas Portugal would surely flaunt its rowdy whites and blues.

It was nearly eight in the evening by the time I turned the Jeep into the barnyard, just in time to bring the horses in, check them, and feed them. However, instead of the orderly line of hungry creatures I'd usually find waiting at the gate (in descending rank order), there were loose horses running around in every direction. *What is going on?*

From where I stood at the Jeep, I could see that the entrance gate had been lifted off its hinges and was now lying on the ground, on top of someone...I bolted in the direction of whoever it was, my thoughts an incoherent jumble of worst-case scenarios. Robert raced to my side as we arrived by the limp, cowering figure beneath the gate, who seemed to be wearing *my* smelly horse jacket. *What the hell?*

Robert had been introducing the woman on the ground to the horses and showing her the ropes the best way he knew. However, my stinky and familiar horse jacket hadn't fooled them. *No, sir.* Far too smart. The horses had copped her inexperience immediately and literally walked all over her. Horses are like that. They pick up on our every vibration and know instantly if we're not in tune with them, or with ourselves, for that matter.

Before Robert was able to help her, the woman sprang up, brushed herself off, and got back to what she'd been doing before we'd found her: attempting to stop the entire herd of horses from knocking down the fence. On her own. *Good luck.*

Who the hell was this person? And what on earth was she doing?

I moved as quickly as my muscles would allow, ducking through a different part of the fence and heading toward the lead mare. She was prickling, sensing tension and probably enjoying the havoc. I was able to catch her and calm her, and soon Robert and I had all the horses secured in their right spots, fed, and checked.

I caught the smell of fresh sweat trickling down Robert's face, darkening his short hair so that it stuck up crew-cut style. Sensing me, he turned round quickly, slit eyes now a dark cobalt blue. I glanced at the woman, who seemed remarkably calm after her ordeal. Before I could open my mouth, Robert spoke.

"Sheila, this is Nova—she's just arrived."

Before she uttered a single word, I knew we were going to get on. It wasn't the fact that we were similar in height, weight, or age. Nor was it her shoulder-length hair and straight fringe that framed her oval face, or her calm eyes that took in every detail. And neither was it her precision and economy of movement and the obvious athletic fitness she possessed. But rather it was a feeling that this person was entirely comfortable in her skin and safe in her authenticity—something that hasn't changed some thirty-odd years and many lifetimes later.

"So good to finally meet you, Sheila. I've heard so much about you," she said as her gaze moved to the horses, now safely tied up and eating their dinner. "Sorry about that earlier. I guess we'll all just have to get to know each other a bit better."

"No worries," I replied, already disarmed by her. "Great to meet you too, Nova. Welcome to the *Alentejo*. Come on, I'll show you your new home."

Now that the ice had been broken and we were walking away from the horses, Robert began rolling his tongue in his cheek.

"It's pure luxury, Nova, just the way you like it," he said. "Remember the last place you lived down in Galway by the outdoor pursuits center?"

Nova's eyes shone with amusement as memories came alive between them.

"You mean, when they made me build my own house?" she said, erupting into laughter and prompting Robert to stop walking and laugh heartily from the pit of his belly. There was obviously more to this story that I'd do well to ask about later. "And do you remember when it rained that first season and all the kayaks got washed away into the lake?" she went on, the two of them in hysterics now. "It took me three days to find them all!" Tears streamed down their faces. "I can't believe I actually put up with that for so long. What was I like?"

I had to admit it, it was oddly comforting to hear another Irish twang. Peas in a pod, they certainly had lots of catching up to do, which was evident by the nonstop banter as we settled into the Jeep. I just hoped the modest little caravan we'd prepared for her would do the job.

Our small rented house on the outskirts of the village was charming to look at, but cold and damp in the winter, hot as an oven tray in the summer, and the ferrous tap water always left us looking browner after showering than before. The cottage was built on a field, which we had now arranged to rent for our horses so we could have them close to us, rather than the "overnighting in a cowshed down the road" scenario. That situation hadn't working well for anyone. Only a week earlier, as I was giving the horses their morning feed, I'd moved my hand along one of the long mangers and scooped out all the old hay and straw to replace it with fresh feed. But my hand came away warm and sticky, covered in fresh blood. After the strange moment it took to realize the blood wasn't mine, the real source of the gory mess clicked into place. Two of our dominant horses had been able to stretch toward each other across the mangers the previous night, and one of them managed to bite off a piece of the other's nostril. *Charming.* In the same way that humans have many blood vessels in the mouth and nose, horses have a similarly large network of vessels in the muzzle area, and so it bleeds profusely.

We were hoping to move the herd over to our home field within the week.

Now, as the three of us got out of the Jeep and walked toward our little house, I wondered if Nova would fit in. Would she mind living in the tiny caravan that had been set aside for her? Robert had told me that she'd traveled extensively all over the world and was well used to roughing it.

"Let's get you set up in your new home, and then we'll show you the highlights of *S. Luis* city," I said.

I glanced at the darkening sky; it was time to get ready for dinner. I wanted to give Nova a real feel for Portuguese life, beginning with its food.

In the local library in *Odemira*, I'd recently been learning more about the region. The first settlers in the area dated way back to the Bronze Age, circa 3300 BC. Only twenty kilometers from the coast, and on one of the country's main trading routes, *S. Luis* had also been occupied by Romans, and then later by the Moors. The most recent census showed its ageing population to be hovering around the two-thousand mark, with residents making their living mainly from agriculture, pig farming, and cork production. However, there were signs of younger generations returning to set up small new businesses. The church, which dominated the town, watching over it from its elevated vantage point, dated from the sixteenth century and was listed as a national heritage site. Popular legend had it that it was built on the promise of a devotee.

I knew that Nova would be interested to know that over seven hundred and fifty kilometers of pristine hiking routes had recently been set up in the area. One of them, the *Historical Way*, was two hundred and sixty-three kilometers long, and took in much of the local culture and nature trails. Another favorite was the *Fisherman's Way*, over two hundred kilometers long and much closer to the coast and its wild, unrelenting nature.

The church bells were just chiming the half hour when Nova emerged from her caravan home.

"I love it," she said, now changed into her jeans. "Thanks for making it so cozy."

I could sense from her tone and natural expression that her remark was entirely genuine.

"Let's go to our local for dinner, shall we?" I suggested. "You'll get a real taste of Portuguese food." I noticed a quick glance between Nova and Robert.

"Hopefully, you'll like it," said Robert, not looking too confident.

"As long as there's plenty of beer, I'll be grand," said Nova.

Please, God, make her more adventurous than Robert. It had only taken me *three years* to get him to enjoy a beautiful freshly grilled fish.

To get to the village center, we took the ten-minute walk through orange groves and cork forests. A drove of long-snouted black Iberian pigs grunted while trampling and rooting round the bases of the trees. Nova did a double take—these guys weren't like the short-legged, snub-nosed pink pigs she was used to back home.

"Another thing I'll have to get used to," she noted, and then pointed at a rectangular building we were passing. "Please tell me that's not what I think it is."

Looking over the low wall, she'd spotted the pre-cast concrete sinks, washboards and drainers, and an ancient water-pulley system. Above were two signs, indicating two very separate spaces. One read *Doentes*, the other *Outros*.

I was both saddened and surprised by Nova's apparent knowledge.

"Yeah, it's a public wash house. Come by any morning and you'll see the village women doing their washing right there. Many houses in the area still don't have electricity, or if they do, the residents can't afford a washing machine. This particular wash house was built in 1940. *Doentes* means 'sick'—it's where any tuberculosis or plague victims' clothes had to be washed. And *Outros* means 'others.' Anyone who wasn't sick could wash their clothes on that side."

Nova's raised eyebrows said it all. "Honestly, it's like going back a hundred years. Please tell me you have a washing machine?"

Robert didn't miss a beat. "Nope. In fact, that's one of your new jobs out here. Scrubbing."

She just shrugged her shoulders and smiled at him. Walking through the village, we passed the many older people sitting on small chairs outside their front doors, enjoying the cool evening air and watching the world go by. *"Boa noite como vai!"* was the common greeting.

The main village square was lined beautifully with orange trees. It had a swing at one end and wooden benches all the way round. While small children ran around playing catch and hopscotch, the older girls played the "elastic game," which consisted of two girls standing three meters apart with an elastic band doubled and stretched between and around their ankles. A third girl could then jump into the middle space between the bands and use her legs to create intricate patterns and designs by jumping in and out through the bands.

While Nova and Robert got lost in watching the elastic spectacle, I made my way into the small *Restaurante Nascer do Sol* and ordered a real treat.

For starters: A plate of *caracóis*—snails—cooked in olive oil, salt, garlic, laurel, and piri piri. Extracted from their shells with a toothpick, they were perfect with beer. Small plates of *tremoços*—lupini beans—and a delicious vegetable soup completed our appetizer course.

Mains: *Choquinhos fritos com tinta*—baby cuttlefish—fried in their own black ink, stuffed with garlic, and utterly divine. *Salada de polvo*—octopus salad—prepared with onion, coriander, olive oil, and vinegar. And on the side, we'd enjoy a red-and-green pepper, tomato-and-onion salad, diced small and delectably seasoned.

Dessert: Now this just had to be an *Alentejo* specialty. *Sericaia*. Traditionally prepared with eggs, sugar, flour, lemon, cinnamon, *and* cinnamon sticks, then baked to perfection, and served with *Ameixas de Elvas em calda*—marinated plums from the city of Évora prepared by nuns using a three-hundred-year-old recipe—it was my favorite dessert in the entire world, and quite simply, heaven on a plate.

Our table, which was covered by traditional paper place mats, faced the square, and soon we each had our *Imperial* in hand, a small local draft beer. With "*Saúde*" and "*Sláinte*" to one and all, I was nearly giddy with the anticipation of sharing the *Alentejo* delicacies.

I watched Nova's face closely as the steaming *carcóis*, *tremoços,* and soup arrived. Not entirely the reaction I'd wanted. While she was able to summon the strength to move beyond looking to actually tasting the soup, each and every one of the other carefully chosen dishes were customarily pushed to my end of the table. Seemingly, the *caracóis* "had eyes on them" and the *tremoços* "looked like bird shit." *Oh, dear.* How was this possible? Robert made a valiant effort to enjoy the food as much as me, but...

When the mains arrived, matters unfortunately did not improve. The *choquinhos* in ink were "disgusting," and as for the *polvo* salad, there were simply too many tentacles for one to consider trying it. The salad was "edible," I was happy, albeit briefly, to hear. The cuisine was so uniquely Portuguese (and delicious!) that I felt to reject it was tantamount to contempt prior to investigation.

Years of training Robert to expand his palate were paying off, and I felt embarrassingly proud as I watched him manage to try a small amount of each dish. But he simply had to—he knew his life wouldn't be worth living otherwise.

Well, I thought, *things surely can't get any worse. The sericaia has to be huge hit.*

Oh, how wrong I was.

"Please, what can I get you, Nova?" I said, almost in tears. "Is there nothing you can imagine eating?"

Nova leaned in conspiratorially with a twinkle in her eye, and in nearly a whisper said, "Do you think they could rustle up a burger and chips?"

I must have looked aghast.

"I'm sorry, I'm just not used to this kind of food. It's different in Ireland."

That jocular energy between Robert and Nova was still swelling beneath the surface. Nova turned her twinkle toward Robert.

"Any chance of a Magnum ice cream for dessert?"

The two of them burst out laughing as if it was the funniest thing they'd ever heard. And it was difficult to not join in. It would be fair to say that I'd got my comeuppance at that dinner. Up until that point in my life, I'd unknowingly fostered the misconception that if I loved something, then surely others must share in that love. That night I learned to think differently.

A moment's conversation with the horses in the field before they come in for the day's ride.

The view of our home base for Caminhos do Alentejo–the lodge and barn. Samoqueirinha means "the little fig tree," and there has been a settlement here with this name for over four hundred years. The feeling of the place was so special and timeless. It was a paradise for our horses, who loved living in the carefully designed, well-sheltered fields. They came into the stable three times a day for meals and attention, but mostly they lived outside in natural herds.

In the dunes of southern Portugal the vegetation is able to grow on the sand as it has a high water table. The sand is not too soft and not too hard for riding. It is just right. The horses' hooves sink in about two centimeters—almost perfect footing.

There were so many special places on our rides, with fields of flowers and "secret" waterfalls only accessible by foot or horseback and full of wildlife, including wild boar. The Atlantic Ocean where we rode had no real continental shelf and the water got very deep very quickly. This kept the ocean temperature very stable, in turn keeping the air cool in summer with afternoon sea breezes even on hottest days. The farther south we rode the smaller the beaches and the more dramatic the cliffs. The cliff below (Carvalhal Beach) shows how twisted the rock strata are from the fault line close by.

In the distance you can see our second group of riders. We usually timed the groups to depart ten to fifteen minutes apart. This ensured guests and horses were conscientiously organized in appropriate numbers for periods of trot and canter, but allowed us to gather all together for meals and socializing.

By Day Two of a ride, the guests began to really understand their horses and get to know each other. (Above, Maya has finished her lunch and is helping herself to mine.) The shepherd in the background (near right) is waiting patiently for us to finish our lunch and move on so his flock can clean up behind us. Nothing was wasted on the trail (and there were often very happy goats). Robert and I would discuss the ride plan at "drinks stops" (far right). These mini breaks were a good time to check the horses, adjust tack, and when necessary, share a riding tip or two that I knew might help a guest when we set off again.

The sunset beach ride was always unique. As the sun relaxed slowly into the horizon the breeze would stop and the light show would begin. The riders listened to the sound of the waves as the cool Atlantic embraced the horses' legs after a long gallop through the dunes.

More than anything, a relationship with a horse is about mutual respect and absolute trust. To make that link, we must let go of our egos and lose the inconsistency we often have between the actions of our bodies and our minds. To a horse we are then communicating clearly without mixed messages, and he will want to be with us.

From a young age, I felt I understood horses and they understood me. It allowed me to be balanced and relaxed on almost any horse. Those some called "difficult" were just misunderstood.

A group coming up from the beach near the Roman fort at Isla de Pessegueiro (far left) and on the Blue Coast Trail near San Luis in the cork oak forests (left and below).

With Antonio Banderas and Guineu, our "movie star," during the filming of The House of the Spirits *(above).*

I bought Akbar (right and far right) as a four-year-old stallion from a horse dealer on an island in the middle of the Tejo River. Maya, our lead mare, let him think he was in charge of everything, even though it was she who was obviously managing the herd. But Maya was smart enough to let Akbar have his thunder, and he was smart enough not to question her too much.

Akbar demanded respect. Once, at a lunch break, Robert got impatient with him because he would not do what Robert wanted him to do. Akbar just pulled up his tie-stake and trotted away, up the hill, Robert running after him. Eventually, Robert gave up chase and sat down on the track. Akbar then showed up beside him and licked him on the ear. Akbar had made his point: they were both equal, both free.

Our horses were happy to go anywhere: Bonita, admiring the view (top left), guests scaling the dunes (far left), and passing Fort Nossa Senhora da Queimada at Porto Covo (above). Robert would often lead a group (near left). He mostly walked beside his horse, jumping on for the trots and gallops. This habit gave him a special kind of place amongst the horses, who then seemed to listen carefully to every word he spoke.

Menina and I lead our group down onto Malhão Beach just before sunset on the most perfect of all perfect days.

The Golegã Horse Fair (Feira da Golegã) is held near Lisbon every November. The most beautiful Lusitanos in the world are shown by breeders and riders in traditional clothing to demonstrate the Portuguese horse's abilities. The kind, large, olive-shaped eyes and beautiful long mane, braided for display at the fair, are typical of the breed. What we cannot see but know is there is the Lusitano's bravery and loyalty, which our amazing horses demonstrated over and over again.

People mix closely with the horses at the fair. It is common for riders to enter the bars on horseback and order drinks while chatting with each other and others attending the event (near right).

I found Tippex in Golegã, very young, skinny, and dragging a hind leg. We fed him during our stay for the fair, but it was clear his injuries were serious, and I could not leave him behind. Into the van he went! Four operations and a month later, Tippy was walking again. He followed the trails with us for the next ten years.

During the December 1995 trail ride, our group was caught out in terrible flooding. In places, the track had been washed away and streams had become rivers. Robert had to help riders navigate a very deep culvert where the wooden bridge was submerged (above), and when I was knocked off a narrow wall while leading Joia across, he had to come to my rescue (left).

By the end of seven days on the trail, a group of horses and a group of people immersed in nature come away as friends—some for life. All are changed forever. Whether it was toasting to the horses on top of the cliffs at the "end of the world" in Sagres (far left), celebrating a well of cool water on a hot day (near left), or recognizing the many years the Riding for the Disabled Association (RDA) came to us from the United Kingdom (above), all were special to us. When our guests got in the saddle, all were equal. Always, the horses knew how to handle each person, demonstrating the depth of their emotional intelligence.

Words can never hope to describe the freedom and energy a group of horses and riders share when galloping across open spaces of spectacular beauty. We tried to vary the places along the trails where we trotted, cantered, and galloped, so the horses were never sure when to expect a change of pace.

Group gallops were a joyful celebration of being alive. No leg contact was needed to direct the horses. We simply placed our trust, absolutely, in a large powerful animal, and in doing so, were rewarded over and over.

Our horses ran like the wind in the company of their friends because they felt good.

Filho do vento—"son of the wind"—is how some refer to the Lusitano horse.

The view from the clubhouse terrace across our little valley at one of the fields where our horses enjoyed their afternoons off.

With Robert

18

*Friendship isn't a big thing.
It's a million little things.*

PAULO COELHO

OVA AND FÁTIMA MADE AN IMPRESSIVE PAIR: resilient, grounded women who always gave their all. Every day, they reminded me that whatever happens, it's not where we are in life, it's who we have by our side that truly matters.

So many moments of Nova's time with us have imprinted themselves on the canvas of my mind and flash before me at the most unexpected times. It's funny how seemingly inconsequential details or exchanges between people can stick. With Nova, it was the way she emboldened those around her that made me smile.

By the time Nova had been working with us for about six months, Fátima had taken over all cooking duties, and Nova was in charge of collecting and delivering guests, making sure their never-ending demands were met, helping with the horses' care, and setting up camp at each ride's night and lunch spots. No matter what she was asked to do, nothing was ever too much for her.

By May we were heading into our busiest time of year. The *Alentejo,* Portugal's breadbasket, was starting to lose its vibrant colors. Flamboyant jacarandas with their explosive purple blooms were fading, mounds of bright-yellow mimosa flowers coated the roadsides, and the polychromatic expanses of blood-red poppies and their neighboring white, pink, and yellow wildflowers were being replaced by rippling waves of ripening wheat and barley. The dams were only half full, with the summer still ahead of us.

Since the previous year, when we'd spent a week riding with the owners of our American tour agency, the number of guests from the United States had multiplied. And now twenty-two American teenagers, ranging in age from thirteen to eighteen, and their guardians, were set to be our most challenging group yet. They all rode at a well-known academy in northern Connecticut, and every year they were taken on an "abroad holiday." Although they were all accomplished riders, the agency warned that "they wouldn't be easy to deal with."

I wondered what that meant exactly.

That Saturday, Nova and I were doing the Faro airport run, and my pickup was an hour before hers. As I was driving back to *Milfontes* through the *Monchique* mountain range with a bus full of our new American arrivals, I happened to pass Nova on her way to the airport. Hanging flagrantly out her minibus window were her khaki shorts, flapping wildly in the wind. ("Drying," she told me later.) I wondered, as we motored by, when she was going to put them back on...and hoped it would be before she arrived at the airport.

As Nova and I waved at each other in passing, a bemused-looking teenager sitting near the front of the bus said, "Do you actually know that person?"

In hindsight, I see how massive our workload was in our busy period, but at the time, it seemed like there was nothing Nova couldn't do. She and Fátima were well able to deal with Robert's demanding miltary-style running of operations. This took masses of pressure off me. Being able to concentrate solely on the horses' and guests' well-being was a blessing.

Funnily enough, Nova's Magnum ice cream tradition caught on. At the end of every long hard week, the first thing we did after dropping the guests at their hotel was sit around on any hay bale in sight, dusty and sweaty, with an ice cream in hand. (Though we all enjoyed one, Nova never had any trouble putting three away!) This was our special moment. *Dissection time.*

Robert unwrapped his ice cream while leaning against a bale and opened up the discussion. "Well, what did you all think of our young Americans?"

Despite the warnings, it had turned out to be easy enough.

"They were all decent riders," I said. "They even found Pash easy. He didn't roll on them in the sea. He didn't even run off with any of them."

Robert sat down and listened with chocolate smudged round his mouth, straw stuck to his torso, and dust streaks striping his face. *God, he's tempting.* I had to make an effort to stay focused on the conversation. I caught Fátima exchanging glances with Nova, who was on her second Magnum by this point.

"Yeah, and they were all light," said MC. "Not an elephant among them. The weigh-in strategy is working a treat." She'd finished her own ice cream and had now stretched out her long lithe body: arms reached overhead, her lower legs drooped down over the other end of her bale. I watched her shut her eyes and drift off. *She warms my heart, that girl.*

"Well, I'm glad *you* all had a good experience," said Fátima with her arms crossed tightly in front of her. I could see what was coming.

Nova placed a restraining hand on her arm. "Leave it," she said. "It doesn't matter now."

"No," said Fátima, dark eyes flashing. "Some things must be said! Explain to me in what country in this world do people eat the way they did? I've never seen anything like it. The meat on their plate couldn't touch the potatoes, the rice couldn't touch the vegetables..." She brought her hand to her brow and seemed genuinely close to losing it. "The lovely fish...had to be deep fried," she said slowly, as if recounting a crime, before pausing. Then, "...and the vegans and vegetarians! Don't even get me started on them."

"But you soon took care of that, Fátima," said Nova. "I was watching you."

Robert and I glanced at each other with more than a little apprehension in our eyes.

"What did you do?" I asked, noticing abstractedly how Nova had seamlessly moved on to Magnum number three. *Go, girl.*

"Simple," said Fátima with a mischievous glint appearing in her eye. "They were starving after all the riding, so I just said to them, 'This is Portugal, not America. Here, kids eat everything they're given. Children in Africa are starving to death. This is all you're getting.'" She smiled triumphantly and sat down beside Nova. "By day three," she went on, "they were eating everything. Even those vegans and vegetarians!"

Robert sat up very straight with a sharp intake of breath. The guest reviews might just land us all in a lot of trouble with our American agency. I tried not to think about how hard he'd worked to connect and bring them onboard.

"Don't worry about that now, Rob, I'm sure it'll be fine," I said, and then putting my placating hat on: "Fátima, good for you. They needed to hear that lesson."

Rob looked away, not convinced, while Fátima beamed, her point proven.

"Actually, you don't know the worst of it," said Nova. "Every evening, I had to take them to dinner to the fanciest restaurants in town—"

"*We* did, you mean," interrupted Robert.

"Okay, okay, *we* did," Nova agreed. "Anyway, we ordered them the fanciest foods, just as agreed with the agency—grilled lobster, tiger prawns, the best steaks—and guess what? They wouldn't touch any of it!"

"Ha!" I said, giving her a friendly shove. "What goes around comes around."

"Yeah, I get it," she said with a concessional smile. "On the upside, we brought back loads of edible goodies every day. Have you enjoyed lobstering it up all week?"

"Ah, it all makes sense now," I said. "I was wondering where all the lovely food came from. Not complaining, are we, Fátima?"

Two thumbs up from her.

After our intense American week, I decided it was time to get Nova up on a horse. Being such a sportswoman would be a real advantage, and Maya, one of the lead mares, would be the ideal teacher. Twelve years old, Maya was purebred Lusitano. Her coloring was the old-fashioned *Milflores* ("a thousand flowers")—a much finer description than the English translation "flea-bitten." She was a creamy canvas with flecks of brown. We'd bought her from a well-known breeder in the northern *Alentejo*, on the recommendation of our trusty blacksmith, Zé.

"You can't go wrong with that one," he'd told me. "She's six years old, untouched, not traumatized in any way. Just bring along a saddle and bridle, and hop on. She'll be just fine."

And so it was. When Robert and I went to try her out, she walked right up to us in the field, nuzzling and sniffing us all over, before standing totally still as we gently brushed her and slowly placed the saddle and bridle on.

Robert looked doubtful. "Are you sure it's safe to get on?"

The first time mounting a horse, especially one you've never met, is always a risk. Anything can happen.

"Zé said she'll be fine," I said. "She looks so relaxed, doesn't she? As if she knows she's coming home with us. Are you okay with this?"

He nodded, maybe not eager but resolute.

"Just hold her head there and talk to her," I said before putting some weight into the left stirrup, holding the saddle with both my hands, and gently hopping up and down alongside the mare. She turned her head round to the left for a brief instant then relaxed again. I took my foot out of the stirrup, patted her all over, then started again. This time, I lay across the saddle with my full weight—no reaction. Again, I removed my foot from the stirrup and patted her all over again.

"Okay, this time, if she's still calm, I'll swing my leg over and sit up," I said quietly to Robert. "Can you then just lead her forward for a few steps, and we'll see how it goes? Just breathe..."

"Sure."

Every time I've had the huge privilege of sitting on a new horse for the first time, my senses are engulfed by a wave of gratitude and amazement. How can such large powerful animals actually allow humans to sit on them?

I had a brief flashback to one ride that hadn't gone as planned: a jet-black, four-year-old stallion. I'd spent two months handling him, longeing him, and putting the saddle and bridle on him. The day I planned to swing up for the first time, my instructor at the time held the horse at his head while my riding companion stood beside me on the horse's left. We patted the saddle, then I placed my left foot in the stirrup and hopped up and down beside him. The horse was used to this and didn't react. *Time to mount*. My instructor nodded. Taking a deep breath, I got up slowly, lifted my right leg over his back, and settled in the saddle.

For five seconds, nothing happened. The horse stood like a statue. Then I gently touched his neck, and he exploded. All four legs took to the air, his back curling into a coil. I was chucked off far into the distance.

You just never know.

As soon as I was up on Maya, however, she obediently followed Robert and seemed oblivious to the extra weight on her back.

"Can you let her go now?" I said to Robert. "She feels good."

He glanced up at me, unclipped Maya, and continued walking alongside us for a few more meters. Then he stopped, and she just kept going.

Six years later, Maya was one of our kindest, most trustworthy, and most comfortable horses. She intuitively guessed what each of her riders wanted. No force was ever required. She was perfect for the start of Nova's riding career.

19

The most beautiful things in the world cannot be seen or touched, they are felt with the heart.

ANTOINE DE SAINT-EXUPÉRY

M Y MEMORIES OF RAIN have always been a source of solace. There have been numerous occasions when I've been caught in spectacular rainstorms, and I've loved them all. But sometimes a storm comes along that shakes you to your core.

Over several weeks, pillars of brooding cumulus gathered on the horizon, blotched with hints of purple, until they progressed into a heavy dark-gray blanket. Robert and Leonel cleared all the storm drains, taking extra care with the huge one that went round the back of the stables and under the main driveway. They cut all the hanging branches from the cork and eucalyptus trees and moved the nine assorted vehicles into a clearing, far from all the trees and buildings.

I could feel the horses getting nervous as the sky hung ominously low and the air bristled with static. They clung together in tight groups, nose to tail, snatching mouthfuls of food.

Standing next to Robert and the rest of the staff in the hay barn next to the stables, I felt calm and protected. The U-shaped barn lent a feeling of connectedness and safe harbor.

"Robert," I said quietly. "Shall we bring the horses in? You know the two old girls, Maya and Boneca, hate thunder. I don't want them to send the whole gang into a panic."

Just as Robert opened his mouth to answer, a cracking boom drowned out his voice completely. A streak of pure white light ripped the graphite sky while huge drops of lukewarm rain tumbled down, bouncing off every hard surface and sending clouds of dust flying. I grabbed his arm and started to run toward the horses.

"No, wait, wait!" he shouted, holding me back with both arms. The girls, who were poised to run out after me, halted to listen. "They may be better off outside. They can move around more. Wait, guys!"

We all stood close together while the rain hammered ceaselessly on the stable roof. *The poor horses! We should have brought them all in.* Trickles became rivulets, and gullies became streams, which gushed with hurried water. Leonel braved the rain to check the storm drains and gave Robert the thumbs up. They were already full, bubbling fiercely with brown runoff from the horse fields, but they were holding and not overflowing.

The dense blur of water closed in all around us, cutting visibility to a few meters. I looked at Robert, whose furrowed brow signaled fervid calculating as he counted the time between flashes of light and crashes of thunder.

"Twelve—that's only four klicks away," he said. "Eight, nine...only three...holy shit, it's moving fast. Okay, everyone, it's nearly here...one, two, three..." On cue, a deafening boom crashed right above our heads. "One kilometer... hold tight!"

Forked flashes bounced furiously all around us now, deafening claps of thunder in immediate concord. I glanced at everyone. The girls had their eyes closed, hugging each other tightly. Fátima and Leonel stood side by side, clasping their elbows. Robert's eyes were wild, his hair on end. Had he been struck by lightning? He paced the length of the stables madly, then stepped outside, constantly looking up into the collapsing lake of water above us. I stood in front of him, took his hands in mine and made him look at me. The curtain of dense water was lifting slightly, and shapes were re-emerging.

"Robert, stop! There's nothing you can do now." He stopped pacing and listened closely. "Listen... seventeen, eighteen...it's moving away." The storm was leaving us as dramatically as it had arrived. Leonel and Fátima gathered up halters, getting ready to bring the horses in.

"Yeah, yeah, you're right," said Robert. "Jaysus, that was something else!"

The rain was falling more haphazardly now, rhythmically drumming the stable roof.

"Okay," I said. "Let's get them all in now. Check everyone."

Fátima went round putting out the feeds while Leonel opened all the side gates. And the horses came rushing in on their own, right over to their stalls.

"Bela, will you please scrape the water off them? And MC, can you please help me blanket them? We'll stuff straw in under their blankets, that'll warm them up quickly."

Bela winked at me and went off for the scraper.

The horses were steaming and shivering, way too unsettled to eat until we had them all dried and calmed down. All except Maya and Boneca.

"They're too upset to eat," said MC. "What shall we do with them?"

"We'll keep them in overnight, nice and warm, and we'll rotate so one of us is always beside them. What do you think, Robert?"

He looked up at the dark sky and then at the row of horses.

"Yeah, I think that's a good idea. I'll do the first shift." He shook his head, invigorated. "I can't believe that storm. Never seen rain like that in my life, Sheila. And I'm from Dublin!"

Totally in his element, I went over and just held him for a long time. He smelled of horse sweat, salt, and hay... perfect.

20

Life is too short to drive boring cars.

ELVIS PRESLEY

ROBERT LOVED CARS and looked after them really well so they'd be up to the endless dusty kilometers we demanded from them. In his mind, everything was fixable—no thanks to our local mechanics, who were either permanently drunk or perpetually stoned. He opted instead for buying all necessary parts in Lisbon and doing the work on the cars himself.

When I'd first met Robert, he'd been driving a snazzy sports car—his pride and joy. But horses have always had a way of eating us out of house and home, so before he knew it, the car was sold to pay for horse food. *He really should have seen it coming.*

Once the business was starting to go well, we were running seven different vehicles. I remember driving to the north to pick up our first secondhand Toyota HiAce van, a cream-colored nine-seater with little checkered curtains. The second one was the same but in a dull golden color. We used these cars for years before selling them on to Angola, where they were fitted with a third bench seat so they could transport twelve people total. (It seems such vans were hugely popular for transporting mercenaries around that part of the world.)

"Thing One" and "Thing Two" were the staff cars—two tough old Renault Fives that were able to go anywhere a Jeep could, except into fast-flowing rivers. My beloved *Umfi* was replaced by real workhorses: a white Toyota GR and a dark blue Mitsubishi Pajero—my prize possession.

On countless occasions, when Robert was researching trails for our rides, he'd managed to get a Jeep so badly stuck in a river, or in mud, or even in quicksand, that the only solution was to get it pulled out by an excavator, which was not always easy to find in the middle of nowhere. I was along on one of these exploratory trips when the mud came up to the Jeep's windows, so we removed most of our clothes, wound down the front windows and climbed through them onto the hood, then jumped from there onto firmer ground. That day, Robert lashed a fence post to the Jeep's front wheel, attached it with a rope to the winch, then wound it around a tree to try to pull it out. It didn't work. And to make matters worse, we were being watched by a curious baby donkey, who'd left his mother's side to mock us from below his oversized ears.

Then there was "Cristine," Robert's "private runaround," a car with many stories to tell. Robert had bought her from a policeman in the local town, and she definitely had a mind of her own. The windows would open and shut randomly, irrespective of rain or sun. The sunroof leaked. (It was actually Robert's party trick to drive around a bend so sharply that all the accumulated water would be dumped onto the passenger's head.) But Cristine's most memorable trait had to be her disappearing act. Robert had parked her in the shade of the eucalyptus tree at the top of the property, and she seemed happy enough. When he returned two hours later, no Cristine. No one had seen or moved her. A search party was dispatched, and an hour later, her trail was discovered, winding its way through the trees, heading downhill toward the stream. Fortunately, the thick gorse and gum cistus bushes had managed to halt her escape. By the time she'd stopped, the only part of her that was visible was her tiny antenna.

It was a different vehicle that made one of our two-week trail rides particularly challenging. I was leading the ride on the morning before reaching our long-awaited destination, *Sagres*. It was the last day of a particularly testing first week, and horses and riders were all looking forward to their day's rest before starting the second part of the journey, back to base. That morning it was cold. The clouds were piling up on the horizon and I hoped to arrive at our lunch spot before any downpours. Tom, one of my riders, was a Type 1 diabetic, and I'd been keeping a close eye on him, aware that his lunchtime insulin was in the Jeep. Tom had explained to me at the start of the week that if he missed a single shot, *hyperglycemia* would set in, causing tiredness, thirst, and a very dry mouth. After a delay of three to four hours, he added, the body started making ketones—that is, it would break down fat stores and generate acids. It could be life-threatening. *Another hour to go*, I thought. *We shouldn't have a problem.*

Nova had been driving the Jeep with the horse trailer and all the supplies that morning, while Robert was in charge of backup in the other Jeep. As she drove down a long hill on the main road, Nova realized that the weight in the trailer was too far toward its back end. When she braked slightly on the downward slope, the trailer snaked frantically behind her for about a hundred meters before finally overtaking the vehicle and jackknifing into the Jeep's driver-side door, slamming it into the metal guardrail. The force of the impact not only caused a crate of beer to rocket from the trunk and smash into the front windshield, but also propelled the Jeep into an oncoming car being driven by tourists. Being so much heavier, the Jeep's weight crumpled the front of the tourists' rental car, causing its unfortunate, innocent driver to break his leg.

An hour later, Robert found Nova sitting by the side of the road, rocking herself backward and forward as she hugged her knees. Luckily, she was totally unscathed.

It was as I rode with my tired group of riders into the chosen lunch spot and the first fat drops of rain started to fall that I realized something must have gone terribly wrong. There was no one there. Nothing was set up for lunch. Such a thing had never happened before.

I glanced at Tom, who was due his next insulin shot in twenty minutes, and saw that he was already perspiring and looking very pale. With no way to communicate with either Nova or Robert, I decided to risk it and continue with the whole group to our next meeting point, nearly an hour away, and just try my best to keep everyone's spirits up.

The sky dimmed, the clouds darkened and closed in on us, and the taunting drops of rain became a heavy downpour. I looked at Tom. His face was a grim mask. He held onto the front of the saddle with both hands while his upper body swayed from side to side. His horse was carrying his head completely sideways to stop the rain from going into his ears.

What the hell has happened? Where is everyone?

We trudged on through the cork oak forest at a walk, as I dared not go any faster. I had Tom's horse now clipped to my own as our guest leaned forward over the horse's neck with a glazed look in his eyes. Rain and wetness had trickled into all our crevices, and judging from the moues on everyone's faces, I knew I wasn't the only one with soggy underwear.

It was with relief that I spotted a familiar sign: Looking down at the trail, an arrow made of branches pointed us sharp left, toward an abandoned farmhouse. My heart flipped, and I turned to my group, giving them the thumbs up.

We were going to be okay.

21

*I've spent most of my life riding horses.
The rest I've just wasted.*

AUTHOR UNKNOWN

THE LETTER I'D BEEN DREADING FOR WEEKS arrived the morning after the big storm. As soon as I saw it, my heart sped up. I immediately folded it and hid it in my bra. I desperately wanted to read it…and I never wanted to read it.

Robert had called for a staff debriefing and for a thorough check of the property for any storm damage. The letter, which had me feeling like a snared rabbit, would have to wait.

Swishing their tails, stamping away the flies, the horses ate their breakfast slowly, all wearing that faraway look of contentment. They snorted in pleasure while we brushed them, checked and oiled their hooves, cleaned out their eyes and inspected them for bot fly eggs. The tiny yellow specks deposited on the horses' legs by these creatures had to be removed every day using a razor blade, or they risked being ingested and developing in the horse's gut.

It had taken till three in the morning for our two older mares, Maya and Boneca, to finally calm down, and only now had they started eating. As planned, we'd all done our two-hour shift to keep them company throughout the night. Looking around now, I could see I wasn't the only one with dark circles and straw in her hair. But it had all paid off.

"Let's give them all a day off today," I said to the girls. "They deserve it. You too. Take a break. I'll feed them later on."

While the girls happily made away, Robert looked at me curiously. I shaded my eyes from the sun and looked back at him.

"You know," I said, "there should be great surf on *Malhão* Beach after the storm. Why don't you go in for a blast? Go on. I'll be fine."

I needed to be on my own with the horses. But I wasn't going to tell him that.

"You sure?" he said quickly. I smiled and nodded, knowing full well there was no way he could resist the sea, especially when the surf was huge.

When they'd all left, I walked slowly up to the house, the dogs following behind me single file, their heads close to the ground. *They knew.*

With the envelope in my hand, I curled up in my special snug and took a deep breath. I opened the envelope and took out the letter. On the left-hand side, there was a long list of tests, which meant nothing to me. On the right-hand side, every box was ticked. My heart raced. What did it mean? A letter slipped out from the back and fell to the floor. I picked it up. Key words leaped out at me: *All levels normal...No reason to suspect any problem conceiving...NORMAL.*

I jumped up and punched the air. *Jesus!* A coffee cup smashed on the ground. I danced round the room. I hugged the dogs. I bounced up and down on the bed. I couldn't believe it. Laughing and crying at the same time, I grabbed Tippex and twirled him around in circles.

I reread the letter over and over. My heart was achingly full.

I stopped suddenly. *Shit.* What would Robert say? Was he ready for this? Would he run away? *Oh, God.* I slumped onto the floor. *No, he'll understand. Or will he?* He knew my biological clock was going crazy. That I salivated every time I saw a baby. That my breasts ached whenever I saw a mother breastfeeding.

I flopped onto the bed.

The dogs inched closer and licked my ears. I buried my face in the duvet, clasping both arms tight around my head.

"Stop it. Go away!"

They took this as a good sign and leaped onto the bed and licked my face and pulled at my sweater. I pushed them off the bed gently. Then I laughed.

"Okay, you're right! Let's go up the mountain."

Climbing always helped me put things in perspective. I gathered the dogs, a backpack, and water, and marched toward the base. Half an hour later I was on all fours, crawling up the near-vertical slope. Focusing totally on my footing, I scrambled up the narrow rocky trail that had been gouged into the mountainside. Cool sweat dripped down my forehead, neck, and back, and stung my eyes. The dogs looked down at me, waiting patiently on a stone outcropping above. I licked a trickle of blood off a graze on my hand while my lungs ached for oxygen.

Finally, I hauled myself onto the flat rock. *Halfway there.* The second part of the climb was a little easier, and thirty minutes later, I'd reached the summit. Breathless and bloodied, I looked around for my favorite rock, placed my folded jacket onto it, and dropped. Earlier I'd felt like I was on the mountaintop, as I'd jumped around my room...but now I actually was.

I sat motionless with my eyes closed. Just being. Breathing. In the eternal now.

I sensed the dogs edging closer and within moments, they were licking the blood off the backs of my hands and ankles. The touch of their tongues was soothing and healing. Eucalyptus essence wafted invasively, yet welcomely. I looked out to the horizon, the world at my feet. The aroma around me broadened to include a woodsy and balmy aspect, scented with pine and a trace of wild mint. The rain had rinsed and cleansed the countryside, painted and polished it bright. Aquamarine sea was fringed with golden dunes. Further inland, the green tapestry was interrupted by fields of blazing sunflowers, their big round faces turning with the sun. And *Milfontes* glistened white in the distance. I had a bird's eye view of the farm below. Everything in its perfect place. Even me.

This was where I wanted my ashes scattered one day.

I breathed out and smiled. I now knew what to do. *Talk to Robert. Tell him my good news. Explain to him that now is a good time. The best time.*

The track wound its way down the mountainside, following its contours. The dogs raced off baying, doing their imaginary hunting thing. They'd never once caught anything.

When I arrived back, there was still no one around, so I brought all the horses in for their lunch. I noticed that Akbar, the unquestionable alpha male, was shaking his head and laying his ears back at any other horse who approached one of his new mares, Simpática. He was clearly trying to tell me something.

I went over and felt her all over, took her temperature and ran my hand down her legs. Nothing unusual. I'd bought her only a month ago from a breeder who'd guaranteed she wasn't pregnant. *Hmm.* I decided to get the vet up in the next few days to double-check. I hadn't yet mastered the art of feeling for life inside the equine womb.

After they'd all eaten, I kept Akbar and Simpática in. He calmed down by rubbing his head quite violently against my back, so much so that I had to hold the wall for support. The two of us went back such a long way.

I'd bought him as a four-year-old stallion from a horse dealer, who kept his herd of youngsters on an island in the middle of the *Tejo River* (to prevent horse thieves, apparently).

A group of four of us crossed over in a small motorboat, and lassoes in hand, went looking for the herd. Within minutes, we heard a rumble of hooves thundering toward us, and just had time to run for cover and watch forty wild stallions gallop past. Blacks and grays, chestnuts and bays, snorting and squealing, they stopped in the clearing. As one, they turned to face us. A dark steely gray with black tips, wide-set eyes, and a massive presence stood in front of the herd. He stamped the ground, challenging us, his mane blowing in the wind. Not for the first time with a horse, the clock stopped for me as I took in his powerful majesty.

"That's the one," I'd said to the horse dealer. Lassoing him and bringing him back with us to land, as he swam furiously behind the small boat, had been the beginning of a long adventure for both of us.

Akbar had kept his wildness during all these years, but slowly, we built a wonderful relationship based on mutual respect and trust. He was now nearly eighteen and had only in the past year or two allowed someone other than me to ride him. Completely white now, his thick tail trailed the ground and his wavy mane fell to well below his neck. I rubbed his forehead and separated his forelock, putting half behind each ear so I could see his eyes, which were full of light and rimmed in natural black eyeliner. I put him and Simpática out in the small field by themselves, just in case. He'd be protective of her if she was pregnant. I left the girls a note, asking them to keep the two of them away from the others.

We didn't need another foal right now.

Back in the clubhouse, I hoped there'd be some food somewhere. Fátima had left a plate of chickpea and salted-cod salad in the fridge. Typical of her to remember, even on her day off. She'd probably suspected something was up with me. I smiled. She'd been into witchcraft and astrology since she was a child and made all her big decisions when the moon cycle was just right. She even wore a good-luck talisman around her neck, close to her skin. I'd trusted her and her uncanny instincts from the first day we met.

I sprinkled some fresh coriander on my fish, picked a couple of oranges from the tree, and sat outside on the terrace. A date with myself.

22

I had been riding horses before my memory kicked in, so my life with horses had no beginning. It simply appeared from the fog of infancy.

MONTY ROBERTS

T HE SECOND I HEARD the phone ring, I knew it was him.

"Robert, that'll be Zé. I need to go shopping again."

Robert took a deep breath, raised his shoulders, and exhaled loudly as the phone continued to ring. "How can you possibly know it's him?"

I contained a smile, prompting him to narrow his eyes and laugh through his nose.

"It's the witch in you. I should have known the night we met."

I shrugged and picked up. "Hello?" I put my hand over the mouthpiece. "He has two possibles he wants to show me."

As I listened to Zé, I watched Robert walk over to the open window in the kitchen and rest both his arms on the upper ledge. His bleached blond hair brushed his shoulders as he leaned his head into his arms. Then I was swallowed back into the conversation.

"Yeah, okay, I'll be there. See you at one."

Robert turned from the window and raised his eyebrows.

"Well, are you off shopping?"

"Yeah," I said, biting my lower lip. "If that's okay? I'll meet him tomorrow."

"You know, 'shopping' with you has taken on a whole new meaning," he said, walking slowly toward me, his dark blue eyes intent. "It used to mean food or clothes, or even shoes. But now I know you'll come home with two or three new horses."

I went over to him and hugged him tight. And listened to his heart.

"And the weird thing is, now I think it's totally normal." I could feel him smile to himself. I just stood there, breathing him in. Did he know how I felt about Zé? Did he sense the unspoken bond we shared? Did it worry him that it nagged deep in my mind, a constant insistence looking for its niche?

WHILE PREPARING FOR THE DRIVE, I remembered every detail from the first time I met Zé. In his local town, *Ferreira do Alentejo*, everyone spoke of him with admiration. He was held in such respect that he'd been granted an honorary citizen's award, and a high-profile bullfight had been arranged in his honor.

I'd parked the Jeep outside the first *taverna* I'd noticed, realizing I probably should have made an appointment. *Surely, he'll be too busy to see me.* I mounted the hand-carved stone steps and entered through the small doorframe. As my eyes adjusted to the darkened room, my nose adjusted to the smell of bodies laced with the local fire water, *bagaço*. An ancient whirring fan hung from the ceiling at an odd angle, while old men sat in pairs, lining the walls, huddled over their drinks and dominoes. I approached the rough wooden counter, pockmarked by a hundred cigarette butts. All conversation stopped. Old eyes swiveled to follow me. I leaned an arm on the sticky bar surface, but as no one appeared, I turned back to the customers.

"Can anyone tell me where *Mestre Zé* lives?"

The wrinkled faces looked at each other blankly, then back to me.

"Who wants to know?" said one of them.

"I might have some business for him. Can you help me?"

Then they all wanted to talk to me.

"Where are you from?"

"Did you drive the Jeep yourself?"

"Why do you speak Portuguese?"

"You don't look Portuguese."

And finally: "He's just across the street. Just listen. You can't miss him."

The narrow alleyway across from the main street had cobbled stones that were worn smooth and shiny. Small whitewashed houses crowded the sides, their tiny doorways and window frames featuring the traditional blue-and-ochre-colored bars.

Then I heard the hammering calling me like a harbinger, and around the next bend, I spotted the oversized arched doorway. The street was jammed by a throng of about twenty men, who looked on with crossed arms while an assortment of mules, donkeys, and horses stood patiently, tied up to well-placed rings, awaiting their turn. I squeezed my way through to the arched doorway and peered in.

The vaulted chamber had been blackened by soot and Father Time. At the back, a roaring forge glowed deep orange with raging red sparks spitting out. Silhouetted against the blaze was the anvil, a blacksmith on either side. They beat the red-hot metal strip in turn and in perfect rhythm until it was the exact fit for a particular hoof. Then they cut out the holes for the nails: seven per shoe. I watched, mesmerized, as each newly molded horseshoe was dipped, sizzling, into a bucket of cold water.

Rivulets of sweat ran off their faces and elbows. Finally, they stopped for water. I looked at the one I was sure was Zé.

"*Mestre Zé*? Could I have a word with you?"

He turned toward me, wiping his hands on his suede farrier's apron. I hadn't been prepared for his presence. I took a step back, feeling his pure energy blast into me. A tall man with closely cropped dark hair, huge forearms, and calloused and scarred hands like vice grips. His black eyes were set wide apart and looked right into me. But the life in those eyes.... It was like he'd walked through the centuries to be there, connected to the earth and those around him as naturally as he breathed.

"How can I help you?"

TEN YEARS AND MANY HORSES LATER, every time I met Zé I still felt my stomach flutter. Not only because of his intuitive feel and profound knowledge of horses—it was something much deeper than that. It was our visceral understanding of each other. It happens so rarely in life, but when it does there's no mistaking it: a familiarity with someone that defies logic and the handful of times you may have met, but a connection so strong, it's as if you were intimately connected in another life.

I sometimes wondered, *What if?* But life, after all, is about choices, and though the current between us was undeniably strong, my heart belonged to Robert.

As arranged, I got to the café at one, and he was already inside having his *bica*—a tiny espresso. Zé had that rare gift of time. He was never late and always totally in the moment, like he'd made some deal with time itself.

"Where are we off to today?" I said, smiling up at him. "It's so damn hot!"

"Inland. It'll be much hotter. Nearly forty," he said. "You won't like what you see, but keep an open mind."

For the hot hour-long drive, we relaxed deeply into the comfort and pleasure of each other's company. The line between us was never straight, and yet somehow, we never crossed it.

"So, are you going to tell me about the horse...or horses?"

He smiled, keeping his eyes on the road. "There are two of them: one's a total basket case, and the other's a skeleton."

I burst out laughing. "They sound really promising! Just what we're looking for."

THE VILLAGE OF SANTA CLARA crouched beside a dried-up dam. What remained of the vast expanse of water was a sorry sight: just a few dirty ponds.

The first horse was kept in an abandoned carpentry yard. When he spotted us, he moved cautiously in our direction, stepping over stacks of discarded rusty intruments, rubbish, and piles of wood. I held my breath.

"How can people treat horses like this?" I said, shaking my head. Zé gestured to a sheltered alcove.

"Well, at least he's got water and a pile of hay to eat in the corner."

"That much itself," I said.

"One of the lucky ones."

Zé ran his hands all over the horse while I checked his teeth and the thickness of his jawbone. I'd learnt over the years that unlike teeth, the jawbone couldn't be filed down to make the horse appear younger.

"I figure he's about twelve," I said, "what do you reckon?"

Zé stood back and absorbed the feel of the horse. "Yeah, bang on," he said, and then with a broadening smile: "Let's get you on board for a tryout. This could be interesting!"

The horse stood deceptively still as we carefully tacked him up, and even when we led him out of the builders' yard, he seemed relatively chill. But the moment I gathered up the reins and put my left foot in the stirrup, all the muscles in his neck and back tensed. He tried to gallop around Zé, who was still holding his head. I stood back.

"That went well!"

"Okay, try again. Be quick. I won't let go."

This time Zé covered the horse's left eye so that I could get on without upsetting him as much.

"Okay, can I let go?" Zé asked, once I was sitting lightly in the saddle.

I nodded and pointed the horse in the direction of the path leading down to the dam. He stretched his head forward and we were off like a rocket, his hooves pounding the dusty trail like he was on fire. I tried to use the reins to slow him down, but it only made him go faster. *Keep calm, Sheila, and think*. I glanced back over my shoulder. Fine orange dust swirled in a long column behind us. Peering forward through his whipping mane, I saw that the track ended at the edge of the empty dam. My eyes widened as he leaped into the dust basin and continued his frenzied gallop straight through the middle of it. I leaned slightly to the left and he responded immediately, galloping round the outer left side of the hollow dust bowl. Then I leaned forward, way out of the saddle, and stroked his neck with my right hand. His ears flickered forward so I continued patting and talking to him.

A dormant memory of a childhood trauma flashed through my mind: a sunset ride on a beach with a friend, a swim in the sea, his horse swimming off into the distance. I'd screamed at him to let go, to hold on to my waist, and he did. His horse was never seen again.

My runaway lowered his head slightly, as if suddenly noticing where he was going. The frantic gallop turned into a loping canter, then a rhythmical trot, and at last, a swinging walk. I leaned slightly to the right. He turned immediately, back toward where we'd started. While I continued speaking and stroking him, he snorted repeatedly. He was starting to relax. He'd turned steely gray with sweat, and thick foam crusted the edges of his saddle blanket as we came to a halt. He stood still as a statue as Zé held him. I dismounted. I felt Zé scan me all over.

"Are you okay?" he said. "My God, I did not see that coming!"

I looked up at him. "He's so fast! No brakes. He's traumatized, there's no doubt about that. But, somehow, I think we can turn him around."

Zé smiled, his eyes dancing. "Your problem is you just can't say no to a horse. But yeah, I agree, he'll be fine." He handed me the reins. "Here, put him away. I'll call the owner and let him know."

A COOL DRINK LATER, Zé and I drove inland for another half hour. The rolling hills flattened out into an ochre plain while small herds of sheep clustered around the trunks of mushroom-shaped cork oaks. As their heads touched the ground, they shuffled along in a trance, following the tree's inching shadow.

Scanning the monochrome landscape, Zé turned abruptly onto a narrow track.

"We'll follow this for about two kilometers, then we should spot her," he said, narrowing his eyes as clouds of orange dust streamed in through the open windows. I was dizzy from the relentless heat and sun, but Zé seemed impervious to it. He always said there was no point in talking or complaining about the weather, as you could never change it. Wise words. "Look, there she is." He pointed to the left.

"You're joking," I said, bringing both my hands to my face and rubbing my eyes. "That's not a horse!"

A skin-covered structure of a horse was tied up and didn't even glance at us when the Jeep stopped and we stepped out. One end of the rope went round her scraggy neck and then around her front legs, hobbling her, while the other end was attached to a stake, which had been driven into the bare ground five meters away. I looked around.

"There's no food or water anywhere. How is she surviving?"

Zé glanced under the horse.

"And she's got a foal somewhere. Look, she's full of milk."

The mare turned away from us and whinnied. The effort exhausted her and her head dropped back toward the ground.

"Maybe the foal starved to death," I mumbled to Zé, wiping tears into my shirt.

"No, he's around," he said. "See the tiny hoofprints over there?"

We poured her a bucket of water from the container in the car. She whickered and drank slowly.

"I have never, ever seen such an emaciated horse," I said, looking at the mare. Her coat was stretched tight over her protruding ribs, hips, and backbone. Deep hollows hooded her eyes, and her matted mane hung off her in felty clumps.

"How do we bring her back from that? What do you think?"

Zé walked round the back of the mare, keeping his distance.

"I think maybe a year from now she'll be fine. Look at her bone structure—big, square, and strong."

"What about the inside of her head?"

"If anyone can connect with her, you can," he said gently. "Hey! Here he comes!"

Cloaked in dust, a tiny foal galloped past us and dived straight under his mum, pushing his little muzzle into her udder. He started suckling.

"Okay," I said hesitantly. "You know, I really don't need a foal."

Zé just laughed and crossed his arms and looked from the foal back to me.

"Ah, look at him. He can't be more than three months old. She's already given him all she had!"

The chestnut colt still had his fluffy baby coat, and was standing now, front legs splayed, slurping and swishing his bushy tail. Zé knew he had me.

"Okay, we'd better come and collect them right away—tomorrow."

I wondered what Robert would say.

By the time we got to a café, the cool sea breeze had got up. Shadows grew taller as the sun started dipping toward the ocean. I felt Zé's dense presence beside me. *So intense...*

"Okay, I'll have the horses picked up tomorrow," I said. "Then the real fun will start."

"I'll check their feet this week." He paused and took a deep breath. "You're sure you're happy to take them? It's your call."

"Yeah, I am. Anyway, I can't just leave them there."

I drove home slowly, trying to lock away the feelings Zé had stirred up inside me. When the car bumped down the dusty drive and came to a stop in the yard, I spotted Robert, sitting cross-legged in the middle of the closest horse field. Beer in hand, he was surrounded by about ten horses, who rimmed him like giant flower petals. Some were nuzzling his hair. Others were touching his shoulders with their rubbery lips. And others were sniffing his bare feet.

I crawled under the electric fence and moved slowly toward them, cooing in a low voice. No one moved away. I squeezed in around their backsides.

"Hey, how was it?" he said, blue eyes smiling. "We're having our Zen moment here. Any luck?"

I sat down on his lap, facing him, and clasped my legs round his back and my arms round his neck.

"Well, they're long-term projects. One's in terrible shape and has a baby," I said, "and the other one has no brakes and is a bit of a headcase." I held my breath, waiting for his response.

"Okay," He squeezed me closer to him. "Do you think we can turn them around?"

I relaxed and closed my eyes. Someone seemed to be nibbling at his t-shirt now.

"Yes, I do," I said. "Six months?"

I untangled myself from him and we got up slowly, pushing back all the intruders.

"How was Zé?" he asked, out of the blue.

I looked away and bit my lip hard.

"Really good. Took his time. You know how he is."

THANKS TO ZÉ'S INSIDE INFORMATION, buying the two horses and the foal that day proved invaluable to our trail-riding operation. We named the first horse Pash, and within a year, he'd settled down and became a hot favorite with all our speed lovers. The mare we called *Joia*—Jewel. She turned out to be our most reliable and safest horse. Powerful and empathetic, she kept food at the top of her priority list. Her foal was Lucky Luke.

Four years later, Robert was key to second recoveries of both rescues. On a searingly hot ride, Joia tripped on hard stony ground and ripped the skin off both her front knees so badly that the tendons were exposed. She hadn't yet fully regained her trust in humans and was extremely hard to treat. Every evening, Robert would sit in front of her stall, sipping a cold beer. One day, as he sat there, she allowed him to do a thorough cleaning, and medicate and bandage both her knees. She made a complete recovery and was back to work within six weeks of her accident.

Around the same time, I'd noticed that Pash had started to eat even more slowly than he usually did. We checked his teeth and lifted his bowl onto a chair so that he didn't have to stretch his neck down to the ground to eat. A large soft mound developed along his neck, just down from his right ear. Within five days it erupted. Thick green pus seeped out and crawled toward his chest. The fetid stench was overwhelming.

The vet lanced it further and we flushed it out daily with distilled water and hydrogen peroxide. Then one day Pash stopped eating. His eyes became dull and listless. The vet recommended we put him out of his misery, unless we could somehow create a sterile environment for him to live in. By this time, we were allowing him to roam free around the farm and gardens, picking at whatever he felt like. We'd fashioned a large net sleeve which stretched from his head to his withers, to keep off the flies.

It was Robert who turned one of the guest rooms into a sterile pad. He removed all the furniture and curtains, whitewashed the ceiling, floor and walls, and unhinged the doors and windows, replacing them with disinfected netting. The thick bed of straw was kept immaculate. Kilos of carrots and apples were blended and mixed into a bran mash daily, which we fed to Pash in small quantities throughout the day. In the evening, we took turns sitting on his straw bed and reading out loud to him. He'd stand close by, head hung low, long eyelashes closed, ears twitching. This continued for two weeks.

Then, one day, he decided to live.

23

*Some horses will test you,
some will teach you, and some will
bring out the best in you.*

AUTHOR UNKNOWN

MAY WAS COMING TO AN END and so were our weeklong trail rides. They'd start up again in September when the weather was cooler. In June and July, we offered our "star-ride program," during which we rode out in a different direction every day, returning home at the end of the ride each night. As usual, we planned on being in Ireland for the month of August when the horses would have their yearly break.

After an article about us made it into the Portuguese papers, a group of riders from Lisbon got in contact. They wanted to ride with us as far as *Sagres* over a six-day period. They'd bring their own horses and grooms, and we'd guide them and provide all meals en route. We met with the group leader and agreed on all the details of the ride, such as where the horses would be overnighting and how our team would supply the safety backup, meals, and transport to the hotels they'd chosen to stay in. My main concern was the fitness level of the riders and horses. I was assured this was not a problem, that they all rode regularly and their horses were in good shape. The ride was planned for the last week of May.

The horses, we were told, were all purebred Lusitanos. The main qualities of the Lusitano horse, such as his explosive spirit, agility, bravery, loyalty, beauty, and ability to stop abruptly, are showcased impressively in modern-day bullfighting. But Lusitano horses first became famous around the time of an alliance formed between the Celts and the Iberians—who became known as *Celtiberians*—in 800 BC. It was around this time that the Iberian horse became renowned as a warhorse. One legend has it that the horses are so swift because they're sired by the wind. Another holds that the myth of the centaur was born at this time, because these horses and riders formed the perfect bond and were as one on the battlefield.

This maneuverable and quick equestrian style of warfare even impressed the Romans, as their empire expanded into Iberia in 206 BC, so much so that the Lusitano horse was adopted into their realm. The horse's loyalty, beauty, and docile nature later made him a favorite with all the royal courts of Europe. The Lusitano is truly a horse fit for a king.

That was a time when human lives depended on horses, not only on the battlefield, but also in our day-to-day lives. Today, so many of the skills born of that relationship, and the corresponding respect for the horse, have been forgotten or neglected. In some respects, it feels like we've lost our way.

AT THE START OF OUR CUSTOMIZED six-day trail ride, I still hadn't chosen which horse to take as my lead. Spoiled for choice, in the end I decided on Pash, now eighteen. With his light, fit build, Pash, out of all our horses, wouldn't be the least bit upset at leading a group of horses he'd never met before. He had nothing to prove; there was no ego involved.

The forecast for the week was for dry weather; temperatures moderate. As Robert finished having breakfast with the group, I went down to the stable yard to make sure everything was ready. The group's horses had been trailered in from Lisbon the day before and were being tacked up by the attending grooms. They were all stallions, and judging from the impressive brands visible on their right flanks, all from renowned studs. I noticed that most of the horses were being ridden in a double bridle, and when the group of riders walked down the driveway to join us, I was surprised to see that they were all wearing spurs and carrying whips.

Pash walked through the stallions without batting an eyelid, long and loose, as was his way, just wearing his comfortable snaffle. As soon as we were out of the main gate, however, the riders pushed their horses forward, cantering off in all directions. *Where the hell are they going?* I decided to continue at my own pace, warming my horse up slowly in the hope that I'd soon catch up with them. We were due to ride thirty kilometers on that first day, and we needed to rate the horses as much as possible.

Half an hour later, I found them all standing at a crossroad, their horses already spattered with thick white foam and breathing heavily. I reined Pash in gently and stood still, facing them.

"Listen, what are you all doing? You hired me as your guide, then you all galloped off. You don't know the way and your horses look tired already. Come on—let's all get off for a bit and give them a breather."

I slid down and crossed my stirrups, waiting for the other riders to do the same. No reaction.

"You don't expect us to walk, do you?" said the group's organizer. "We have grooms, you know. We have more horses. We'll send for them when these get tired."

"Suit yourself," I said, leading my horse out along the track. *What are these people thinking? How can I make them tune into their beautiful horses so they can enjoy the spectacular ride we have planned for them?*

Ten minutes later, I mounted my horse again as the coastal plain opened up in front of us. Long white sandy tracks stretched out in all directions, bordered on one side by a thick eucalyptus forest, and a series of high dunes on the other, creating a natural barrier with the sea. Saltiness enveloped us as the cool sea breeze drifted in.

Pash's steps got imperceptibly higher as he started to coil. He was ready to run. I turned in my saddle toward the group.

"Look at this! It's a perfect track to let your horses have a gallop, if you want. It's safe, and all you need to do is slow them down before the path winds into the forest again."

Before I'd finished speaking, they were off, legs flapping and whips whacking the horses' sides. I eased Pash into a canter and soon he was cantering past them all, not engaging in the race, but just enjoying himself. When I leaned forward and whispered to him, he slowly dropped back down to a trot, and to a long relaxing walk. He kept himself aloof.

An hour later, we approached our planned lunch spot in a place called *Cabo Sardão*. We clattered along a short stretch of tarmac before turning off it onto a soccer field perched right at the edge of the cliffs. I raised my hand and turned again to face my group of riders.

"Okay, we've arrived at our lunch spot," I said. "This is *Cabo Sardão*, which I'm sure most of you have already visited. It's between the beaches of *Almograve* and *Zambujeira*. That lighthouse behind us was built in 1915 and is seventeen meters tall."

I wasn't getting a single reaction from any of the riders. They looked like they wanted to die right there and then, leaning across their saddles, all of them sitting at really odd angles.

I ploughed on. "They say this is where the world slows down so much that it nearly comes to a standstill." This comment usually raised a smile. *Nada.* I tried again. "These sea cliffs are between sixty and seventy meters tall. From the top, you can actually look down and into the nests of the white storks. They're all balancing on cliff peaks and pinnacles—it's amazing! As far as I know, they're unique to this part of the world."

Someone spoke up. "Can we just get off, eat, and rest now? It's enough."

"Yeah, you can, of course, but now I'm going to ask you again to get off and lead your horses for the last bit. You'll feel so much better."

A general grumbling followed, which I totally ignored as I dismounted, loosened Pash's girth and rolled my stirrups up. Then I just waited. Five minutes later, we were ready to move off. There was no point mentioning the fact that apart from the storks, these spectacular cliffs were also home to peregrine falcons, gulls, sea doves, robins, wagtails, sparrows, cormorants, and shrikes. Or that the cliffs were formed by a distinctive geology of twisted and folded shale rock formations.

Cool sea spray plumed upward as we walked along above the ocean. Way below us, balancing impossibly on a pointed rock tower, I spotted two oversized stork nests with a hatching stork in each one. But I kept it to myself. *Why ruin the moment?*

As we approached the lunch spot, six grooms jumped to attention and took the horses from the riders. They led them off to their allocated spots where they untacked, fed, and sponged them down. There was no sign of the riders themselves checking in with their horses.

I looked after Pash, checked him over, then walked over to the other horses. Three were already lying down, flat out, and the other three had their heads hanging low, eating slowly. One of the grooms walked up to me.

"Are your horses okay?" I asked. "They look exhausted. I'm not sure they can be ridden this afternoon."

Cap in hand, he looked to the ground. "They're not used to this kind of work, that's all. They're good horses." He glanced at the riders, all sitting at the table now. "I'll see what the *patrão* wants to do."

I walked over to Fátima, who was holding out my plateful of freshly grilled sardines and a seasoned tomato, red pepper, and onion salad. A mouth-watering slice of *pão caseiro*, homemade bread, sat on the side. I was salivating.

"This looks delicious, thank you. How's everything going?"

Her slitted eyes said it all. "Rob's going to have to talk to them," she muttered, turning back to her grill.

I sat on an upturned bucket beside her, listening to Rob talking to the group. It sounded like no one wanted to ride in the afternoon, and the horses were all too tired anyway. It was decided to have them sent back to Lisbon with their grooms, and have the next six horses brought down that evening. The riders themselves were all going back to their hotel for the day to recover. Pash and I would finish the rest of the day's ride on our own, and then the following day we'd all set off on the second part of the ride as a group again. While Robert worked out the logistics with the riders, I went to help the grooms load up the six exhausted horses onto their truck.

"Are the horses you're bringing down later any fitter than these ones?" I asked the head groom. Again, he looked down at his feet.

"No, not really. But you have to understand—it's not the horses' fault. They tried their best."

"I know," I said. "It's never the horses' fault. Look, tomorrow I'll try to help your horses more...I'll try to make the riders understand."

He looked me in the eye with a mirthless smile. "I wish you good luck with that. Anyway, we'd best get going if we're to be back tonight. It's a long drive."

"Okay, safe trip. I'll see you later," I responded, wondering how we were going to solve the problem and make everyone's week as enjoyable as possible. Talk to them? That hadn't worked. Lead by example? Maybe. Explain that horses needed to be given the respect they deserved? Not sure.

But for now, what a privilege to be having two hours on my own in this magical part of the world with *this* perfect horse.

Pash and I set off, walking side by side along the sandy white clifftop trail. A fresh breeze blew tufts of dried-up grass across our path, and after a kilometer or so, the track veered inland and south, away from the clifftop toward the village of *Odeceixe*, where the horses were to be stabled that night.

Sand now gave way to much richer soil and totally different vegetation. Fields of dark-green corn covered the undulating hills, which were watered by a long mobile irrigation system set up to move along slowly from one end of the field to the other. Farther on, I noticed the pretty yellow flowers of a peanut plantation. Although the plants were above the soil, the nuts grew underground, and also needed to be irrigated. Pash and I trotted alongside the two-meter-wide canal, which provided water to this farmland for a nominal annual fee. In turn, these local canals were fed by the Santa Clara dam, only forty kilometers away.

Two hours later, I arrived at our overnight stable in a disused cowshed and checked that everything was ready for the new group of horses arriving in from Lisbon. Temporary box stalls had been set up and the smell of sweet straw was everywhere. I led Pash outside for his roll, then thoroughly groomed and rubbed him down. So far, the ride hadn't taken anything out of him. I'd only just put him into his stall at the far end of the barn when I was being swept up and twirled off the ground.

"Hi, you. I didn't know you'd arrived already," Robert said. "How was your ride?" He held me so tight, I could hardly breathe, and I felt my body melt into his. It always surprised me that shapes always fit like a tight jigsaw puzzle when you're happy but are invariably a pointy and painful mismatch when you're not.

"It was just perfect," I said, clinging onto his big shape. The lingering smell of fresh sweat and sea air was addictive. "But...what shall we do about tomorrow? It was a total disaster of a ride today for their poor horses. The riders just don't want to know."

Robert listened while his mystical Irish eyes took on a calculating quality, and then after a prolonged moment, he nodded. "I've an idea," he said. "I've arranged to go out with them for a drink tonight. I'll see what I can do."

The sound of the horse trailer pulling in naturally punctuated the end of our discussion, and we walked out to greet the replacement batch of horses. Four grays, a palomino, and a stunning blue-black horse were unloaded by the grooms. Again, all stallions. And again, of very impressive bloodlines. I double-checked the brand on the black horse. An oval "O" inlaid with a "C" superimposed on a smaller "O." An *Ortigão Costa*. These magnificent specimens were always black and extremely sought after for dressage and for the bullring. I hoped he'd cope well with the ride the following day.

The grooms quickly took off all the horses' travel wraps, rubbed them down, and set them up in their new stalls. Pash didn't even glance their way, oblivious to their challenging stallion neighs, squeals, and snorts.

THE FOLLOWING MORNING, the riders looked refreshed and were full of chat as their beautifully presented horses were led out of the stables by the grooms. Pash purposefully took an extra-long detour around the prancing black stallion. I was magnetically drawn to him, though, as always happened with black horses—maybe a link to that previous life in Florence. Although the riders all still carried their whips, most of the spurs had been lost. *A good start.*

Then, for a good kilometer, they all walked on foot with me along the trail, the grooms leading the horses for them, until we found our tree mounting block. The whole group felt so different, I wondered what Robert had said to them the night before when they'd met up for a drink. I left Pash grazing while I went to help them mount, and to check their girths for a last time. Then, before mounting myself, I addressed the group.

"So—it's great to see you all back again and with such magnificent horses. I'll try to be extra careful so you, and they, can enjoy the beautiful ride we have planned for you." They all seemed to be listening... "We'll continue riding south firstly through *Aljezur*, then onto the wild coastal plain. The going is really good for the horses, and it should be great fun." Still no complaining... "And we'll try to do some more walking on foot today—you'll see, you'll get used to it." Again, no grumbling. *This was all going far too well.*

I called Pash over, mounted, and we all set off at a walk. The new horses were very eager, prancing about and all trying to get into the lead.

"Try to relax them," I said. "Just talk to them, keep your legs off their sides and pat them. They'll calm right down."

The riders seemed to be listening and trying to connect with the horses. The black stallion was the most agitated and kept throwing his head about, trying to stretch his neck out.

"Look, put him in front of me," I said to his rider. "Loosen his reins and see if you can get him to extend a bit. I'll be right behind you."

The rider turned to look at me. Her hands were white from gripping the reins and she was holding her body up straight and rigid. "But he'll run off with me then. You don't know what he's like."

"You're right. I don't, and I wish I did, but if I was riding him, I'd try to talk to him, relax, and enjoy him. He's a dream horse. What's his name?"

"Marengo. Like Napoleon's horse."

"Okay, Marengo, I want you to lead us now in a trot. Nice and steady. You okay to do that?"

She nodded, I raised my hand and signaled the others to stay behind me as we wound our way through the pine forest. The going was perfect, and glancing back, it seemed like all the horses were settling in. Two kilometers later, I could hear the traffic.

"Okay, bring him back to a walk now, we have a road coming up," I said to her. "Just put him in behind me while we cross."

Robert was there as backup. He walked alongside me, as we continued on the next trail.

"Everything okay?" he said, his eyes holding a whisk of a lingering smile.

"*Mmmm*, so far so good. They're like a completely different group. What did you say to them last night?"

He just grinned like a cream-fed cat. "Just keep doing what you're doing, and I'll see you at lunch in about an hour and a half."

My curiosity would have to wait to be sated.

Marengo seemed happy to walk alongside Pash, who totally avoided eye contact with him and spent most of his time looking the other way. He was sensing my attraction to this beautiful black stallion—I had to be less obvious. Our path now dipped sharply toward the bridge and the village. Instead of dismounting, I asked all the riders to lean back and let their horses find their own footing, and to try not to interfere with their balance. Again, I put Marengo in front of me.

"Okay. Relax, lean back, let him have his head, nice and slow," I said to his rider. "He'll be fine."

The black stallion leaned way back onto himself, awkwardly straightening his front legs out in front. The rider froze.

"Look," I said, "I'll go ahead. You try to copy what I'm doing, okay? You'll be fine."

Pash sidled by as if it was nothing. Such a *showoff.* I slowed him down and looked back at the other riders slowly sliding their way down the steep incline. They were all leaning way back, gripping the back of their saddles with their spare hand. But it worked, and soon we were all at the bottom, ready to continue. I gave them all a thumbs up. "Great work. That's not easy!"

"Um…" came a voice, the *patrão's*. "Can we walk a bit now? I think we all need a rest."

"Great idea," I said. "It'll be good for all of us."

This time they watched as I ran up my stirrups and followed my lead.

"We're just coming up to the bridge in *Odeceixe*," I said. "Don't worry, it's not very long and our backup car will be there. You'll be fine. The bridge also marks the border between the *Alentejo* and the *Algarve*."

The *River Seixe* was still flowing, flanked on each side by drooping willow trees. Nesting egrets clumped and smothered the trees like sticky candy floss, the overladen branches dipping with the extra weight.

As one we all stopped. Mesmerized.

The transformation had happened.

Our ride carried on to the next lunch spot, and eventually to *Sagres*—"the end of the world." A few more horses were replaced, but it was different than the first day. Respect had replaced disregard and abuse.

When I finally asked Robert what he'd actually said to the riders that night on the town, he just smiled a rogue's smile and winked at me.

"Sure, that'd be telling."

24

A horse is a beautiful animal, but it is perhaps more remarkable because it moves as if it always hears music.

MARK HELPRIN

ATURDAYS WERE MY "TURNAROUND DAYS," and I loved them. They gave me a chance to spend quiet time with all the animals and to mentally prepare for the week ahead. The new group of riders—with all their mental, emotional, physical, and spiritual baggage—would arrive later in the day, and I would meet them in the evening for a chat and a meal. It never failed to astound me that people from opposite sides of the globe were so similar underneath their exteriors. Horses, with their lack of bias and full-on honesty, usually ironed everyone's problems out. They made riders confront themselves.

Robert and Leonel left for Lisbon with the two vans at ten in the morning. As Robert was leaving, I caught sight of his eyes in the rear-view mirror and noticed the crow's feet spreading deeply from their corners. The constant stream of visitors and the 24/7 workload was taking its toll.

I'd thought the past week had perked him up. There'd been a honeymooning couple from Australia, six high court judges from the United States in their late sixties, and a group of four singles: two French girls in their early twenties, and two Irish barristers who'd driven up from Gibraltar. All bonded over their love of horses, and all of us basked in the infectious glow of the newlyweds. The older American judges had found the physicality of the riding itself challenging, but they came into their own at night.

Robert joined them every evening for dinner in town and was fascinated to learn that one was an ex-astronaut and another owned an underwater hotel in Florida. They all had strong views on everything and delighted in each other's company. Topics ranged from philosophy to crime to politics to current affairs. Robert, who could usually talk anyone under the table, had been in his element.

I'd thought he'd seemed happy.

The French girls had been on a manhunt...and successful in their quest. (Both the barristers had missed out on a day's riding. To recover.) More importantly, they'd also been exceptional riders. One of them had ridden Pash, our speed-freak rescue. I spotted him in the field now, rolling and stretching out in the sun.

The dogs' excited barking outside tore through my thoughts. I cursed as three shiny black Jeeps braked in the middle of the courtyard, spewing dust everywhere. The tinted windows of the first car rolled halfway down to reveal a bushy beard topped by mirrored shades. "Do they bite?"

I called the dogs off. The beard emerged, rapidly closing the door behind him.

"Sheila, I presume? I'm Tony. It's a pleasure," he drawled, holding out his hand. He was all shiny shoes and greased-back hair. Skin-tight black leather jeans, a wide black leather belt, and a silk black shirt opened just a bit too far. I winced at the sight of the thick gold chain embedded in chest hair and his shiny Rolex.

Tony was a film producer and was scouting horses for a film. Isabel Allende's book *House of the Spirits* was being filmed in the area. Seemingly, our open plains and mountains were similar to those in Chile, where the story was set.

"We already have most of the horses we need," said Tony. "Just looking for the last piece of the puzzle—a real showstopper for the main role."

I felt reeled in already. *Do I have what he wants?*

"What do you say?" he said, avoiding my gaze and reaching for a cigarette. "Do you mind?"

I put my hand on his. "Actually, I do. The horses hate it. What type of horse do you need?"

Tony turned to the Jeep and beckoned with his hand. "You can speak to the man yourself."

A huge heavyset guy got out of the passenger side and went around to open the first car's back door. A man in his early thirties, wearing faded jeans and a loose black t-shirt, stepped out and looked around. As he walked toward me, my mind raced. *I know him...What the hell is his name?*

Loose black curls framed his oval face. His black eyes narrowed as he tilted his head sideways and beamed a disarming, winning smile.

"Hi, my name is António Banderas. I am so happy ju can help me."

Of course! It all came to me now. I'd seen him recently in a *Pedro Almodóvar* movie. I nodded dumbly, shaking his hand. He was stunning. He smiled from the inside out.

The other car doors opened and the rest of the cast stepped out. There stood Jeremy Irons, tall, slim, elegant, and so distinguished-looking. Then from the next car stepped Winona Ryder. Young, waif-like, and beautiful. Glenn Close appeared next, clutching two small yappy dogs to her chest. And then...*Oh, my God, this can't be real.* One of my all-time favorite actresses stepped out. *Meryl Streep.* There she stood, in the flesh. Scenes from *Out of Africa* and *Sophie's Choice* spilled through my mind.

I pinched myself as they made their needless introductions. *What the hell is going on? And where is Robert when I need him?* He'd know exactly what to do. He'd say, "Relax, they're just people."

The cast of the film made it easy. We walked around in a group and talked about horses. They all seemed so *normal* and genuinely interested in what we did. Jeremy Irons and his silky clipped voice were obviously at ease with all the animals. (I'd learn later he didn't have a stuntman on *House of Spirits* and did all the challenging riding scenes himself.) Winona and António looked just the part. They played the young couple in the movie. *Dream casting.* Glenn Close was very friendly, but more concerned about her two dogs than anything else. And Meryl just seemed so calm, taking everything in and listening to all the horse talk.

Too soon, most of my surprise visitors left in two of the Jeeps, while António and Tony came up to the clubhouse to talk. They needed a safe but striking-looking horse for António to ride. He had a stunt double but was planning on doing all the riding himself.

"But the problem is," he said, "I cannot ride. Would ju be able to teach me?"

Inside, I was screaming, *Ai! Ai!* He was totally impossible to refuse anything.

"How long do we have?" I said out loud, trying to sound normal, business-like, and unsmitten.

"Two weeks, tops," said Tony. He smirked, enjoying the effect his star was having.

What? Impossible! "Okay," I said to António. "But you'll need to train every day. It's really not a lot of time."

Is this really happening? I turned to Tony. "Come and see the horse I'm thinking of. I think he'll be perfect for you."

I felt like I was in a dream as we wandered together into the field. *Concentrate. Where is the horse, anyway?* A tight-knit group of three grays started walking slowly toward us. I knew they were assessing the newcomers and would sense my excitement. I crossed my fingers and tried to control my breathing. Two of them stopped about ten meters away, but one kept walking toward us. Ash gray with a flowing white mane and tail, he really was a showstopper. He was only five years old, but he had the kindness and patience of a horse that had never been traumatized or starved or mistreated.

I turned to António. "This is Guineu. I hope you like him." *And especially vice versa*, I thought.

Guineu, on cue, sniffed António and took a step closer to him.

"I think he likes you," I said, amazed at the horse's perception. Tony stood back, lifting his shades. He looked the horse over, nose to tail.

"You know, he'll do just fine. Just fine."

We walked back slowly to the clubhouse to work out a rider training program, and quite naturally, while sitting together having a coffee, everything suddenly seemed entirely normal. I didn't hear the van pull up in the yard, and the dogs, over their earlier excitement, said nothing. Robert rushed into the clubhouse and stopped in his tracks when he saw us.

"What the feck?"

25

*The snort of the horses as they cleared
their throats, the gentle swish of their tails...
little sounds of no importance, but they stay
in the unconscious of the memory.*

WYNFORD VAUGHAN-THOMAS

WHEN MY MOTHER WAS A TEENAGER in Sweden, she used to train racehorses, and so naturally she was my first great riding influence. As a young child in Portugal, I always tagged along behind her when she went riding. There was instruction, sure, and of course osmosis played its part too. But really, it was in my blood.

All my teachers gave me at least one significant takeaway. From my first teacher, *Senhor Fernando*, I got a great foundation based on balance, which he instinctively passed on to his adoring and terrified students (funny how they often go hand in hand). From Carlos Pinto, the great Portuguese Olympian, who I trained under for three crazy years when I was twenty-one, riding or training seven horses each day, it was his consistency, his calmness, and his singular connection with any horse he sat on.

It was between the ages of twelve and fifteen, however, that I had riding lessons from a very special master. Lord Henry Loch was a connoisseur of Lusitanos, dashing in a way that only a certain type of handsome Englishman can be, and responsible for transforming my horseback riding. He singled me out early and told me I had the gift, that I could communicate on a special level with horses, and that I must never stop being in touch with them. He impressed upon me just how important touch is. That any horse will respond to even the most sensitive of touches. It calms them down, especially when you're sitting on them and they're frightened or out of control.

"No one needs to see you doing it," he'd said.

I've kept that with me to this day.

A defining moment in my life came one day when I was fifteen. I was watching Lord Henry ride when he thought he was alone. He sat perfectly still. No whips, no spurs. His reins were loose, almost hanging. And the horse seemed to somehow not touch the ground but rather float just above it, such was the ease and grace of his movement. It was such a powerfully beautiful moment for me that I couldn't stop the tears flowing freely down my face. This kind of riding is called self-carriage, where the horse and rider are so in tune and balanced that the horse carries both himself and the rider as if they're one being. In that moment, I had the crystallizing realization that the whole aim of riding should be to have the horse perform all his movements with the same grace, balance, and power as he would if he were riderless and free. That's what I still strive for with every ride; it's pure magic when it happens.

Besides great teachers, there are sometimes great students, too. António took to riding like a bird takes to flight.

YOU CAN DO ANYTHING WITH A CAMERA. A ten-centimeter windmill becomes a looming tower. The magnificent family home? In reality, only a shell. (The interior house scenes from *The House of the Spirits* were apparently filmed in Copenhagen.) Even the gory, blood-stained train crash looked real. But beyond the staging and artifice, the acting was raw and genuine.

Robert and I were invited to watch the filming on the days that our star, Guineu, was being ridden by Antonio's character, "Pedro." In the scene, Pedro sprinted across an open field, then vaulted onto the back of an old mule cart. *Cut.* Makeup then sprayed him with cold water before he, as a revolutionary, tried to rally all the farm workers against their master, the fascist landlord (Jeremy Irons' character) "Esteban Trueba."

"He must be frozen," I whispered to Robert. "That's his tenth take. And he's as passionate every time." He was also drop-dead gorgeous. *Cut.*

I prodded Robert in the arm. Bille August, the director, was beckoning us over.

"Can you please help?" he asked earnestly. "You know your horse best."

I loved his lilting Danish accent. It was so like my mother's. He explained that in the next scene, blank gunshots were to be fired close to the horse's head. To keep Guineu calm, he asked us to plug his ears with large soundproof cotton pads.

"Is that okay with you?" he said, his bright blue eyes twinkling behind his rimless oval glasses. "The last horse who worked with us on this scene couldn't handle it. He suffered a kind of horsey nervous breakdown and is having a month off."

I glanced at Robert, who stood beside Guineu with a protective hand on the horse's shoulder. I knew he'd never allow this horse to suffer any pointless stress or pressure. He looked directly at me.

"What do you think? Will he handle it?" he asked while Guineu grazed beside him, oblivious to everything else.

"Yeah, I think so. If he frets at all, we'll pull him out."

I gently inserted the soundproof pads in his ears without any resistance. He seemed to be enjoying his newly acquired star status.

Bille then told António exactly how he was to run up to and approach the horse from the side and mount while dodging Esteban's bullets.

Then Bille turned to us: "Would you mind being as close as you can to the horse? Just out of shot, in case he freaks." He smiled and jerked his chin at António. "I just can't have anything happen to this one."

António looked nervous. I gave him the thumbs up and leaned toward his ear. "Breathe. Talk to him. He'll be fine."

Against the director's wishes, he'd convinced his stunt double that he'd do this scene himself. We'd been practicing it at the farm for the two weeks, building a strong bond between him and Guineu. For the first week, we'd worked with António on the longe line until he'd felt secure and could ride and control the horse at a walk, trot, and canter. Then we let him ride on his own until he felt totally confident with Guineu. It made it so much easier that both horse and rider were of such good temperament. António wasn't only a talented pupil who was able to look like a professional rider in two weeks, he also had a lovely laidback way about him. Although I was still smitten, it got easier to think of him just as *him*. Robert took him totally at face value, and they enjoyed each other's company whenever they were together. As for Guineu, he seemed to know he was on a mission, and he was beginning to feel that little bit self-important.

Next, we had to teach Antonio to run up to the horse at full pelt and mount as quickly as possible. He practiced it over and over again until he seemed to fly up onto the horse.

As Robert and I crouched down behind some bales of straw, I snuggled into his shape, cupping both my hands round his.

"This is it," I whispered. "He's practiced it enough. Oh, God, I hope the horse behaves!"

> *Take One:* The farm workers start gesticulating and pointing. António looks around and sees Jeremy Irons, who's sworn to kill Pedro, approaching at a gallop while taking aim with his shotgun. António leaps off the mule cart and runs, crouching and zigzagging, toward Guineu, as shots ring out around his head. He goes behind the horse, places his left foot in the stirrup, pushes himself up and hooks his right knee over the saddle, so that only his right calf is exposed. His hands grab the leather strap around Guineu's neck. He turns the horse and gallops off, as more shots burst around him, and Jeremy's horse runs in hot pursuit. *Cut!*

The take was good. No repeat was needed. We jumped up and Robert lifted me high, twirling me around.

"You did it! It was perfect."

"We all did. Especially Guineu."

António was beaming as he led Guineu back to us. "Thank ju, *professora*. I could never have done this without ju."

Oh, that heart-melting smile.

We were due back on set the following week. As we loaded Guineu into the trailer, Bille came over to us with a grateful smile.

"That was perfect, guys, thank you so much. I wish everyone had such great horses. Look, the next scene will be a bit more difficult. It's set in an old warehouse full of boxes and crates. There'll be more gunshots. Do you think your boy will be okay?"

"We'll give him a few days' rest," said Robert, "and then, if it's okay with you, I'd like to show him the place, get him used to the smell and stuff." He turned to look at me. "What do you reckon, Sheila?"

"Yes. It'll really help him."

Bille agreed to our plan. As we drove off, cast and crew were gathering around a huge red catering truck. The beers were already flying. I'd heard they were serving over five hundred meals a day.

"Aren't you glad we're not in the catering business?" I said. Robert smiled a small one and nodded.

Three days later, we loaded Guineu and his best buddy Tango into the horse trailer and headed for our "dummy run" to find out how the horses would cope. The set for the next scene was a huge barn with a high beamed roof and a wide, but low, entrance at one end. Wooden pallets piled high with sacks of grain and flour covered about half the floor space. Sharp blades of sunlight pierced the dusty interior.

"He won't like the musty smell," said Robert. "Let's scatter some hay and food around, then try to get them both in."

Tango was smaller, so I led him in first, figuring he'd go more easily through the low doorway. Robert waited at the entrance with Guineu. The entrance was so low that even unsaddled, Guineu would have to crouch to fit. Instead of trying, he backed away, lifting his head to its full height. *Great.*

I tied Tango to a ring on the wall and gave him some hay. He settled in, content.

"Hang on, Robert," I called. "Let's try him with food to start with."

It was pointless fighting with a horse. I'd learned that a long time ago.

For the next hour, we slowly coaxed Guineu into the warehouse. One of us stood inside with Tango while the other held Guineu on a long line, offering him a mouthful of food every time he moved a step forward.

Finally, he crouched down, and rushed under the low doorway and into the barn. We then took both horses back outside and repeated the exercise ten times, until Guineu was relaxed enough to go in ahead of Tango.

"Come here," said Robert at the end of it, giving me a hug. "Jaysus, I'm glad we did this today. Bloody horses! This acting thing has gone to his head."

THREE DAYS LATER, we were back on set. There were no crowd scenes, so along with Guineu, there were only the two main actors, their doubles, and the director and crew.

Bille greeted us, then explained the scene: "Look, I've tried to keep this simple, but the horse part will be difficult. I need your boy to be tied up close to the main door, and I need him to keep real quiet. When Esteban comes in looking to kill Pedro, can you somehow get him to warn his master? A neigh? A banging of hooves? Something?"

"Yeah," I said immediately. "No problem."

"Can you also hide close to him like last time? Just in case. We'll start in twenty minutes."

As Bille moved back behind his camera, Robert raised his eyebrows, looking right at me.

"No problem?" he whispered.

"Come here," I said. "I need to show you something."

A few weeks earlier, in one of our training sessions at the farm, António's body double, Juan, had noted that Guineu might have to perform a particular trick sometime during the filming. He'd showed me how to encourage the horse to turn his head around to his side by bribing him with a carrot. The bribe coincided with me lifting one arm, so that Guineu would begin to associate that particular movement with the reward. Next, we had gently tapped the horse's lower leg with a whip until he banged his hoof on the ground to try to make the tapping stop. *Carrot.* Within a week, Guineu had learned the trick to look around and bang his hoof when I raised my arm.

Guineu performed his trick for Robert perfectly.

"Amazing what bribery can do," Robert said with a wink.

We led Guineu into the barn and inserted the sound-proof pads in his ears. After tying him close to the low doorway, we crouched behind the nearest pallet, piled high with flour sacks. I hoped I had enough room to move backward and catch my horse's attention to give him the signal without being caught on camera. *Fingers crossed.*

And action! Pedro is sleeping on the floor behind some empty boxes. Esteban, who's been tipped off to his whereabouts, quietly opens the door to the warehouse. Rifle in hand, he silently searches behind all the pallets and piles of grain. Guineu is standing motionless by the door, as if he knows they don't want to be caught. Behind one of the last pallets, Esteban finds his sleeping target and takes aim. *I stand up silently, step back into Guineu's line of sight and raise my hand, mouthing NOW.* Incredibly, the horse turns his head right around to his side, toward Pedro, and bangs the cement floor repeatedly with his hoof. Pedro hears the commotion, leaps up, and runs at a crouch over boxes and pallets, dodging Esteban's bullets. The noise is deafening. *Guineu is getting very anxious. His ears are back, and I can see the whites of his eyes.* Pedro runs up to him, pulls the quick-release knot, and the two of them escape dramatically through the door. *Guineu thankfully remembers to duck.* Pedro gallops off while Esteban reloads his rifle. *Cut!*

By the time Robert and I got outside, António was leading a clearly distressed horse back to the set. Dark with sweat and snorting loudly, Guineu was throwing his head up and down.

António's face was serious. "What is wrong with him? Is he okay?" he said, voice full of concern. "He was fantastic in there."

I took the reins from him. "He's just stressed out. The gunshots were so loud in that space." Removing the pads from his ears, I turned to Robert. "I'm just going to walk him for a bit...try to calm him down. Can you pick us up down the road?"

I was aware of the film crew watching us.

"Sure," said Robert, stepping in to give me a big hug. "Take your time. I'll finish off here."

As I turned to go with Guineu, I felt a hand on my shoulder.

"Hey, Sheila, thank ju. Thank ju so much. I learn so much. A hug. Please."

I turned to that smile. *Irresistible.*

"Goodbye, António. Take care. It was such a pleasure."

I hugged one film star...then led another away.

Talking quietly to Guineu as I held his reins, I walked with beside him for a good hour before he relaxed into his swinging walk. Eventually, he lowered his head toward the ground, and the white around his eyes—a sign of fear—disappeared. He breathed out in contentment.

I understood now why the other horse they had tried to use on set had had a breakdown.

Many months had passed when we received a DVD of the finished movie, including all the deleted scenes. Portugal, I felt—and in particular, Lisbon—were the perfect replacements for Chile and Santiago, where the story was based.

And five years later, António Banderas played "Zorro" in the hit movie *The Mask of Zorro* alongside Anthony Hopkins and Catherine Zeta-Jones. I heard that he did most of the riding scenes himself.

26

Meu cavalo, meu amigo
Es um ser tão especial
Quero percorrer contigo
Os campos de Portugal

My horse, my friend
You are such a special being
I want to travel through
The fields of Portugal with you

GUSTAVO PINTO BASTO
&
ANTÓNIO PINTO BASTO

GOLEGÃ, HORSES, TRADITION, NEW WINE, *fado,* and chestnuts are tightly entwined in my being like a thick immutable braid...and have been since I was ten years old. Somewhere deep in the recesses of my mind, memories of November and *Golegã* play out like a black-and-white film reel: Flickering pictures of dense crowds, jostling through the narrow cobbled streets, dodging horse-drawn carriages, sidestepping street artists, and avoiding horses galloping by. And the same crowds contouring street vendors, sampling the small glasses of *água-pé,* scoffing roasted chestnuts from newspaper cones, ogling the flamenco dancers in the corner cafés, and listening longingly to snatches of *fado* filtered through gaps in the clamor—the pounding and the shouting.

This is *Golegã,* the small town northwest of Lisbon known as the "capital of the horse" (*Capital do Cavalo*). Every year around the eleventh of November, the Lusitano horse is celebrated with a festival that's become a national institution—the best for this breed of horse in the world. The most renowned Lusitano breeders gather there to show, present, and sell their finest specimens.

As time has gone by, the images in my mind have grown more vibrant. And now, twenty years later, I was bringing Robert there, but in full color.

The Toyota HiAce was our camper. With a big mattress covered in quilts and pillows filling the back, and "blackouts" lining the windows, we were good to go. The plan was to park in the campsite in the center of *Golegã,* close to all the action.

As we got closer, butterflies filled my stomach. I snuggled closer to him, slipping my hand under his thigh, and watched him glance my way.

"Are you okay?" he said. "You've gone all quiet suddenly."

I closed my eyes before answering, breathing in and out slowly.

"Yeah, I am. I really am." I looked around us at the familiar narrow streets, the central church dominating the old square with its ancient quality, the throngs of horses and people streaming toward the center of town. "I just hope you'll love it here as much as I do. For me, it's magical—look, turn right just there."

We parked up at the far corner of the campsite, set up our bed, hid our belongings, and set off into town.

We were immediately swallowed up by the loud clatter of metal horseshoes on cobblestones as dozens of stallions rode by, all tacked up in ornately decorated bullfighting saddles with glittering box stirrups. Robert stood, slack-jawed, as four grays riding abreast trotted by.

"This is medieval," he said. "They're like moving paintings. And their riders—what are they wearing?"

The ladies wore stylish wide riding trousers, which covered their leather riding boots, and embroidered white shirts, tight-fitting corsets, and waist-length jackets, over which a long flowing coat was worn that spread out behind them, covering the horses' kidney area. A flat wide-brimmed hat completed the outfit. The men were just as sophisticated, wearing sashes in their family colors tightly wound around their waists and the same flat-topped hats as the ladies. They all carried long riding whips in one hand in front of the saddle, pointing straight up in the air.

Rather than saying anything in response, I just watched Robert soaking in the wonder as more and more immaculately presented horses rode through the growing crowd. As each horse passed, the crowd immediately closed in around and behind, making horse and rider disappear. I threaded my arm through Robert's and pressed him toward the closest roast-chestnut stand.

"You've got to try these now. It's tradition."

Gray smoke belched out of the clay roasting pot and clung to our hair and nostrils. *The comforting smell of autumn.*

"*Uma dúzia, por favor*," I said to the vendor. *The same old rolled-up newspaper cone; the same twelve roasted chestnuts, slightly cracked and seasoned with sea salt.*

We rejoined the river of horses and people, all headed toward the main square, stepping aside as yet another group of riders strode by.

"They're stallions, aren't they?" said Robert, looking a little worried.

"Yes. They're incredibly well behaved. You'd never know. It's the breed. There's never any trouble," I said. "Look over there!" I pointed to one of the bars with an unusually high arch entrance. "Can you see them?"

We walked over and looked through the bar's entrance. Standing at the raised counter were three riders on horseback, making a toast, and shoulder to shoulder with them were patrons on foot, doing the same thing. Perfectly normal in *Golegā*.

"They're drinking *água-pé*. It's a kind of 'poor man's champagne.' So yum. Here, let's have a glass," I said, walking inside and ordering two.

"That's far too easy to drink," said Robert with a cheeky smile, downing his immediately. "One more, please."

We were now at the high bar, wedged between two stunning gray stallions, who stood perfectly still, ears pricked forward, seemingly listening to their riders' conversation. Their long wavy manes, tumbling halfway down their shoulders, complemented perfectly their dark almond eyes, lined in natural kohl behind abundant forelocks. With his third glass of *água-pé*, Robert looked totally at home in the "horse sandwich."

I wanted to tell him about the legend of Saint Martin and why we celebrated the eleventh of November. I wanted to explain that the legend speaks of how the saint found a freezing homeless person and cut his cape in half to give to the poor man to warm him up. As a reward for his kindness, God created a "Saint Martin's summer," not unlike the "Indian summers" often experienced by those in the northern hemisphere. But all this storytelling had to wait—I was no match for the two beautiful horses Rob was talking to.

By the time we left the bar, the old streetlights were coming on, transporting us back to varying shades of monochrome. Robert stood still for a moment, just feeling it.

"We've just time-traveled backward around three hundred years, haven't we, to when all this began?"

"That's right," I said, clasping his hand in mine, "way back to the eighteenth century. Come on—I have to show you something."

The focal point of the whole *Golegã* fair was the *Largo do Arneiro*, the central square, where horse rallies, equestrian games, dressage, in-hand showing, carriage driving, and all the main equestrian exhibitions took place, all free to the public, in a huge rectangular area. Around this circulated the *Manga*—a ten-meter-wide track with a low wooden fence on both sides, where any rider, appropriately dressed, could ride his horse— everyone going to the left to avoid collisions.

I caught my breath as a forgotten memory lit up my mind.

It was the first time I'd competed here in the national dressage championships. I'd arrived in town the day before with the horse's owner, and the horse. After settling Duque into his temporary stall, we'd decided to take him into the *Manga* to get him used to all the action.

A highly strung chestnut, the horse grew taller the moment I slipped my leg over the saddle, and all his muscles bunched up as he inhaled the excitement. His ears twitched back and forth, taking in the cacophony around him: neighing, galloping hooves, people shouting, bells ringing from horse-drawn carriages. His nostrils flared while he tossed his head up and down as we pranced toward the *Manga*. Horses cantered past us on either side, but it was when a four-horse team trotted past that I felt him about to explode.

I turned him gently into the *Largo,* the arena, where there seemed to be fewer horses. But his nerves went into overload. Dark and slippery with sweat, he turned into a bucking bronco and careened round the outside of the *Largo*, lashing out at the metallic sandwich boards set up all the way round the fence. The crashing and clanging of metal shoes on metal signs drove him into a further frenzy. By some miracle, I managed to stay on, and eventually he settled into a canter, and then to a trot, and finally a long, loose walk.

The owner and I prayed fervently that Duque would be sound to compete the following day. As it happened, we did our dressage test in the morning in the pouring rain, which calmed him down, and we came second. *What a star.*

On this night, the Manga and the main square were lit up by tall spotlights, drawing the crowds like moths to a flame.

"Come on, Rob," I said as he stood at a vendor's stand, trying on one of the fancy wide-brimmed hats.

"Suit me?" he asked, tilting his head just a little too much.

"Can you get it later? We don't want to miss the show. Hopefully, we can still get a seat."

Dragging him behind me, I made my way toward the *Manga.* Placing both hands on the flimsy fence, Robert stopped dead.

"What's going on here?" he said, looking genuinely astonished. "How can so many horses be together like this? How can those tiny children ride such huge horses? This is insane!" He turned to me as a carriage trotted past, ringing its bells and somehow fitting through the masses. "Are there ever any accidents?"

"I've never seen any in all the years I've been here." Out of the corner of my eye, I spotted something else I'd never seen before. I tugged on his arm. "Rob, look over there—the gray with the elderly gentleman. The horse doesn't seem to be wearing a bridle!"

The beautiful horse walked by us, behaving perfectly, his rider sitting in the saddle, totally relaxed, with one hand resting in front of him and the other gesticulating while he talked to his riding companions. And then they were gone in the crowd.

Robert shook his head in amazement. "How is it even possible?"

"I don't know. Maybe we'll see him again later and I'll ask the man about his training methods. Come on! Let's cross over now while no one's galloping past."

You had to get your timing just right to cross the *Manga.* We dashed toward the central arena and the stands. *Maybe we'll still squeeze into a seat...* The performance of the *Escola Nacional de Arte Equestre*—the Portuguese School of Equestrian Art—was about to begin.

Just as we found a seat, a collective hush descended on the main *Largo,* and those on the *Manga* became respectfully silent as the spotlights followed eight identical bay stallions, trotting in single file down the center of the arena. As one, the eight riders raised their black felt tricorn hats, signaling the beginning of their exhibition. They were dressed in stunning velvet claret-colored long jackets, and beige waistcoats, outlined in white by their shirts, long gloves, and stockings that came to just above their knees. Beige riding breeches, black leather gaiters with boots, and flat spurs in yellow metal completed the traditional costume.

The stallions were so similar in build, size, and color that at first it was hard to tell them apart. Their beautiful manes and tails were plaited Portuguese style, interwoven with the traditional white-and-yellow silk ribbons, their manes set in a long-running braid. Their saddles were, again, Portuguese-style and similar to the bullfighting saddles, but in a natural suede color. The ornate stirrups were hoop-shaped and bore Portugal's coat of arms in gilded metal. And every horse wore a breastplate and a tail crupper.

We huddled up together on the wooden bleachers, and although I'd seen the performance many times, the magic and timelessness of it always took my breath away.

"This is impossible to put into words," said Robert in a whisper. "I've got goosebumps all over, don't you?"

"Always." I snuggled in closer. He was a big heater.

"It's like watching a horse ballet," he said in a state of pure wonder. "Look at their timing. Their precision. It's so beautiful. I wish I knew more about it."

Oh, you will.

The eight stallions performed their quadrille movements to perfection. Not a hoof out of place as they walked, trotted, cantered, did their half-passes, passages, piaffes, and tempi changes. As they finally filed out, the lighting changed to a single yellow spotlight.

Robert leaned forward on his seat. "How can anyone top that? By the way, when did all this start—last century?"

"It was actually founded by King Dom João V way back in 1748," I said. "The school is always giving presentations here and abroad. It's really helped to put the Lusitano horse on the world map. Our kind of traditional national heritage..."

"*Shhh*, here they come now," he said, utterly enthralled.

Two riders, now on foot, came in, long-reining their horses. This involved walking right beside the horse, and by giving subtle instructions with the two long lines and a long whip pointed straight up in the air, getting the horses to perform what are known as the *airs above the ground*. Not only did the riders pace calmly beside the horses as they walked, trotted, and even cantered, but they were also able to show off jumping and leaping movements like *caprioles* and *levades*, to name but a few.

Robert looked bewitched as the horses seemed to sit on their haunches and raised two front legs in the air where they stayed immobile, then leaped high in the air, kicking out with their back legs simultaneously.

"What's that fancy move for?" said Robert. "It looks impossible."

"It's a *capriole*. Apparently, it was developed when horses were used on the battlefield. The movement has them jump so high, they could kick the enemy in the face."

"Amazing," said Robert, shaking his head.

As the spectacle ended, all the lights came back on, and we were transported back to the twentieth century again, in full color.

"My hairs are all still upright...thank you," Robert said. "You were right—it has to be seen to be believed."

I was choked up, unable to speak. *He felt it all.*

"Come on, let's go and get that dang hat for you. Everything starts getting a bit wilder now. You'll see."

We took our life in our hands as we looked for a safe moment to dash across the *Manga*. All the horses had gone up a gear, and many of the younger riders were racing each other.

"Quick, *now*!" I cried, pulling his hand. "Before the next one comes racing by."

"Coming!" And then, "Need to eat! It all smells too good."

We now had to push through the crowds. Every café and vendor was packed.

"Look, there's a spare table in the horse bar, over in the corner." I rushed toward the upended wine barrel and two empty stools. "Quick! Sit down. Ready for your next *água-pé*?"

"Absolutely. What can we eat?"

"I'll order the dishes of the day for us." I decided to get him roast spare ribs marinaded in garlic and laurel, served with *migas*—crumbled up bread cooked with olive oil, garlic, and coriander. For me, the eel stew with onion, garlic, white wine, red peppers, tomato, and garlic.

Just as our dishes arrived, in walked three horses with their riders, all with girls sitting side-saddle behind them. They walked right up to the bar and stood there, totally relaxed, as their riders and their dates ordered drinks.

Robert ate his food, mesmerized by the scene.

"What do you think?" I asked. "Yum?"

"Yeah, too good. And just everything else. It's amazing." He turned to face me fully. "I'm so glad you brought me here. Time to join the horses at the bar now. Coming?"

It was many glasses of *água-pé* later when we eventually left and zigzagged our way back to our trusty HiAce. I felt that for Robert, it couldn't have gone better.

We ended up bringing our riding guests to the *Golegā* horse fair for the next fifteen years.

27

"Is there anybody there?" said the Traveller, knocking on the moonlit door; and his horse in the silence champed the grasses of the forest's ferny floor.

WALTER DE LA MERE

ELLA WAS THE MOST SENSITIVE DOG I've ever met. A labrador mix, she was completely black except for the white tip at the very end of her tail. A serious and sensitive soul, she was the first one to pick up any changes in our facial expressions, body posture, or tone of voice. If an argument broke out, she'd immediately disappear down the road into a field until she sensed that everything had calmed down.

But it was on the night of an earthquake that she came into her own.

At around two in the morning, five minutes before the quake started, Ella quietly made her way to Robert's side of the bed, and, shoving her snout into his face, scratched at his arm, and whined into his ear until she had his full attention. He realized immediately that something was wrong and rushed around waking everyone, getting them outside and into the open, away from any buildings.

She knew Robert was responsible for his tribe.

Turned out to be a 5.8 magnitude earthquake—the biggest one in Portugal in a number of years. Ella's ability to predict the earthquake was an example of how we perceive only fragments of life's rhapsody while she could feel the larger rhythm section. It also reminded me of the another big earthquake I'd experienced way back in 1969. At four in the morning, a dove, who lived free in my bedroom, had perched on my bedstead and cooed loudly until I woke up and rushed to my parents' room to warn them. That was the biggest earthquake Portugal had experienced for a hundred years, reading 7.9 on the Richter scale.

From my experience, we should always listen to what the animals are trying to tell us. It's when we shut out their signs and signals that things can go badly wrong.

When I was thirteen, my friend and I were riding home after a full day's exploring along the coastal plain. We'd decided to take a short cut home through a wide-open field, criss-crossed by small narrow waterways. *No problem*, we'd thought, figuring the horses could just jump over them and we'd get home an hour earlier. My friend was riding her big gray mare Serrana, while I rode bareback on my small pony Mascote. As we approached a slightly wider canal filled with murky brown water, both horses slowed down, and then Serrana stopped dead in her tracks. No amount of cajoling or encouragement was going to make her jump this one.

My friend decided to listen to her horse and ride the long way home. I was determined to carry on with Mascote. We trotted up to the canal as I encouraged him to jump the narrow waterway. After skidding to a halt, he suddenly leaped into the air, missing the far bank and landing with a thud in the murky water. I instantly scrambled off him onto the bank, and with the reins twisted tightly round my hands, turned to look at him. All that stuck out from the muddy water was the top of his neck and head. And that's when I knew it wasn't just water we were dealing with, as both my shoes had been sucked off my feet.

The dried-up fields stretched off in all directions, and as far as the eye could see, there wasn't a soul around. Every time Mascote tried to free himself, he sank deeper into the quicksand. *He is going to die, and it is all my fault.* Consumed by feelings of utter helplessness and loneliness, I looked about and saw part of an old tree stump lying on the ground. I rolled it toward the edge of the canal and tied my pony's reins around one end of it, thinking it would keep Mascote's head out of the water and I could run and seek some help.

My gut-wrenching screams floated off on the breeze. Standing up on the stump, I tried to see farther. *Nothing.* It was one of those moments when my life, short at that point, flashed before me. There and then, I promised myself that I would never, ever again ignore an animal when, in that animal's own subtle way, it tried to tell me something.

When I spotted a group of men walking together in the distance, I yelled at them as loudly as I could, waving my arms above my head and sobbing. They turned as a group and ran to me. Soon they had dug a tunnel under Mascote's belly, pushed some thick ropes under him, and then, bit by bit, hoisted him out of his near-death situation.

We arrived home sometime later, caked in thick sticky mud from head to hoof. It was a lucky day.

Darkness, moonlight, and water have long been used in Portugal as a method for calming and focusing nervous, unpredictable horses.

Zé told me of another horse he'd spotted in a field that he thought might be useful for us. He filled me in on her background while we drove to where he'd last seen her: a ten-year-old bright bay mare, possibly an Anglo-Luso cross, who'd spent about five years in the hands of the *ciganos* (Portuguese Roma), pulling a cart. She was then sold to a sheep farmer, her current owner, who found her too difficult to handle.

Here we go again, I thought. All the horses we'd bought from *ciganos* so far, while always quality horses, had so many issues, and sometimes needed years of rehab before settling, so I was expecting the worst.

The *ciganos* I'd met in southern Portugal told me that they'd originated in northern India and had been living in Portugal for the past five hundred years. They'd reckoned, at the time, that they numbered well over fifty thousand. But because of their nomadic existence, poverty, and refusal to conform to conventional societal rules, they still found themselves shunned, outsiders in their own country, and denied their past, present, and future. Theirs was such a punishing existence. In the winter, living under a plastic sheet, their possessions strewn about, and in the summer, taking cover beneath a stretched tarpaulin, if they were lucky. It was little wonder they seemed to have such low regard for the animals in their care.

(As an honor, I was once invited to a Roma wedding and asked to be a witness for the matriarch, who was in charge of checking the virginity of the bride-to-be. To everyone's great relief, everything was intact, and a great dancing session followed around an open fire.)

The bay mare Zé wanted me to see didn't allow us anywhere near her, but pointedly turned away and raised one of her hind legs toward us. Zé picked up the rope she was tethered to and inched closer, being careful to avert his gaze and keep his body at a non-threatening angle. Her eyes opened wide, showing white rims around the edges, and she snorted constantly while stamping her front legs, challenging us. She had a fat star drawn on the center of her forehead, a black mane and tail, and black tips extending down all her limbs. Her coat, though dusty, was silky-looking.

Time stood still as we both tried to absorb the horse's terror and anxiety. Silence, our greatest ally, connected us to the present. To her. After what seemed an eternity, her breathing slowed down, her eyes softened, and she dropped her head. She allowed me to touch her shoulder, and I knew we had to take her home. Our *Estrela*, our star.

"You know what will help with her?" said Zé, piercing the moment with his knowing gaze. "To ride her at night. She'll have to learn to trust you, to listen to you, to rely on you. And when it's warm enough, just gently shower her legs and body with cold water—it's soothing and will help her focus on you. But...you have a long road ahead with this one."

He was right, as he usually was with all things horse. For the next six months, I rode Estrela out at night as often as possible, and slowly, her mindset changed. She started to trust me. She learned to enjoy the cold-water treatments, and by the time a year had passed, she was one of our most popular horses for the most experienced riders. She ended up retiring in the United Kingdom with a very special guest of ours.

Our moonlit horse.

28

*Let a horse whisper in your ear
and breathe on your heart.
You will never regret it.*

AUTHOR UNKNOWN

I T'S FUNNY HOW ONE EXPERIENCE can open the door to another, even if they happen to be years apart.

The owners of the biggest agency we worked with in the United States had heard about our involvement in the making of *The House of the Spirits*, and wanting to meet us in person, decided to come to us for a week's holiday. Mali and Bryat owned one of the biggest dude ranches in Montana and were absolute professionals. We all agreed that mid-October would be the perfect time of year for their Portuguese experience.

As usual, before a special week, we invited all the staff to a dinner and a general briefing at the clubhouse. I had our favorite meal ordered in from our local fish restaurant in town. When the steaming pot of *arroz de marisco* arrived, I could sense Fátima, Leonel, MC, Bela, and Robert salivating, probably because I was salivating myself. The traditional shellfish rice dish was cooked with mussels, clams, prawns, onions, garlic, white wine, and piri piri, and was topped with fresh coriander. *Vinho verde*, or "green wine," was served on the side, and to finish off, we had freshly cut cubes of honeydew melon with a lime mousse.

Afterward, Leonel settled back into his chair, totally sated, his forever grin even bigger than usual, never mind the morsels of lime mousse that had dripped on his shirt. Fátima took her time explaining in detail to MC and Bela exactly how to cook this *arroz de marisco*. She made it sound so easy.

As Robert ran through all the details of the coming week, I sat back and observed. It quickly grew into one of those moments where I became acutely aware of just how special these souls around me were, so much so that a little lump formed in my throat, prompting me to look away into the flickering fire. I was so privileged to be working with this amazing group of people. They were all two hundred percent committed to the horses, to the job, to us. At times we entrusted each other with our lives. It couldn't be any other way.

The next day, Robert and Leonel drove the two vans to Lisbon to pick up the group of American guests. We'd limited the numbers to twelve for this week and would be riding in two groups of six, giving us plenty of spare horses.

That evening, I went into town for the first dinner with the guests. Prior to their arrival, we'd been sent a "stats sheet" on each rider from the agency. This included their age, height, weight, riding experience, and fitness level, for example. The riders were aware that on the first morning they'd be subjected to a "weigh-in." Ten percent over their given weight, and they could be asked not to ride.

I cringed as I remembered why we insisted on the weigh-in. About a year before, a group of eight friends from Manchester, England, had booked a group holiday. On paper, they'd looked fine, but upon meeting and speaking to them all on the first evening, I knew they were lying about their weight, and my heart dropped. They were *big*. Seriously big. And I knew we didn't have the horses to accommodate them. After our dinner, I'd gone home in floods to Robert.

"It's very simple," he'd said. "We just weigh them after breakfast. If they're over our limit, they won't ride. We'll tell them we always do this. To protect the horses."

I'd hardly slept that night.

Standing in their jodhpurs the following morning, they looked set to burst out of them. After breakfast, I gave Robert a nod, indicating the weighing scales in the corner of the room, and slunk off to check on the horses. Suffice to say, the fat group were not impressed. They ended up riding for just an hour a day, and then only at a walk. Afterward, they tried suing us through their agency for ruining their holiday. As it happened, they didn't stand a chance. Word got out to all the other agencies and outfitters we worked with, and within a year, everyone was using the dreaded scales.

I got to the restaurant early, chatted with the staff, and worked out the menu with Manuel, the head waiter.

"Sheila," he said. "For starters, would you like some marinated octopus with green olives and sheep's cheese on the side? And some of our fresh bread?"

I nodded. "What about the main dishes?"

"Well, I thought you'd like our fish of the day: grilled sardines or sea bass. As a meat choice, I suggest the *carne de porco à Alentejana*. You know our special pork dish served with fresh clams. They always love the garlicky coriander sauce it comes with. White rice on the side."

"Perfect," I said, and then ventured, "What about the vegetarians?"

Manuel's face was a long grimace topped with black eyebrows.

"Okay, okay," I agreed. "Omelette it is."

In Portugal, vegetarians were still regarded with suspicion. *What do they make of vegans?*

"Will you have the usual wine selection? You know your green wine is a big favorite with our riding guests."

Manuel nodded and smiled. "Of course: red, white, and green wine. Then your usual desserts, coffee, and a port for the road."

After my chat with Manuel, I stood by the window, looking out over *Milfontes Bay*, nearly lost in its beauty. The *River Mira* widened and flowed into the sea in front of me, while white sandy beaches edged the sparkling blue water. In the distance, crispy waves peaked where the river married the ocean.

Every new group was always a new journey. I learned so much about human nature and different cultures through the riders who came to us from around the world. Mostly good.

Loud American chatter brought me back from my reverie. I turned to see Mali and Bryat leading the new group in. With a glance, I mentally weighed everyone. *All good.*

Bryat came straight up to me. "A pleasure, Sheila. So good to finally meet you." Tall and lean, he wore a Stetson casually, just slightly to the side. I imagined he also slept in it. I shook his weathered hand.

"The pleasure is all mine. This is weird—you look so familiar."

Bryat smiled, mostly with his eyes. "Dang, I get that all the time. The Marlboro Man? We look like twins. Darrell was their top guy and ended up being their poster boy for twenty years. My best friend. Of course, like all of them, ended up dying of lung cancer." He gestured to the woman beside him. "This is my wife, Mali."

I felt her scanning me, as horse people always do. She had a slight build, was about my height, and had deep hazel eyes that looked straight through you. Everything about her was economical and efficient: her movements, the way she dressed, even her speech. I could sense the contained energy simmering below the surface and knew instinctively that we'd work well together.

As the group enjoyed the meal, I chatted with each rider individually, and tried to feel not only which horse their personality would be best suited to, but which horse would live up to their dream for the coming week. Throughout the evening, I could feel Mali watching me, taking mental notes. She'd been a trail guide in Kenya, and I was looking forward to hearing her adventures. Trail riding in Africa had to be a totally different experience.

After dinner, I walked them back to their hotel and made sure they all had bottles of water. Because of sporadic cases of cholera, consuming tap water was not advised.

Robert was fast asleep on the bean bag in front of the dying fire when I got back. The dogs, splayed out on the floor beside him, gave me a perfunctory tail wag without even opening their eyes. I left them to it and tiptoed to bed with my cup of herbal *cidreira*. I was only aware of Robert again at dawn when outlines began to form in the bedroom.

"Come here, you," he said, reaching out for me. "What did you think of our new guests? Real horsey people, aren't they? It's good to see. Should be a great week."

I snuggled up to him while he held me close. "I really hope so," I whispered.

Had I known.

The first two days of the trail ride went smoothly. We left our base and traveled south, covering about forty kilometers a day. The horses and riders gelled well together, and apart from the extremely loud and more inexperienced Janice, were well prepared for the long gallops and fast pace I'd set for the week.

Then on the third night, the heavens opened, and rivers poured from the skies.

The following morning, before we set off, Robert made sure everyone was well equipped. Waterproof jackets, ponchos, and chaps would keep the worst of it off. I set off with the first six riders, which included the brash and very talkative Janice, Bryat, Mali, their son, Ralph, and two others. Our route veered inland through the traditional village of *São Teotónio*.

Because of the threatening weather, the town looked deserted. As we led the horses with their clattering hooves through the empty streets, I glimpsed only one old woman peering out at us from behind the lace curtains of her tiny window. The heavy black clouds hung oppressively close as we approached the next valley. Somehow, we'd managed to keep dry, so I decided to up the pace. I put the annoying Janice directly behind me and set off on a two-kilometer canter, thinking that was the safest place for her. I could instruct her as we went along, and I knew her horse, Tango, would respond to my voice commands. So far, she'd been coping reasonably well.

I kept glancing back at her to make sure she was okay. As orange, pasty mud went flying, she closed her eyes, stood up in the saddle like a committed jockey, grabbed the strap around the horse's neck, and abandoned her reins. It was in that moment I realized she'd totally overestimated her level and her riding ability.

In a flash, I decided it was safer to just keep going. When I eventually put my hand up to slow down, I got a thumbs up from a grinning Mali.

"Good call," she mouthed across to me.

Even as we relaxed into our walk, I could hear the rumbling river. *Please, God, make sure Robert is there.*

He was.

The once knee-high stream had swollen to a roaring torrent about five meters wide. To the right was a small wooden bridge, which at this point stood about half a meter above the water's surface.

Thank God Robert had parked the Jeep on the far side and hadn't attempted to drive through. I wouldn't have put it past him; it was the kind of challenge he loved.

"How's it going?" he called over the rumbling. I signaled for him to come over to us, as we could hardly hear him over the raging river. He crossed the rickety bridge and came straight to me, keeping his back to the other riders.

"What do you think?" I asked.

"It's pretty deep—at least a meter twenty. I suggest you and MC ride all the horses across for everyone, and the riders can all walk over the bridge. I'll carry anyone who's too nervous..." He paused, locking into my gaze. "... before it gets washed away."

MC appeared just then with the other group, and we explained the plan to everyone. Bryat and Mali elected to ride their own horses across, which Robert seemed perfectly happy with.

I went first with Mini. Monster horse that she was, she just ploughed through, leaping onto the far bank easily. Mali and Bryat followed, their experience showing as they calmly leaned forward, grabbed a handful of mane, and didn't interfere in any way with the horse's forward movement and balance. While Robert helped the other riders over the bridge, giving the odd piggyback, MC and I kept riding the horses across until only Tango and Janice were left.

I should have known leaving her last was a bad idea.

As I approached her to have her dismount so I could ride Tango across, she suddenly kicked him into the river. He slipped slightly, and she yanked the reins in an attempt to keep her seat. Tango promptly stood up on his back legs, trying to regain his balance, and Janice was immediately washed off his back. Both of them disappeared under the bubbling, swirling water.

Before I'd fully realized what had happened, Robert was in the river, hanging onto the far side of the wooden bridge with one arm. He ducked under for an eternal moment, then resurfaced, his free arm wrapped around Janice's chest.

Facing his back into the current, he created a space for her to come up and get some air. MC rushed on to the bridge beside him, and between the two of them, they carried and dragged the semiconscious Janice to the far bank.

Meanwhile, Bryat and Mali made a two-man chain, and as Tango's head re-emerged farther downstream, they grabbed his reins and coaxed him out of the roaring river. I rushed across the bridge, straight to the horse. Completely drenched, he was shaking his head, trying to dislodge the water from his ears. I got a towel from the jeep and rubbed his head, drying his ears, while talking to him, comforting him. From the corner of my eye, I saw Robert and MC had Janice on her side as she lay coughing and spluttering. *I never want to see her again.*

Mali came over to me. "You okay?" she asked in that slow, still voice of hers. I kept rubbing the horse. She patted him, then patted my hand. "You know, in my experience, there's always one of them. That was a terrific performance by Robert back there. He's quite the guy. You're a lucky lady." She winked, and for the third time in as many days, I felt a deep connection with this woman. Like we'd traveled the same road together before.

Tango was trailered home. He'd done enough. Janice, who'd banged her head underwater, didn't feel like riding for the rest of the week. And, truth be told, that wasn't such a bad thing.

29

Horses don't speak, but they communicate through body language. If you look very closely, you will find out your horse has been trying to talk to you every day.

SHEIKHA HISSA HAMDEN AL MAKTOUM

ROBERT AND I FINALLY GOT HOME at ten o'clock that night. The horses had been stabled in a warm, dry barn in the rural town of *Odemira*, while all the guests had repaired to the comfort of their hotel in *Milfontes*. Driving home, we'd stopped in a café to catch the weather forecast. The main news was still on, which showed a new shopping center in Lisbon whose roof had collapsed under the massive weight of rainwater. Miraculously, no one had been killed. It was the highest rainfall in over seventy years, they said. A weather alert was issued for the following day.

ROBERT CAME OUT OF THE SHOWER with a skimpy towel wrapped around his waist and collapsed beside me on the couch. Steam curled and drifted up from him, prompting me to close my eyes and inhale his scent. Lolling with both hands behind his head, he stretched his legs out toward the dancing fire. As we coasted in silent contentment, I inched instinctively toward him, savoring the flame burning in my belly. Time was dough in my hands, and I kneaded it gently, rolling it out to stretch the moment. I pressed my curled-up back into his side, aware again of our perfect-fit body jigsaw puzzle, and began to doze.

"Come here, you can't go to sleep on me now," whispered Robert as he pulled me up and led me to bed. *That always works for me.*

Later, as Robert slept, my old nightmare of the boy's horse swimming off to sea returned. Water all around me as I desperately dragged Mat back to shore, and his horse's head and ears becoming smaller and smaller until they disappeared under a black wave. The rain hammering the glass skylight in the bedroom became the pounding sea. I suddenly awoke and sat bolt upright, sweating and shaking.

Without altering his sleep pattern, Robert reached out and pulled me to him, holding me tight until I let go and came back to the now, to the safe and snug sanctuary of our bedroom.

I didn't want the night to end, and of course the morning arrived too quickly. Robert was up before I knew it. I could feel the energy beaming off him like laser lights as he dressed briskly in his military gear, heavy boots, back support, and headband. *This looks serious.*

"Where are you going?"

Rambo eat-your-heart-out stopped at the door. "I'm going to *Odemira* to check the ride route. Take your time with Fátima. Be really positive with the guests. Don't let them know you're worried about the floods. I'll see you there." And he was gone.

Fine.

To their credit, even after plenty of wine the night before, all the riders looked fully recovered. Mali sidled up to me with a conspiratorial wink.

"Apparently, Janice has decided to stay in bed to rest today."

"That's a shame," I said, biting my lip.

Bryat grinned at me and pushed his forever Stetson toward the back of his head.

"You know, I always thought that Montana, the land of deer, bears, and wolves, was where it was all at," he said in his signature drawl.

"You were wrong, honey," said Mali, hazel eyes alight.

"What adventures has Robert got in store for us today?" asked Bryat.

"Your guess," I said, smiling back at him, "is as good as mine. With Robert, you never know!"

During the twenty-minute drive to the horses, I could feel the riders' eagerness and anticipation pumping up the van like a balloon. In the end, I had to lower the window to let it all pour out. As we approached *Odemira* from its south side, dropping down into hairpin bends shaded by giant eucalyptus, I spotted the swollen fast-flowing river. Overnight, its banks had become crowded with collected trees, bamboo, rubble, and all manner of debris. Mali, who was sitting in the front of the van beside me, seemed to be evaluating the width and flow of the river along with me.

Our crossing that day was planned for farther downstream across a minor tributary, so I said nothing. I prayed Robert had been able to work his magic and sort out a safe way back home. Fátima and I drove in convoy, following the contour of the river along a wide track, then up to the farm where the horses had spent the night. The view was spectacular: *Odemira* in the distance embraced by low-lying hills, its castle and kaleidoscope of houses gleaming white after the deluge.

Robert was deep in action-man mode. I spotted the brown Jeep he'd taken earlier parked behind the barn, only now it was totally camouflaged in thick orange mud with a small round peephole cleared in the front windshield.

"Looking good, everybody! Ready for your final day's ride?"

I sensed everyone's relief as they gravitated toward him, and the confidence he always projected. As he chatted with Bryat and Mali, I checked all the horses and caught up with the guides. Bela, who'd been getting more confident every day, was down to lead the second group today. She didn't look up as I approached.

"Sheila, I'm sorry," she said. "I just can't do it. Robert said there's some kind of crazy footbridge we have to cross..." Her horrified eyes met my gaze briefly. "...over that flooded river! I just can't." She was blinking back the tears.

I glanced at MC, who just raised her shoulders and eyebrows a fraction.

"Okay, I haven't spoken to him yet," I said gently. "But don't worry, Bela, you don't have to ride. MC, are you up to it?"

"Yeah, should be okay. As long as we all meet up on this side of the river."

Out of the corner of my eye, I saw Robert coming toward us, all mud and sweat. He narrowed his eyes at me for a second. *There is definitely an issue.*

"Are we good to go?" I asked.

"Yeah, do the ride as per normal. We'll deal with the river bit when we get there." He touched my arm briefly, turned, and was gone. No mention of the "crazy footbridge." I heard the Jeep roar off a few moments later. This had to be serious. *Why didn't he fill me in properly?* I decided to send MC ahead. Her group of horses was calmer than mine.

Twenty minutes later, I headed out with the second group. Mali walked ahead on foot as we all led our horses out along the trail for the first five hundred meters. This was a perfect time for horse and rider to reconnect and check each other out, although over the years, I'd realized it was the horses who did most of the assessing.

Menina seemed to feel my uncertainty. She gave me a get-a-grip nudge and strode off on her own, passing the line of horses. As each of them stood aside to let her by, she dealt a quick nip or push with her muzzle.

Bryat waited for me to come alongside him, his smiling eyes deeply set in his weather-worn face. "Looks like your girl's giving them all a message. Wish I had such an alpha mare with my horses back home. By the way, anything we should be aware of?"

"To be honest, Bryat," I said, lowering my voice, "I don't know. I'm playing it by ear. Robert will have something worked out, don't worry." I breathed out slowly as I walked to the front of the line.

We all mounted and started walking along the sticky mud track. To our left, the *River Mira* was flowing fast, gushing and spluttering as it dragged along its load of bamboo canes, logs, trees, and detritus. The usually bright-green rice paddies were totally submerged by the dark-orange river water, the perfect setting for the congregated muster of storks to enjoy a frog-eating party.

I glanced down, listening to the swooshing sound the mud made, sucking at the horse's hooves, and started trotting. *Lucky me.* The front rider never got plastered by the sludge. When, unexpectedly, Menina bounded to one side to leap around a landslide, we slowed it down to a walk.

I spotted MC's group waiting for us about a kilometer ahead. By the time we joined them, Robert was there, all smiles, chatting with the riders. I noticed there was no sign of the Jeep. Nor of our footbridge...

"How's it going, guys?" he said brightly. "We have a slight change in our riding route today." He smiled openly at everyone, then focused in on me. "As you can see, our normal route has been washed away."

I held my breath as I realized what his plan was. A few meters downstream there was a sluice gate, generally used to control water flow. A wall had been built over the top of this gate, spanning about twelve meters. *But it is only forty centimeters wide.*

"Don't worry, we're nearly home. First, I need you all to dismount. We'll hold your horses for you. Then, if you could just walk over that wall, over the sluice gate, and wait on the other side, one of us will lead your horse over and hand him to you. Just stay relaxed. It'll be fine."

I took another deep breath, acutely aware that all the riders were watching my reaction. He'd constructed a thick rope barrier on either side of the wall with reinforcements of poles and ropes every three or four meters. *How the hell had he done that?* I noticed that the rope barrier on the upriver side was triple-layered and very taut. The one downriver side was only one layer thick and strung quite loosely. Better, then, to fall in on the downriver side, away from the choking sluice gate. The water, about three meters below, was a violent flow with debris clogging up the entrances to the sluice.

Robert went on, as relaxed as if he were giving directions to the bathroom. "If you all dismount now, Sheila, MC, and I will lead the horses across for you. Any questions?"

Everyone just looked at each other, too scared to say anything. I could feel Bryat evaluating.

"Okay, it's your call," he finally said. "You want us to help?"

"No, it's okay," said Robert. Then, he reconsidered. "Actually, if you could go across first, Bryat, then help everyone remount, it would really help. Keep everyone together."

The riders all dismounted, the sound of roaring water thumping loose logs against the sluice wall in the background.

Robert came up to me, put both hands on my forearms, and made me look at him.

"You'll be fine. The ropes will help the horses to focus straight ahead. I'll go first, then MC, then you."

"What if they slip and fall into the river?" Terrifying images flashed before me. "We could lose them."

"Get a grip, Sheila. Come on, you can do this. Let's go."

Here we go again. How many times had he drummed it into me that "life is either a daring adventure or nothing at all." *Oh, God. Get a grip, girl.*

But what if the horses fall in?

One by one, the riders walked across the narrow wall, using the thick ropes as handrails. Then Robert led the first horse, Boémio, the ex-bullfighter superstar, who, without batting an eyelid, walked slowly across. MC went next with Calema. This steel-gray, big-boned mare was usually ridden by our most nervous riders. After a slight hesitation, she walked slowly across.

"Just don't look down," MC said to me when she walked back over.

I led Menina now, feeling her power and confidence wash over me like a flood. *Don't look down, don't look down.* I looked straight ahead, focusing on the far bank. *No problem.*

One by one, we walked all the horses across, leaving Joia, the most laid-back horse for the end. By now, all the riders on the far side had mounted and were standing quietly, chatting and waiting for Joia. Robert stood at the far end of the wall, keeping an eye on me.

Just as I started to lead the horse across, I heard a loud splash from the opposite bank, followed by a female cry: "Crocodiles! Run!"

As one, the group of horses galloped off and Joia instantly leaped onto the middle of the narrow wall, pushing me off its side. In my peripheral vision, I registered Joia making it across as I fell backward toward the froth and mud and spear-like sticks. I was aware of the thick rope behind my back, which I gripped with both hands, and tensed up, preparing for impact. Just before I hit the water, I felt myself being catapulted back up again. The thick rope had held and was now acting like a bungee cord.

I erupted into helpless laughter. Robert lowered himself down to hoist me up, but I couldn't stop laughing. His face was white.

"Are you okay? Let me look at you, come here. Stop laughing, it's not funny."

He hoisted me up and held me so tight.

"Where are the crocodiles?" I gasped as my laughter turned into sobs.

"Oh...for a minute Mali thought she was still a guide in South Africa, and when a log rolled into the river...she thought it was a crocodile."

I was still sobbing. Out of control.

30

For to be free is to live in a way that enhances the freedom of others.

NELSON MANDELA

THE GERMAN SINGER-SONGWRITER Marius Müller-Westernhagen says in his song *Freiheit* that *"Freiheit, ist das einzige was zählt"*—freedom is the only thing that counts. I'd always felt that we are afforded freedom for the short time we have the privilege of sitting on a horse's back. Maybe that's what our guests felt when they returned to ride with us time and time again. The record was set by one particular lady who returned *eight times* during *one year*. She always rode the same horse—*her* horse—and after arriving extremely stressed from her busy life, she'd leave recharged and at peace with herself by the end of the week.

Are we genetically wired to ancestral memory, to a time when we were intrinsically reliant on and connected to our horses? In today's busy world, where each small section of time is so controlled and compartmentalized, we often find ourselves rushing about frantically and not absorbing the tiny beautiful threads of the tapestry that make up our rich and wonderful life. The sound of birdsong trickling through the forest. The round white spotlights sunlight makes as it meanders through the leafy trees and settles on the ground. The velvet caress of a horse's muzzle gently blowing his secrets at you.

I often imagine an old man, "Mr. Timeless," in a robe and a long pointy hat that droops over his shoulder. His spine is curved with age. A multicolored gunny sack is slung over his back, and he wanders through time zones, collecting fragments of moments, which will eventually help him figure out the eternal nature of time itself: a sliver of moonlight; a newborn's first cry; the cresting of a wave before it smashes to the shore; the first clock ever invented; a smidgen of moon dust from man's first moon landing.... One day, I picture him laying it all out on a blue silk sheet and piecing it all together.

There's a Portuguese saying that goes, *Vai devagar para chegares depressa*—go slowly so that you get there quicker.

Enjoy the journey.

THERE ARE SOME FIFTEEN-ODD BIRD SPECIES that utilize three of the elements around us to their full advantage: they can fly in the sky, swim in the ocean, and walk on the earth. Some of these include the bald eagle, cormorants, the horned owl, petrels, gulls, and swans. It seems they have a true union with freedom.

For me, freedom and gratitude are twin spirits that walk around hand in hand. The times in my life when I had very little were always when I felt I had so much, and that feeling brought with it an empowering sense of freedom and deep gratitude for this astonishing life. Less, it seems, is always more.

In a tangled and convoluted way, the older I get the more I realize that physical and mental suffering is empowering and liberating. When the trickle of tears has carved grooves in your face, then there's no more need for pretense. It's easier to totally assume and inhabit one's own skin without worrying about how other people feel or think about you.

Müller-Westernhagen sang in *Freiheit*, *"All who dream of freedom shouldn't miss the celebrations, should also dance on graves."* My sister Monica had an unmarked grave, which I was finally able to trace some fifty-odd years after. Now we can celebrate her life and dance on her grave. She'd been shadowing and peering over my shoulders for a long time, waiting for that closure to happen. It brought liberty to her, and to us all.

According to author Arnaud Desjardins, *"Life is movement. The more life there is, the more flexibility there is. The more fluid you are, the more you are alive."* I feel that the more we're open to life's opportunities and the more accepting we are of all the new adventures waiting out there, the more we'll benefit and grow as people. It seems to come down to being in the flow, to being fluid and flexible, and to letting it happen.

31

Horses change lives. They give our young people confidence and self-esteem. They provide peace and tranquility to troubled souls. They give us hope.

TONI ROBINSON

I TIPPED MY HEAD DOWN and shoulders forward to fit through the doorway and into the darkness inside. I stretched my hand out in front of me to probe the dense blackness as the stench of mold and urine clotted the air. The presence of terror swirled around me, veiling my head oppressively like a murky smog while a raw metallic smell assaulted me from every angle. *Pure fear.*

"Where is she?" I whispered to Zé. "I can feel her so close. Jeez—the smell!"

"Wait a minute. I've got a flashlight here somewhere."

I sensed him shuffling through his pockets; then a murky beam pierced the thickness. Behind me, an old shutter clanged open, tossing off generations of cobwebs shrouding it.

A hoof scraped the grimy floor. Zé put his hand on my arm.

"*Shhh*. Listen. Look, she's standing in the corner."

The horse had frozen into a silent sculpture, straining back against the thick rope that bound her to the wall. Another rope hung down and seemed to tie her left front leg to her right back leg, pulling them close together. Her ears were flattened, flush with her skull, and the whites of her eyes gleamed in the half-light. She was terrified. My heart sank. Another victim of ignorance and abuse. *Why did it have to be like this?*

The mare snorted and stamped her free leg, her spirit challenging us. I shook my head. Where did this one come from?

"Look," said Zé, "why don't you go wait outside? We're crowding her." He led me to the door. "Go on. This one's best on my own."

He took forever. I walked away and sat under the circular shade of a solitary palm tree, the shack behind me, a wretched oasis in a dust desert. A place where silence had taken a lease.

What gives humans the right to have animals? To treat them this way? In reality, we can never "own" an animal any more than we can "own" a house or a thing. We have the privilege of caring for it and looking after it the best we can. But we can never *own* anything or anyone. I closed my eyes and waited, and concentrated on my breath, on slowing everything down.

A scratchy rustle interrupted my meditation. I opened my eyes to see a perfectly round ball of dung rolling by my feet. Behind it, a dung beetle was pushing it with its hind legs by walking backward. With that, he stopped and climbed on top of the ball, and waving his short antennae around, did the dung-beetle dance, like he was celebrating freedom itself.

A dung-beetle fact sheet flashed before my eyes: *thirty million years old; essential to our ecosystem; eat and bury animal waste; navigate by the sun and stars; stand on top of their dung balls to orientate themselves; prefer the taste of exotic dung.*

A couple minutes later, the little guy finished his dance, climbed down, and started reversing his dung ball in the opposite direction.

One muffled clatter later, and Zé materialized from the hole in the wall, leading the tiny gray mare on a loose lead. She sniffed the air, then stopped suddenly, buckled her knees and rolled over again and again in the dust. She just wouldn't stop.

I wondered if we'd ever be accepted by her. Maybe. *But only on her terms.* I looked at Zé.

"Zé, she's tiny! She's complicated. You know what Robert will say: 'We need big horses.'"

He just stood there, smiling that inimitable smile of his, his arms crossed in front of him. His look brushed over me, then the mare. "You know that all good things come in small packages, don't you?"

I shook my head.

"Well, believe me," he said, "she's a purebred. She's had a terrible start in life. No food. Beatings. But she's a braveheart. Trust me, you won't regret it." His black eyes blazed into mine, and again, he looked from me to the horse. *Were we that similar?*

"What shall we call her?" I said softly.

"*Alma. Minha alma.*"

My soul.

IT TOOK US TWO YEARS to earn Alma's trust, though touching her head would never be allowed. She was perfect, compacting everything we could want into her small frame. She challenged experienced riders and was an expert at reassuring our more nervous riders. She gave back all the love we gave her. Twofold.

It was nearly two years after that when we were finalizing the arrangements for our upcoming RDA (Riding for the Disabled Association) week. Lady Gladstone had been in constant contact with us through that wet stormy winter. We were ready to help the UK's RDA celebrate its fiftieth anniversary by hosting a week's riding for a group of its members and helpers.

Several weeks before the start of the event, details on all the riders arrived. I panicked. *This is a huge mistake. What was I thinking?* Our horses were strong athletes, difficult at times for able-bodied riders, let alone...

I ran off to find Robert. He was in the middle of the stable yard, putting the finishing touches to the special mounting block he and Leonel had built. Fashioned from wooden pallets, it was a solid structure with a wheelchair ramp on the left of it and low matching steps on the right. The whole platform was three meters long and two wide.

Our horses and staff had been in training. We'd led each horse up to the side of the ramp, one by one, and mounted them from the block on both their left and right sides. Alma would have none of it. Each time we led her up to the ramp, she snorted, eyed it suspiciously, and leaped sideways. Bribery, cajoling, patience, and insistence had all failed miserably. I'd decided to give it one more try. I'd put a bucket of food and water on the platform itself, fenced off the surrounding area, and left Alma loose in the area overnight. In the dawn light, I found her standing *on* the ramp, looking down at me in her special way.

"Okay, okay. You win," I said, and we walked down the wheelchair ramp together and around the whole mounting block. *Not a bother.*

"Rob!" I called to get his attention over the loud banging of his hammer. He stopped and turned to face me with nails in his hand and dust stuck to his sweat lines.

"What's wrong?"

"The list from Ros has come. Look. I don't think we can do this..."

He put down the hammer, sat on the mounting block and started reading the list aloud:

> *"Marina, now in her thirties, blind since birth; Patricia, a teenage girl, was in a terrible car crash just two years ago and has lost control of one side of her body. She speaks through an automated talking machine into which she types her answers..."*

"Do you see what I mean?" I interrupted, wringing my hands and hopping from one foot to the other. "It's just not possible."

Robert put his hand up and continued reading:

> *"John and Peter, both in their twenties, have developed MS and walk slowly on crutches. Their condition is deteriorating rapidly; Samuel has a form of ALS, Amyotrophic Lateral Sclerosis, a motor neuron disease. He has single-handedly fundraised the entire cost of his holiday. His speech and balance are seriously impaired; Adrienne, in her teens, only has the use of one side of her body. She is a dressage rider, training to represent the UK in the forthcoming Olympic Games; Samantha and her friend, Joanna, both in their early forties, are amputees and are bringing their wheelchairs; Gary has a rapidly progressing type of muscular dystrophy."*

He held the piece of paper in one hand and pushed his wet hair back off his face with the other. As he focused in on me, I caught that tangy fresh smell of sea and sweat. He licked the salt off his lips and glanced briefly at the list again.

"So what's the problem?" he said.

OUR EDUCATION IN THIS NEW WORLD of fearless, wonderful people started at the airport in *Faro*. Loading the nine riders, their six helpers, and luggage into our two nine-seater minibuses was Robert's first challenge. The group split their sides laughing when the wheelchairs ended up tied to the roof racks.

The first part of the journey was on a highway. While following Robert in the other van, I tried my best to listen to Ros, who sat in the front, beside me. Her azure blue eyes were just as twinkly as I remembered. I sensed she was taking in every detail of our road trip, but we could hardly hear each other, such was the delight and squeals of joy bouncing round the van.

"Don't worry," she said. "They'll settle down soon. They're so excited!"

Half an hour later, we veered northwest and left the highway to follow the narrow and twisting road toward the village of *Saboia*.

"We've now left the *Algarve*," I said to Ros. "Welcome to the beautiful *Alentejo*."

"It's like stepping back into the last century. It's so untouched," she remarked.

Nursey, the gang's medical go-to, leaned over the seat from the back.

"Sheila, my dear," she said in a gentle voice. "Could we have a pit stop soon? I think nerves are getting the better of us."

I glanced at her and nodded. "Of course."

I flashed the headlights at Robert and pulled in behind him under the shade of a giant cork oak. Everyone tumbled out and Nursey delegated helpers for those who needed to go behind a bush, administered Rescue Remedy to others, and made sure everyone had their water and snack.

"Just a couple of drops of 'the Rescue' under the tongue always does the trick," she said, grinning at me. "Great for the plane journey."

The smell of April was everywhere. I sat on a rock watching as Nursey's super-efficient hands got to work. She checked each rider in her unobtrusive way, her kind dark eyes missing nothing.

A little breeze rushed past me as I felt Robert sit down next to me on my rock.

"How do you feel about everything now?" he murmured, leaning his shoulder against me.

"A bit better. Nursey's a scream. She had everyone in stitches on the bus with all her stories."

He gave me a quick squeeze on the arm and got up.

"It'll be fine, you'll see. Come on, let's get on the road again."

An hour and a half and another quick pit stop later, we arrived at the hotel. It had been especially selected as a wheelchair-friendly hotel, situated in the middle of *Milfontes'* horseshoe bay, overlooking the river estuary and the crashing Atlantic Ocean. Robert stayed to help the group get settled and I went off with Mandy, the group physio, to a nearby café where we could discuss all the riders' individual need and decide on the horse allocations for the following day.

"You live in Paradise," she said as we walked toward the café. "Lady Gladstone told me this place was beautiful, but I never expected to be right on the ocean. What a magical view of the estuary."

She was right. It was mesmeric. Never to be taken for granted.

If I were to describe Mandy in one word, it would be *forbidding*. And she was a *real* horsewoman. Tall and physically strong with shoulder-length auburn hair, she had a private feeling about her, like an unmade bed. The kind you look at from a safe distance and don't dare to make or neaten in any way. Words and actions weren't wasted and her smile was slow to surface. I wondered what life had done to make her like that. It was like someone had plucked something from inside her, and she knew how precious time really was.

I ordered our coffees and waited for a moment while she checked her notes, scanning the memo on all the horses I'd previously sent her. We then went through the list, matching each rider to a horse. Each of her pointed questions cut straight to the nub of the issue. "How wide is the horse?" and "How fast is his walk?" and "Is he sensitive to loud noises?" and "Does he mind something like a stick waving in the air beside him?" and "Does he obey voice commands?" and "Will he allow a helper to run alongside him?" and "Will he mind a rider sitting with his weight over to one side?"

Two thoughts collided in my head: First, I was confident that we'd been painstaking and meticulous in our preparation with the horses for this week, enacting all possible scenarios we could imagine. Second, Mandy would ride Menina. It would be a perfect match—the ultimate mark of respect being something you give, not something you get. But I would only let her know tomorrow.

Back in the hotel, Robert had met and spoken to all the riders. I found him sitting on a low wall in front of the hotel with Samuel, looking out over the dunes through a pair of binoculars. Robert said something and Samuel immediately interrupted him. I couldn't understand a single word he was saying.

"What did he say?" I asked Mandy, who was standing beside me, smiling.

"He just corrected Robert. He said the bird sitting on that shrub is a snowy egret, not a little blue heron." She watched my mouth drop. "Listen to him for a while and you'll be able to understand what he's saying. He's actually just been offered a place at college for next year to study theology. He's incredibly bright."

I swallowed hard and bit my lip. The determined mind inside that drooling, wheelchair-bound man was brilliant and incisive. I watched as Robert dabbed his mouth before he spotted me and called me over.

"Sheila, this is Samuel. He's just been giving me a lesson in ornithology. I can't believe how ignorant I am."

Samuel smiled his beautiful lopsided smile as I shook his hand. I felt something so pure and warm in the handshake that I knew I'd made the right decision: for him, it would have to be Alma. Two souls joined by circumstance.

"Hi, Samuel, I'm so glad someone can finally put some manners on him."

I didn't catch his response. I'd have to ask Robert for a translation later.

Sleep skirted around me that night as I tried to tune into Robert's deep relaxed breathing. The scent of jasmine seeped in through the open windows while I slowly untangled myself from his arms and legs and padded into the kitchen. Light from the crisp cut of the moon backlit the clouds and fell onto the floor. Standing on my tiptoes by the window, I could just make out some of the horses' silhouettes relaxing in their fields. The rest dissolved into darkness. *How can Robert sleep tonight?* Then I remembered him telling me once that he'd volunteered at a clinic for patients with severe spinal injuries and how amazed he'd been at their coping mechanisms and positive attitude to life. *Hmmm. But this is different.*

Sometime later, I crawled back in beside him. Fast asleep, he felt for me and held me tight as our breathing synchronized again.

FOR THE FIRST DAY, Mandy and I had decided that each trail leader would have three riders in their group, plus two additional helpers on horseback, and some on foot. We agreed that Samuel was to have a helper on each side to help with his balance. In total, eighteen horses had to be prepared. I'd gone down to the barn early to help the girls, and to have a last chat with all the horses. I explained to them that this was a really special week, that they had to behave, and that I was very nervous.

Half an hour later, the vans arrived and red-logoed sweatshirts were suddenly everywhere. Ros came right up to me with her deep smile.

"Good morning, Sheila. Everything looks amazing. You've even organized a perfect sunny day for us."

It was true. I hadn't noticed the welcoming sun, the open flowers, the feeling of peace. *A good place to start from.*

MC was to lead the first group, which included Samuel. Robert pushed the wheelchair up the ramp, then lifted Samuel out and held him steadily in a bear hug. He nodded at me, and I led Alma up to the side of the mounting block. We walked by once, so she could take in this new scenario, then came round again, stopping just alongside Samuel. I then turned, and holding her on a long rein, rubbed her neck while Robert and Mandy maneuvered Samuel into the saddle. The special box stirrups were adjusted to his length and a long strap, which went round the horse's neck, was placed into his right hand. He had no control over his left hand. That was when I realized how important the box stirrups were—a sort of plastic square that held the rider's feet safely, not allowing them to slip through, which could lead to a rider being dragged behind the horse in the event of a fall.

When everything was adjusted, I led Alma forward while two helpers walked on each side of Samuel. I walked backward, watching him. His huge smile cracked his face open and made the sunny day even brighter.

I was going to have to get the password to that smile.

32

You have three choices in life: Give up, give in, or give it all you've got.

COWGIRL SPIRIT

IT WOULD USUALLY TAKE US FORTY MINUTES to get three groups of horses and riders prepped and out of the stable yard. Today, however, it took us all morning. MC led the first group, which included Samuel, Samantha, and Joanna. Both ladies had suffered above-the-knee amputations and were riding with adapted prosthetic limbs. To keep the prosthetics close to their horses' sides, they had a special modification that velcroed loosely to the girth, holding their legs in the correct position, close to the horse's flanks. They looked so elegant in their beige jodhpurs, dark-brown chaps, and RDA sweatshirts. You'd never have known their challenges at a glance.

Bela's group was next, and included the three boys: John, Peter, and Gary. Mandy had mentioned that they all rode at the same club back home and were good friends. John, who was already mounted, beamed through his thick spectacles and cheeky grin, while Peter discarded his crutches and supported himself on Robert. With wispy black hair and deep blue eyes set above prominent cheekbones, he looked up as Mandy gently lifted his right leg across the horse's back and settled him into a comfortable position. *What a stunner!* Finally, Gary was wheelchaired up the ramp. While his horse Hobie was brought into position, Robert held Gary by the waist. Because of his muscular dystrophy, he was more comfortable mounting from the horse's right side. Horse and rider were well matched. Both were lovely, large, and lumbering, and clearly placed food at the top of their priority list.

Pat, the specialized RDA instructor, accompanied Bela's group as they rode out together. I glanced at Bela as the six horses set off. The intensive one-to-one lessons I'd been giving her had made such a huge difference. To see her smiling and chatting with her riders with such grace and confidence filled my heart with joy. *Just what we need on this first day.* Robert gave her a thumbs up as she passed him, and then looked back at me with a little nod. He was as proud of her as I was.

The third group was now ready to be mounted. Marina, who was completely blind, was set to ride Cladda. As I led the mare out of her stall, I felt the usual intake of breath she always stole from her onlookers. Almost silver, with perfect lines that flowed from her ears all the way to her tail, her large almond-shaped eyes were burnished gold, full of intelligence and empathy. We'd been fortunate to buy her from a well-known breeder of pedigreed Lusitanos, who hadn't been interested in crossing her overly sensitive bloodline into his stock.

Robert was standing on the mounting block beside Marina, ready to help her mount. Then it struck me. I looked up at Robert and then to the horse. Robert smiled and gave me another tiny nod. *That telepathy again.*

"I think Marina should see Cladda before she starts," I said to Mandy, the physio, and the other helpers. "They'll connect better."

Mandy narrowed her eyes for a moment before answering. She immediately picked up on the horse's aura and what I was implying.

"Marina, would you like to meet Cladda before you get on?" she asked gently.

Cladda stood still as a statue as her new rider stood beside her shoulder and put both her hands on the horse's neck. Marina's hands gently traced all the warm contours along her neck, through her mane, down her legs and along her back.

I leaned into Robert. No one spoke.

"She feels like white champagne and poetry. Like a queen," Marina said at last, her hands now moving along Cladda's forehead and around her eyes. I was amazed at how she could see better than most people.

Mandy caught our look. She stepped forward.

"Come on, now, let's get you onboard. I think Cladda is dying to go for a ride!"

Patricia was up next on Maya. She was riding without her automated talking machine, so we had to rely on signing. We'd been advised by Ros to take a mini course in sign language, so we all felt fairly comfortable communicating the basics. Patricia was tall and slim with a mass of burgundy curls that threatened to escape her riding helmet.

Mandy was signing to her. *"Are you ready?"*

"Born ready," Patricia signed back, grinning.

"Cheeky."

"Always."

Robert and Mandy lifted her into the saddle. While I was moving around to adjust her stirrups, Patricia started sliding quickly off the horse toward the right, the side of her body she couldn't control. Instantly, Maya dipped her back and took a step to the right, literally placing the saddle under the tipping rider. Patricia then had time to grab a handful of mane and hoist herself back up.

I breathed in deeply. Robert's color had drained. For once, he looked a bit fazed. He shook his head and turned to me. "How did she know to do that? She did the exact opposite to me. It's not fair."

The previous week, Robert had fallen off Maya twice in a row. He'd been galloping round a sharp corner and lost his balance. The next second he was on the ground. Maya had stopped instantly and turned to look at him. When he tried again, she used the same technique. A lead mare, Maya had always defied Robert's authority. And she won.

Patricia held her specially adapted loop reins in her good hand. Each rein had been fitted with a series of loops, which allowed the rider to hold the reins securely at the correct length without them slipping away.

Adrienne was the last rider in the group. We'd decided she would ride Brida, a stunning bright chestnut five-year-old mare with a distinctive star and long white snip stretching over her upper and lower lips. Also a purebred, we'd bought her from a breeder close to Lisbon. She was just coming into her own, and from the preliminary groundwork we'd been doing with her, she was already showing signs of liking dressage work. It had taken us a year of slow and gentle training to have her ready to do a full week's work. Willing and generous-natured, she had a lively and elevated forward movement, which made her extremely comfortable to sit on. I had hoped she'd match Adrienne's dressage aspirations. I noticed Adrienne was also using the loop reins and held a long dressage whip in her right hand to replace her right leg. Brida made no objecton.

"She really fits you," I said to Adrienne. "How do you feel up there?"

"I love her," Adrienne murmured, "but she's so big! I'm used to riding much smaller horses. I hope she'll look after me."

Robert walked round the other side of the horse and did the final check. He glanced over the horse's neck at me. I knew he'd been nervous about using this very young, inexperienced horse for our riders this week. Against his judgment, I'd decided to risk it. There was something so wise about this mare, as if she'd been here many times before. *Fingers crossed.*

"She will, Adrienne. Brida is one of our new stars," I said, and smiled back at Robert.

All the other helpers were now mounted and getting acquainted with their horses. I went to get Menina.

"You have to behave for Mandy. Do not let me down, I'm really counting on you now," I whispered in her ear. She'd been watching the mounting proceedings with interest, taking it all in. She looked down at me condescendingly as we walked out together. *Butter wouldn't melt.* Maybe, just maybe, she'd control her flightiness and extremely high spirits. I led her once around the mounting block while she and Mandy measured each other up.

"She's magnificent, Sheila. A gift," said Mandy quietly. "We'll be fine. I know it. Don't worry."

Finally, I mounted my own horse, Pash, and our ride set off. The riders beamed, experiencing their new horses, interesting smells, and so much space. We walked up and down valleys and even managed a few trots out on the open plain. Horses and riders gelled so well.

I forgot to tell Marina to duck when we rode under a low branch. She laughed when her helmet got whacked.

"Don't worry, Sheila, it happens to me all the time! I'm fine."

Glancing back from my position at the lead, I sensed that all the horses were taking their responsibilities seriously. Even Menina had switched into a carer and walked quietly in line. It was uncanny.

That evening, we discussed the day with the RDA staff. The first ride had gone according to plan. It was decided that the next day, we'd try to ride for an hour and a half.

ON THE EVENING OF THE THIRD DAY, I went to town with Robert, as we needed to clear our heads. Walking along a cobbled pathway that wound its way through the dunes, Robert took my hand in his.

"Samuel said something amazing to me today," he said, and then he paused. I waited. His hand squeezed mine until it hurt. He looked away.

"What did he say?" I asked gently.

He stopped and turned to face me. "He said: *'In riding, we borrow freedom.'*"

My heart was thumping. We hugged each other tight while our tears intermingled and fell to the sand. *So humbling.*

Having found our way to our favorite seaside restaurant, we indulged ourselves in garlicky grilled prawns and a bottle of green wine. With the gentle breeze whispering around us, I made a decision.

"Let's try and ride to the beach with them. It would be a real highlight."

He looked at me hard, banging his glass onto the table.

"What? How? I really don't think it's possible, Sheila. Think about it—mounting, dismounting, the length of the ride, the safety issues on the beach with horses running off. You know how they always love to roll in the sea and on the sand. Have you even thought this through?"

I had. There were risks. Horses love to roll on the soft sand on the beach with their riders onboard. They find it irresistible. And how many times had our horses galloped off when approaching the beach? But this week, they'd shown such compassion and understanding for their riders. I'd never experienced anything like it before.

"Yes, I have," I said gently. "Please, Robert. Together we can do it. The girls have really stepped up to it this week. The horses are being unbelievable.

You know the riders would never ever forget it." I looked into his heart. "Talk about borrowing freedom."

I got up and went to the bar to order a coffee and left Robert to weigh it all. I waited until I felt him come back into the room. He looked focused. I knew it was a yes.

TWO DAYS AND MUCH PREPARATION LATER, the three groups were en route to the beach. The plan was that the horses would camp there overnight with the staff and whoever else was up to it. Tents were set up in a semicircle. Fátima prepared her special *bacalhau à braz* dinner. She knew this salted cod dish with potato, egg, and onion was everyone's favorite. As some riders wouldn't manage the full three-hour ride to the beach, we'd decided to have their horses follow the group. *Loose.* We'd then mount them up about half an hour before the beach—Robert and Leonel had somehow put together a portable mounting block.

All three groups assembled after we mounted the remaining riders, and the eighteen-strong crowd of horses and riders set off.

We stopped at the brow of the hill, and everyone fell silent. Even Nursey. I turned to watch their faces. The raw, visceral beauty of the creamy dunes and azure-colored sea was overwhelming. Marina tipped her head back and deeply inhaled the whole experience.

We rode slowly down the dunes and onto the beach. Our helpers on foot walked among the horses now, keeping a close eye on everyone. This was where it could all go badly wrong. I spotted Robert walking along with Samuel, both engaged in deep conversation. Samuel had made so much progress during the week that he now required only one helper to walk alongside him.

The tide was out. I rode along the water's edge, looking back, when suddenly, my horse went down and tried to roll over on me. A wave caught me, and I got drenched. The irony of it!

"*Pash!* Get up, *get up!*" I cried, pulling at his reins, and getting back on him at the same time. "It's okay, everyone, I'm fine!" I said to the confused-looking riders. "I wasn't paying him enough attention."

My right leg felt a bit crushed from the horse's weight, but everything seemed okay. The wet sand had sunk in the shape of my leg as we landed and acted as a cushion.

Everyone was now in fits of laughter. Robert quickly handed Samuel's reins to another helper and sprinted over. He held me at arm's length and scanned me all over.

"Are you sure you're okay?"

"I really am. Relax. Nothing happened," I said to him gently, trying to ignore my throbbing leg. It would be fine, I reckoned. It was only my leg.

33

Don't walk behind me: I may not lead.
Don't walk in front of me:
I may not follow. Just walk beside me
and be my friend.

ALBERT CAMUS

ÁTIMA HAD PREPARED one of her picnic specials for our drive to the airport. *Rissóis de camarão* and *pasteis de bacalhau*, the seafood delicacies the group had loved, *presunto* and goat's cheese sandwiches, and mini fruit salad bowls. We veered off the main road, and I pulled up beside Robert's van just below the arch of an old Roman bridge.

A proper feast, the whole gang dug in on red-and-white gingham tablecloths we'd stretched out on the grass. Samuel, as ever, sat beside Robert, who, between forkfuls, gently dabbed the corners of Samuel's mouth.

I could feel Ros watching me. I moved around and sat on a rock, facing her.

"You know, you remind me so much of myself," she said in a low voice. "Here, sit beside me." She made room on the rock beside her. I sat down with my back to the others.

"I don't want to interfere," she continued, looking right at me, "but I don't want you to make the same mistake I did all those years ago. I nearly waited too long." She looked down at the ground. "And then we also adopted. Two more children."

My heart quickened. "How did you know?"

"It's like watching myself in the mirror. Don't wait. Your home is wonderful and perfect for children." Her smile deepened. "And Robert is ready."

I stood and gave her a big hug. "Thank you. Thanks for everything."

WE WERE ALL TEARFUL at the airport. As I hugged Ros goodbye, she whispered in my ear: "We'll be back next year, if you'll have us. And think about what I said."

I held my breath and bit my bottom lip. *No, for God's sake, don't cry now.* On the other side of our group, I could see Robert squatting down beside Samuel's wheelchair. He had one hand on the chair's arm and the other on Samuel's knee as they laughed and chatted. Then Samuel placed his hand on top of Robert's. I looked away, realizing that for once we were the big losers. We were the ones who were going to miss them.

Patricia came up behind me. Tall and still cheeky, her burgundy hair was now reaching for the stars.

She typed into her talker: *"Will you miss me?"*

I nodded. "So much."

She grinned and typed on. *"Can we come back again? Can I ride Maya again?"*

I smiled as the image of Patricia hugging the big gray mare flashed up in front of me. She had leaned in really close to the horse and had just managed to clasp her hands round Maya's neck.

"She's yours. I'll just be minding her for you."

Patricia beamed. We hugged one last time, and the group was off. The airport had emptied.

Robert and I drove back home in our separate vans, full of awe and gratitude for the most special week we'd been so privileged to share. The shortest week with the longest days.

The RDA rode with us for the next eight years. The same wonderful helpers always returned but with a different group of riders. Lucky us.

THERE WERE SIGNS EVERYWHERE. Driving into the farm was always like arriving at an oasis. Even in summer, when all the countryside around was parched and crusty, and you could literally inhale the powdery dust, the farm was always lush. I could see clusters of thick bamboo cane lining the stream. The orange and lemon trees were weighed down with abundant ripe fruit. Even the exotic papyrus were blooming, their small stalked flowers fitting like umbrella spokes around the stem tops.

Anticipation hovered in the air when I went looking for Porsha, the wild barn cat. She'd appeared in the stables early one morning six months ago and had decided to make the hay barn her new home. Because she was feral and untouchable, we had come to a mutual arrangement. We fed her, and she looked after the mice and rats.

The girls hadn't seen her for a week now, and I wondered if she'd been snatched by a wild animal.

I recalled seeing a pair of lynx only a month ago. Doing the last rounds at ten at night with the dogs in tow, I'd got lost in the sparkling lights scattered above the inky vastness roofing and connecting us all. Only the cicada songs scratched the silent canvas. Ella, the oldest dog, had stopped abruptly in front of me and let out a low, unnerving growl. Reaching down to stroke her head, I'd sensed that her body was stiff and her back was spiky with hackles. At that precise instant, the other three dogs had moved warily forward, standing in front of me in a line, staring at some fixed point in the blackness. Slowly, I'd taken the flashlight out of my pocket and shone it in front of me. *Nothing.*

Ella had still been growling, so I'd looked again. This time I'd picked out a flash of light on the fig tree, and I saw them. Two lynx were sitting on the lowest branch, facing each other. I'd gasped, remembering what I'd read about them. Tawny, with a spotted black coat, the Iberian lynx was an endangered species with a bobbed tail and white underbelly. I'd looked again, controlling my breathing all the while. They sat crouched on the branch, their small heads turned toward us. We'd been so close that it was easy to make out their tufted ears and long whiskers. Keeping the light on them, I'd started to back away, whispering for the dogs to follow, who were more than happy to oblige. As soon as it had felt safe, we'd turned and dashed back to the house.

What a privilege.

I'd read that they were usually solitary, nocturnal animals who only paired up in breeding times. Also that they roamed up to a hundred kilometers...and that they fed almost exclusively on rabbits!

Climbing up the laddered bank of hay bales at the back of the barn, I peeped into every dark little space. No death stench anywhere. Just then, the tiniest, feeblest *mew* trickled down. I scrambled right to the top of the pile. Porsha, plus three tiny kittens, lay there, curled up into the safest space she'd been able to find. The kittens' eyes were nearly open, so they must have been born about ten days before. She looked at me defiantly. I went off to get her a big bowl of warm milk. The kittens purred loudly as they kneaded their mum's belly.

There was something still perturbing me. All of a sudden, I remembered Q, our old labrador. Only yesterday she'd excavated a hole in the dog couch, strewing tiny bits of foam everywhere. *So out of character.* She couldn't be making a nest, could she?

Robert didn't notice me as I jogged by him on the way up to the clubhouse, absorbed as he was, fiddling with something in the pool pump outbuilding, his pride and joy. Only two months ago, the ten-by-six-meter prefabricated pool had dramatically arrived. Dangling precariously from the truck crane, it had swung from side to side as the engineers—with Robert in command, of course—measured the size of the hole and the thickness of the retaining walls he'd prepared for the pool's inset. It had slotted in snugly, of course.

MC came running out of the clubhouse with bright eyes and her neck and face flushed. "Sheila! It's Q! Puppies! Three. All different colors. Come quick."

I held my breath. *No.* That dog was far too old to have puppies.

"What? How did we miss that? Is she okay?"

MC looked down, clenching her hands. "I'm not sure. I don't know..."

Q was lying flat on her side and her breath was labored and irregular. She didn't react when I stroked her head. My heart contracted. I tasted metal. *No, not Q. Please, no.*

MC hovered behind me uncertainly.

"Could you get Robert, please. He's down by the pool," I said to her in a low voice. The golden puppy was already dead. The mottled gray one was barely breathing. His limp limbs and tail drooped off the edge of my hand.

But the smallest one, the black one, was whimpering pitifully. I scooped her up and rubbed her along my cheek, inhaling that intoxicating puppy smell.

Robert and MC tiptoed into the room. I glanced at them. MC was pale and had tears spilling down her face. I handed her the black puppy.

"This one's fine, I think. Robert, the other two didn't make it."

"Poor old Q," he said softly, leaning down to fondle her ears. "Will she be okay? She doesn't seem to have any milk, does she?" His face was ashen. *She means so much to him.*

"No, she won't until she gets rid of the placenta. But she's too tired now." I looked up at him, sensing the thick rope that moored us together. He stood very straight and tall, not daring to breathe. This dog was so very special. I squeezed his hand.

"Q's tough. She'll pull through." Sometimes he was just too soft.

We discussed all our options and agreed on a plan. The two dead puppies were buried up at the communal cemetery below the ancient oak tree. Q was to be monitored and accompanied at all times. And *Musga*, the survivor, was to be bottle-fed at three-hour intervals.

Two sleepless nights later, Q recovered her strength and began to bond with her puppy. A puppy who lived like every day was her last.

A few days later, I woke up to the sound of rain falling as quietly as a whisper. I swung my legs over the side of the bed. My heart was pounding. Robert reached over, his big arm encircling my waist.

"What's wrong?" he said in a groggy voice. "Where do you think you're going?"

I wriggled away. I couldn't get rid of a horrible feeling.

"Something's happened," I said, "I can feel it." I tried to pry open the arm. "You know the way things always happen in threes?"

The arm tightened. He tried to open his eyes.

"Robert, listen. It has to be Simpática. Maybe the foal was born early."

"What? No, no, it can't be," he muttered from far away. His breathing deepened. The emotion that had haunted his face vanished as the arm around me loosened. Still, I waited to be sure he'd gone back to sleep. There was enough light coming in through the window now to show me his face.

I knew I could never unlove him.

I threw on an old tracksuit and boots and slipped out quietly. Too early for the dogs; they didn't even look up.

According to our vet, the mare wasn't due for another three weeks, so we'd left her with her own herd. But that had been a guess. The breeder we'd bought her from had sworn blind she wasn't in foal. *It isn't possible,* he'd said. After three months, however, her expanding belly told a different story. The plan had been to put her into her own field just before she foaled. We weren't sure how the others would react to the new arrival.

The field was empty close to the bottom gate beside the entrance to the stables. Usually, the horses would be lining up now for breakfast. I started walking up toward the top of the field, breathing out dense white clouds. My heart thudded. Cold sweat lined my upper lip.

At the top, huge eucalyptus trees grew in a semicircle. With their blue-green leaves and tasseled cup-like flowers, they formed the perfect backdrop. The other half of the circle was made up of the group of horses standing shoulder to shoulder, looking inward. They didn't move. I approached slowly and pushed my way through. The tiny miracle was in the center.

Lying with her legs tucked up under her body, the gray mare nuzzled a shiny black foal curled up beside her. She let me sit. I stroked her head. The foal struggled to stand up, his long legs barely supporting him. He tottered over to where I was sitting and sniffed my face. I waited, felt his tiny lips rustle my hair, and time became meaningless... The foal then tried to turn toward his mum and fell into a crumpled heap. Simpática curled her head round and looked me straight in the eye.

"Don't worry," I said to her softly. "I won't touch him."

She eased herself up and nosed the little foal as he staggered up to his feet. Like a magnet, he was drawn to her milk and started slurping and sucking, splaying his four legs wide to stay balanced.

The mare breathed out through her nostrils and relaxed. She seemed to be saying, *This is our little secret.*

He would be *Segredo*, the secret.

34

Horses leave hoofprints on our hearts.

AUTHOR UNKNOWN

IN MAY 1990, IT WOULD HAVE BEEN HARD to predict which way the dream would flow, or if it would even be successful. Our very first group consisted of just one lady from Switzerland. We spent most of our time talking, getting to know each other, and enjoying long, high-speed rides every day. This lady became a very close friend and was still riding with us fifteen long years later.

Starting out with five horses, our operation grew until, at its busiest, we had twenty-eight horses in work, plus seven that were retired, resting, or too young to be used on our rides.

One of the problems many equine business owners face is what to do with their horses once the animals no longer feel like working, are not enjoying it anymore, or have simply had enough. We were incredibly lucky, as the answer came to us in our first year. A Scandinavian woman, staying with us for a week, fell in love with the horse she was riding. She simply *had* to have her. Within three months, Saffie was on her way to Norway. She was only six at the time and never looked back, ending up competing at a very high level in dressage. For us, for Saffie, and for her Scandi soulmate, this was the perfect solution.

Of the fifty-plus horses we had the pleasure of working and living with over the years, we were able to keep track of most—those who either lived out the rest of their adventures with the guests who fell for them or who retired at our farm.

Alma, our fiercely determined friend to Samuel, retired with a good friend of ours in Portugal. From the shell-shocked rescue she was at the start to being one of our most popular horses, she lovingly tolerated us in her own way, never forsaking her hard-won independence.

Akbar, the leading alpha male, was in control of himself and those around him to the very end. He developed a tumor in his neck, making it impossible to swallow solid foods. All his meals were liquidized in the blender, which made his life manageable, but one morning when I was about to take out a ride, I knew he'd made his decision. With my heart squeezed dry, I hugged him for the last time and walked away. Robert told me later how he'd sat with him in his field under an oak tree, and that *Akbar* had lain beside him, put his head on Robert's lap, and with a heavy sigh, just closed his eyes. His decision. He was twenty-three years old.

Allegra, daughter of *Cladda,* had been given to us as a fiery and wild three-year-old. Unapproachable, I still have an image of her galloping full pelt toward me in the field, then lashing out with both her front legs. She behaved like a stallion. Fortunately for us all, one of our staff members, a professional and highly empathic rider, formed an unbreakable bond with her. Step by step, she worked alongside the horse until she became impeccably trained. Since she was so sensitive and fiery, we only ever used her to give our guests lessons in a controlled environment, or to be ridden by the most experienced guides as a lead horse on the trails. In her teens, she went to live in the United Kingdom with one of our guests where she competed in dressage at quite a high level.

Boneca, one of our first, was in her teens when we bought her. Very gentle and delicate, she usually followed along loose behind the rides as a "spare." Within a couple of years, she'd been retired to Germany with one of our guests.

Bobby was the surprise and unexpected daughter of *Joia.* A bright bay mare, she was Joia's present to Robert on his birthday. A loving, kind horse, she sustained an injury in the field and was retired at fourteen in Portugal as a field companion.

Brida, the compassionate chestnut mare, sister to *Damastor,* came to us as a mentally mature four-year-old. She always accepted whatever was presented with unflappable grace and was a great favorite, not only on the rides but also as a teacher in the school. She eventually retired in France.

Bela and *Boemia* both retired in the United Kingdom.

Bonita, pretty by name and by nature, was a most unusual color. A pale dun, she was tall and dashing, had a dark-brown dorsal stripe, red-black mane and tail, and elegant black stockings up to her knees. She found the trails very tiring and was eventually sold to a lady in the *Algarve*. Amazingly, she escaped and made the hundred-and-forty-kilometer journey back to the farm on her own. Crossing bridges and roads at night, she slept in fields in the daytime, and eventually wandered into the stable yard some four days after she'd run away. One of my greatest regrets is that I sent her back to her new owner when it appeared all she wanted was to come back *home*.

Betsy, the big four-year-old who'd belonged to our blacksmith Zé, eventually went back to live with him. I have an enduring memory of him pulling up at the farm in his small pickup with an enormous horse in the back. She barely fit in the small space with all her legs bunched close together. Her long neck and big head came right over the cab so that Zé was looking at her muzzle as he drove. I never found out how he managed to load her, but she was totally unfazed, and somehow managed to turn around and jump down onto the ground when she arrived.

Boémio, our ex-bullfighter, was a gentleman to the end. One of the kindest and most generous souls I've ever met, I've mentioned that he was the one I felt safe enough to ride when I had my leg in a full cast. (I simply tied it round his neck and off we went.) Ironically, some years later, he had his own leg broken by another horse while on a ride. Honorable to the end, he'd slowed down to let his rider dismount safely before he dropped to the ground. He was buried on the cliffs overlooking the ocean.

Briosa, when she eventually retired, went to live with a good friend and neighbor in Portugal. She died at the age of thirty-two.

Baiona, the gentle chestnut mare with the curly mane and tail, was one of the silent leaders. She was always philosophical about her life and happy for each and every day. A true confidence-giver for our most nervous guests, often I would sit on her facing backward as she was resting at the lunch break, with my lunch spread out on her broad back. When she was close to twenty, she retired in the *Alentejo* where she continued to help and encourage young people to ride.

Caramelo, the little palomino Shetland, moved to the *Algarve,* where he may still be going strong.

Cladda, our snow queen, retired in the United Kingdom and cared for a lady with MS until the end of her working life.

Calema, of the flat feet, also one of our first horses, was bought when she was only eight years old by one of our guests and moved to Germany.

Divina, the golden girl, with endless, unbridled energy, and *Luke*, son of *Joia,* both went to live in Scotland with one of our longest-standing guests.

Damastor, the long-legged purebred chestnut gelding, and one of the guests' favorite horses, was the perfect all-rounder. He ended up with a guest in the United Kingdom where he did some eventing.

Desejada retired in the United Kingdom.

Dominó, the stunning dun, went to live in the north of Portugal, and *Everest*, the biter, retired to Wales. I still have an image of the day I went to buy him from a friend in the *Algarve*. A compact little purebred, he'd been hand-reared and had absolutely no respect for people. The lady who was selling him was at her wits' end—her arms were bruised black and blue. Living in a herd where the hierarchy was well defined by the lead mare helped Everest find himself, and he became one of our most popular teachers.

Estrela, the *cigano* rescue and mother of *Fiesta*, developed a very special bond with one of our guests and retired with her in the United Kingdom. She'd come such a long way from the nervous and unpredictable wreck of a horse she was when we took her in, but being ridden by different people didn't suit her.

Elsa, the big bay mare, was adopted by one of our staff and lived well into her twenties.

Fiesta, the lively little roan, eventually went to live in France.

Guineu, our movie star from *The House of the Spirits*, retired in Germany. Acting, it seems, had gone straight to his head, and he no longer wanted to be an ordinary trail horse.

Galante, the big gray gelding, retired in the north of Ireland with one of our guests.

Hobie, the big Dutch Warmblood cross, whose top speed was not above a fast trot, became a companion to a retired gentleman in the *Algarve*. They were well matched.

Íntima, the beautiful dove-gray purebred, was never sound and became a broodmare with a well-known local breeder.

Índia, the lively chestnut, so named because her long inward-curving ears reminded me of the beautiful *Marwari* breed, retired to France with one of our guests.

Playful *Jivago* retired with a delightful Swiss couple in the *Algarve*. His party trick was to rear up and put both his forelegs on Robert's shoulders.

Joia, the rescue who came to us in a terrible condition, was taken to Ireland by one of our staff, where she lived out her happy retirement.

Jigsaw, the piebald mare, was retired by one of our staff in the United Kingdom.

Kaya, the eye-catching palomino, retired with some friends in the *Alentejo*, and *Kiri*, the small bay gelding with a huge heart, died in my arms. He'd always tried so hard at everything. The autopsy later showed he had severe liver and kidney failure, possibly due to malnutrition and lack of care in his younger life.

Linda and *Luna* were both retired with guests.

Max, the big black gelding, went to live on a friend's farm in the inner *Alentejo,* where he spent the rest of his days occasionally being driven in a light buggy.

Maya, the wise lead mare, colicked—a common and often deadly gastrointestinal trauma in horses—and, despite our best efforts, did not survive.

Mistral, the talented dun mare, went to live with some good friends in Germany, where she competed in dressage to quite a high level.

The magnificent *Menina* retired to France, as did the alluring black *Morena*.

Nero, the black gelding with zero brakes, was one of our first horses. He retired to Germany with one of our favorite guests.

Padeiro, the striking gray gelding, lived out his long happy retirement in the United Kingdom. We'd bought him from a breeder who raised bulls for bullfighting. In his previous life, *Padeiro's* job had been to round up these impressive bulls. Nothing ever fazed him. His looks and temperament had made him one of the most popular horses with our guests.

Pestana, the flighty and difficult gray mare with the longest, thickest eyelashes ever, proved to be too unpredictable as a riding horse and was retired as a broodmare in the *Alentejo.*

Pash, our speed-freak rescue, retired with one of our staff in the *Alentejo* and lived well into his late twenties.

Poeira, the highly sensitive, dreamy gray, got a rare cancer and eventually had to be put down.

Qomplexo, the talented gray gelding, was initially sold to our veterinarian, and then went on to live in the United Kingdom.

Quo Vadis, the purebred gray who was too beautiful for his own good, was eventually retired in France with one of our guests.

Santana, the difficult and often misunderstood bay gelding, did not enjoy being ridden and was retrained as a driving horse by a close friend of ours.

Simpática, the gentle purebred mother of *Segredo*, was never sound and was retired as a broodmare with a local breeder and friend of ours, while *Segredo* was sold to a friend in the *Alentejo.*

Trovão, the bright little chestnut gelding who always made his riders feel that they were riding a huge horse, was retired with a guest in the United Kingdom.

Cheeky *Tango* had a heart attack in the middle of a canter while leading a ride and died before he hit the ground—and was buried on the spot. Others we lost—*Akbar, Maya,* and *Poeira*—were buried at the farm where their spirits could roam and gallop freely in the place they knew as *home.* At dawn and dusk, when the world slows down a bit, you can always hear them.

I FEEL EXTREMELY PRIVILEGED to have been a part of these incredible horses' lives over the years. Each and every one of them left a permanent hoofprint on my heart.

As the Greek philosopher Heraclitus said, the only constant in life is change, and like us, Samoqueirinha, the healing oasis we called our farm and home, has had to adapt and diversify. When life moved us on to a new environment, we weren't able to physically let it go, so we decided to turn it into a small rural hotel. Now it has thirteen rooms, is run very successfully by a local hotel group, and is home to six rescue horses who do short rides in the area, teaching children to ride.

Gratitude, according to John Ortberg, is the ability to experience life as a gift. I was so fortunate to have been gifted this time with these special horses in this most magical part of the world.

35

The voice of the sea speaks to the soul.
The touch of the sea is sensuous,
enfolding the body in its soft, close embrace.

KATE CHOPIN

EVERYTHING IS CONNECTED. Some days I can feel the tendrils of energy that surge and thrive around us merge inside me, and I feel one with the very essence of life. I can feel it, touch it, be it. Like an egoless power that can be harnessed.

Did Robert ever get that feeling? I felt a pang of guilt. While I was living my dream, maybe Robert wasn't living his. I decided it was as good a day as any for a chat.

I spotted his tall figure beside the pool. He'd recently developed a system to run the pool pump off a rotating solar panel, which followed the sun's trajectory, so that it only worked on a sunny day. No doubt he was now inspecting his clever creation. I crept up on him slowly from behind...and then stopped in my tracks.

In his hands he was holding a shattered swallow's nest, and it was full of screaming baby birds. They were only half-covered in feathers. He turned to face me, his eyes dark with emotion.

"Their nest fell. Look, they're still alive." The two parent birds were swooping in concentric circles, emitting high-pitched whistles. "Here, just hold this. I'll make a new nest for them." He thrust the nest into my hands and sprinted off.

As if the kittens, puppy, and foal aren't enough to keep us busy. But Robert had always had a soft spot for birds. He rushed back with a small flowerpot and jigsawed the broken bits of nest into its center, then gently placed the helpless fledglings onto the snug feather bed.

"Will the parents still come and feed them?" he wondered, scanning the trees for a glimpse of them. *Not a bird in sight.*

"No, I don't think so. They smell us. I think you'll have to feed them yourself."

He opened his eyes wide. "Any idea at all what they eat?"

I put my hand on his arm. "It's a long shot, I know, but I heard Leonel once mention a crazy mix that might work. A bit of cat food with a drop of egg yolk. Then add some chopped-up human hair. It helps them to digest, apparently. I've no idea why."

"How does that man know these weird things?" He shook his head, smiling. "Could you go fix that for me, please?"

For the next ten days, Robert was totally absorbed in tweezer-feeding the squawking babies at four-hour intervals. Holding one tiny bird at a time in his left hand, he'd pick up a dollop of the concoction in the tweezers with his right hand. He'd then flap his other fingers and *fly* his hand around the bird's head, and as it opened its beak wide, he'd push the tweezers gently— but far—down the throat and deposit the food.

Within a week, the birds were perching themselves along the rim of their flowerpot home, energetically beating their tiny new wings. Each time Robert's footsteps approached, all seven of them would flap and squawk.

Strange as it may seem, he was their mum.

Two weeks later, and now covered in shiny black-and-white feathers, they were all still alive. It was time to fly.

"There's just one problem," said Robert, "I still haven't seen their parents anywhere. They won't be able to look after themselves on their own."

The night before their scheduled maiden flight, I felt the bird man walking about the house at three o'clock in the morning. I hadn't seen him so immersed in a project since we'd moved to the farm ten years before. Back then, he'd supervised the construction of all the stables, clubhouse, and guest rooms.

But now it was different. I sensed he was outgrowing this space. The ripples of his energy were a rising tide, reaching out. The bird rescue had captivated and funneled his imagination, and confirmed his need to grow outward. I said nothing that night. He was also preparing to fly.

At six in the morning the sun was just creeping up behind the mountain, hueing the valley a pale-pink. Robert gave his babies one last feed before the flight attempt, which would be about three hours later, when they'd be hungry again.

Meanwhile, I helped the girls. We worked together to feed and check all the horses, puppy, kittens, and foal. Segredo, our secret, was growing into his long legs and had taken to galloping around the field at top speed, trying to round up the other horses. Patiently, they obliged this jet-black colt with the diamond-shaped star on his forehead and two white ankle socks.

When the flight time came, we all stood in a semicircle and sipped our coffees, waiting for liftoff. Leonel broke the silence.

"It won't work. The birds need their parents to show them how to fly."

"I hate to say this, but Leonel's right," said Fátima, frowning. She knew how much this meant to Robert.

I looked at MC and Bela. "Do you think they'll make it?"

They looked at each other. MC raised her shoulders and shook her head. "No, I don't. What do you think, Bela?"

"I'm getting good vibes about this," she said lightly. "I think they will."

I smiled at her. She'd changed and grown so much over the past few months. Chatty and friendly with the riders, she was often requested as a guide by our less-experienced guests. And her dress style was all her own. Today, her bright-purple jodhpurs and orange blouse were completed by a black leather waistcoat and a multicolored scarf, which she'd threaded through her unruly golden curls. Beside her, I felt monochrome.

Robert emerged from the pool-pump house with the first baby bird perched on his right index finger. He motioned to us all to keep still and quiet. It was time.

Moving the arm with the fledgling up and down while flapping his other arm, Robert tried his best to motivate the tiny creature to take off. I'd spotted him practicing this move with the birds in our living room for the past few days.

After some hesitation, miraculously, the baby bird took off.

And at that precise moment, the two parent birds swooped down out of nowhere and flew alongside their baby, chirping loudly while guiding him toward a nearby tree.

Robert was speechless. He could only beam.

The same procedure was repeated with the next five, until only one baby was left: the tiniest. He crash-landed after a few meters. Robert rushed to pick him up.

"It's okay, little guy," we heard him whisper as he carried the bird back to the nest. "We'll try again tomorrow."

And the next day, the tiny bird succeeded in flying away and joining his parents.

The following spring a new family made its nest in the same spot.

Maybe now Robert would have time to talk to me.

WE DECIDED TO GO FOR A WALK on our favorite beach, *Malhão*, just a ten-minute drive from the farm. The Jeep bounced along the sandy access track, which meandered its way through the pine forest, perfectly set amidst the extensive dunescape. Random clumps of wild rosemary and lavender grew alongside the stunning santolina with its gray-green leaves and yellow flowers. And wispy, golden festuca was scattered everywhere—all part of the protected coastal nature reserve that would never be developed.

Robert parked on the orange clay cliff overlooking the beach. We sat for a while in silence, watching the surfers, like black seals going for big waves. Unconsciously, my left hand slipped under his right thigh.

"You're dying to be out there with them, aren't you?"

He turned his head toward me and smiled.

"Yes. I should've brought my wetsuit and board. I'll come tomorrow if the waves are still good." He held my hand. "Come on, let's go for a walk."

The salty air stung my nostrils. The sand smelled of heat. The olfactory cocktail from the plants was making me dizzy. I sank down into the white sand.

"Sheila, are you okay?" He lifted me up and held me. "What's wrong? Do you want to rest here a while?"

"I don't know. The smells. Just everything. Sorry, just felt a bit dizzy."

TO BORROW FREEDOM

We walked on the white sand, hand in hand, along the water's edge.

"This is my favorite beach in the world," I said.

He looked back at the impressive dunes rising up behind us, then back out at the sea. The sets coming in were very big now. Seven huge hungry waves, then seven smaller ones, spurring the surfers to paddle hard to get out of the water.

He led me to the empty coastguard hut, and we sat on the sand in front of it and watched the sea. A magical streak of shimmering light reached us from across the water. It was breathtaking.

He turned to me, his eyes as dark as the sea before us.

"What's with your bionic sense of smell?"

I shrugged and smiled. "I can't explain it. It's weird." I started playing with the sand, sifting it from one palm into the other. It was super-soft, gleaming with miniscule shells. "Also...I'm hungry all the time."

I lay back, cocooned between the blue sky, the warm beach, and Robert. He turned toward me. With his weight on one elbow, he gently placed his other hand on my stomach.

"Why didn't you tell me?" he whispered.

ABOUT THE AUTHOR

Born and raised in Portugal, Sheila Greenfield inherited her mother's love for horses, learning to ride at the age of five. Following her passion, she went on to study the art of classical riding, training for three years with the late Lord Henry Loch and a further three years with classical instructor Carlos Pinto, who represented Portugal in dressage at the Sydney Olympics in 2000 and was a former pupil of the late Nuno Oliveira. After training in Portugal and England, Sheila obtained her instructor's diploma in Germany before returning to her home country to be with the Lusitanos she loved so much and set up her own classical riding and trail riding center: *Caminhos do Alentejo* (Trails of the Alentejo), which steadily grew into a leading name in European adventure travel. It was here, along Portugal's idyllic southwestern coast, that Sheila and her husband Robert Lee entertained guests from all over the world every week for 15 years. Their company was spotlighted on the Australian travel and lifestyle television show *Getaway,* the German international news channel Deutsche Welle (DW-TV), and in a feature called "Lower Alentejo at a Canter" by Elizabeth Marcus in *The New York Times.* When the 1993 feature film *The House of the Spirits* was filmed in the area, Sheila was given the task of teaching actor Antonio Banderas the basics of riding.

Sheila's family and friends were heartbroken to lose her to a long and bravely fought battle with cancer in 2024. Her memoir keeps her indelible and beautiful spirit alive.

*In loving memory of Sheila, Mum,
who now writes among the stars.*

Gone from My Sight
(1904)

I am standing upon the seashore.

A ship, at my side, spreads her white sails to the moving
breeze and starts for the blue ocean.

She is an object of beauty and strength.

I stand and watch her until, at length, she hangs like a
speck of white cloud just where the sea and sky come to
mingle with each other.

Then, someone at my side says, "There, she is gone."

Gone where?

Gone from my sight. That is all. She is just as large in mast,
hull and spar as she was when she left my side.

And, she is just as able to bear her load of living freight to
her destined port.

Her diminished size is in me—not in her.

And, just at the moment when someone says,
"There, she is gone," there are other eyes watching her
coming, and other voices ready to take up the glad shout,
"Here she comes!"

A NOTE FROM THE AUTHOR'S DAUGHTER

Witnessing Mum pen the final chapters of this book, often from the confines of a hospital bed, offered a profound insight into the depths of human resilience.

It is undeniably true that my mother, Sheila Greenfield, was an extraordinary individual. Her gentle yet indomitable spirit touched the lives of all who knew her. An unwavering beacon of kindness and sensitivity, she possessed an innate connection with all creatures, particularly horses and dogs, reflecting her deep reverence for the beauty of life in all its forms. This remarkable empathy was the dye with which she painted life. And paint she did—indeed, the tapestry of Mum's life was woven with such a multitude of vibrant experiences that no single volume could ever fully capture its beauty.

Mum departed this world peacefully in March 2024, surrounded by the love of her family, as she embarked on a new and boundless journey in the company of her sister Monica and her recently departed cousin Michal. Mum's unparalleled bravery throughout her prolonged illness left an indelible mark on the hearts of all who knew her, from us—her immediate family—to her devoted brother Sven, her loving extended families spanning Ireland, Denmark, and Portugal, and her vast network of cherished friends. Beyond her immediate circle, Mum's compassionate nature reached countless others across the globe, enriching and transforming lives in profound ways. Her memory will forever reside in our hearts, in the recollection of countless shared moments, and in the wisdom imparted through her written words.

There are certain individuals without whom this book would not have come to fruition. We extend our deepest appreciation to Rebecca Didier and the Trafalgar Square Books family for their unwavering support, compassion, and patience in the face of unforeseen and tragic circumstances. We are also profoundly grateful for the guidance of Jeremy Massey, whose boundless *grá* and dedication brought this project to life. To Helen Ryan and your writing group family, where Mum discovered confidence in her narrative voice, we are beyond words—thank you for everything.

Mum's legacy of empathy and compassion serves as a guiding light for us all, inspiring acts of selflessness in her honor. It will continue to inspire and uplift, echoing her unwavering belief in the power of love, kindness, and the pursuit of freedom.

Nicole Lee
2025